Roderick D. McKenzie

ON HUMAN ECOLOGY

THE HERITAGE OF SOCIOLOGY

A Series Edited by Morris Janowitz

Roderick D. McKenzie
ON HUMAN ECOLOGY

Selected Writings

Edited and with an Introduction by

AMOS H. HAWLEY

THE UNIVERSITY OF CHICAGO PRESS

CHICAGO AND LONDON

Library of Congress Catalog Card Number 68–9728

THE UNIVERSITY OF CHICAGO PRESS, CHICAGO & LONDON
The University of Chicago Press, Ltd., London W.C. 1

Contents

IV. DOMINANCE AND THE REGION

Introduction

VIRTUALLY EVERY scholar is heir to an intellectual tradition having an ancient past and a future that reaches well beyond him. In that tradition are not only certain major themes but also numerous derivations and corollaries, some clear and recognizable, others lurking in an inchoate state. The scholar is guided by that lore to the posture he adopts, the problems he chooses for study, and the way in which he formulates them. Yet, if his is a creative mind, he is not a captive of the tradition. He selects what he judges to be useful, shifts emphases here and there, and adapts the heritage to the issues of his time. He adds further to the tradition through his experience with new data and new situations, with borrowings from here and there, and, of course, by his own reflective ingenuity. The result is an amalgam that resists analysis into the elements of which it was formed. How is one to know whence it all came? It seems that the question is unanswerable. Hence the rendering of a full and fair account of a scholar's contribution to his discipline is an undertaking both difficult and fraught with contention. So it is with the life and work of Roderick Duncan McKenzie. His writings mingle the indisputably original with assimilations to his point of view of the thoughts of others and with amplifications of various features of his heritage. Much more unyielding to cataloguing and appraisal are the spoken obiter dicta, the casually mentioned insights and the critical remarks that enter into the universe of scholarly discourse with seldom an imprimatur of authorship.

McKenzie was born in Carmen, Manitoba, February 3, 1885,

the son of Scottish farm parents of venerable lineage. His self-sufficiency asserted itself early in his life. He assumed responsibility for his high-school education and then for a classical education at the University of Manitoba. Summer work as a rural school teacher and as an employee of a Winnepeg business firm, together with one extended interruption during which he taught at the Manitoba Agricultural College, enabled him to obtain his Bachelor of Arts degree in 1912. Before that event, however, McKenzie had grown dissatisfied with the prospect of a career in the humanities and had begun to cast about for an alternative field of study. As he browsed through university catalogues and periodical literature, his eye was caught by the *American Journal of Sociology*. The articles in that journal disclosed to him a new and dynamic field of great promise. He decided to pursue graduate study in sociology. McKenzie applied for admission to the University of Chicago and entered the University in 1913.

At Chicago he was almost immediately attracted by W. I. Thomas, for whom he developed a lasting admiration. That there was a meeting of minds between the two is evident in McKenzie's continuing interest in interethnic and interracial relations. The arrival of Robert E. Park as a new member of the faculty, in the fall of 1914, must have been instrumental in broadening the horizons of McKenzie's studies. In any case, in his subsequent work McKenzie viewed the meetings and assimilation of peoples from different cultures in the context of expanding territorial organization. Clearly it was the larger problem that dominated his later thoughts. In Park he found an intellect that stimulated and complemented his own, as one may judge from their parallel intellectual careers and the long and intimate association that followed. For McKenzie was much too modest a person to engage in open reminiscences about his private life.

After only two years as a graduate student in residence, he accepted, in 1915, a full-time instructorship at Ohio State University. It was there that he first met Ernest W. Burgess, who was soon to leave for a faculty position at the University of Chicago. Overshadowing everything else was McKenzie's marriage, in 1916, to Eva

Irene Bissett, of Winnepeg, who became his constant companion in all that he did.

Progress toward completion of work for the doctorate was slowed by teaching responsibilities. World War I added further hindrances. In 1918 McKenzie served as director of Civilian Relief, for the American Red Cross, at Camp Sherman. Later he worked as an investigator for the U. S. Food Administration. Then in the Fall of 1919 he accepted an associate professorship in the University of West Virginia. His one year in that assignment was notable mainly for his finally fulfilling all of the requirements for the doctorate. Thereafter (1920) he moved directly to a professorship in the University of Washington. One can but guess at the feeling of achievement he must have experienced on that occasion. Circumstances had denied him opportunity for leisurely study and reflection and had curtailed his associations with teachers and fellow students. His fortitude, his zest for learning and his faith in himself had at last brought him to the road he wished to travel.

McKenzie's ten years in Seattle were his most productive period. The Northwest, though well on its way toward maturity, yet retained many traces of a frontier region—an extractive economy, a mixture of races, and a still developing settlement pattern. Moreover, from its position on the Pacific rim, Seattle looked out over a vast theater of shifting scenes. A more congenial joining of scholarly interest with environment is difficult to imagine. McKenzie responded vigorously to the opportunity to investigate the dynamics of human settlement. Most of the writings gathered together in this volume were produced in that setting. But there was much more than is reported here. The breadth and the quality of his work made their impression on the president of the University of Washington. Consequently, out of the national competition among university presidents for one of their nominees to receive the Albert Kahn Foundation Fellowship for Foreign Travel, in 1925, the high honor came to McKenzie. His report on that very fruitful year of travel and study was published in Paris under the title *L'Evolution economique du monde* (1928). Immediately after his return from abroad he was commissioned by the Institute of Pacific Relations to prepare an analytical report on the Oriental migrant in the United States. The report, published as *Oriental Exclusion* (1927), was widely acclaimed as having set the record straight on the contributions made by the Oriental to this country and on the harsh effects of exclusion legislation. The conference in Honolulu to which McKenzie presented his report was followed by another in Williamstown, Massachusetts, at which he led a round-table discussion on population and race relations. One of his last commitments while at the University of Washington was to undertake, at the request of President Hoover's Committee on Recent Social Trends, a major study of urbanization in the United States. The study was completed two years later and published in 1933 as *The Metropolitan Community*.

McKenzie's distinguished writings on human ecology, regional change and interethnic relations earned him, in the brief span of a decade, a national and international reputation as a scholar. Thus the University of Michigan turned to him in its search for a scholar of note to chair its newly formed Department of Sociology. Persuaded by assurances that he would be fully supported in the development of a first-rank department, McKenzie accepted the appointment and moved to his new position in Ann Arbor, Michigan, in 1930. Unfortunately, the great depression put all of those assurances in abeyance. Instead he was faced with the trying task of eking out slender resources in an effort to nourish a slow process of departmental growth. In the meantime he enjoyed the prestige of a widely consulted authority and occupied his few spare moments in thinking and writing on human ecology.

Although the paths of McKenzie and Park intersected infrequently, the two men sustained a close personal and intellectual relationship over the years. They exchanged thoughts on their common interests in a lively correspondence. An outcome of their long dialogue was an agreement jointly to author a book on human ecology. Their aspirations on that score were to be frustrated, however. Having arrived at the peak of his career, McKenzie fell victim to an advancing illness, which rendered him progressively unable to work. His untimely death came in May of 1940.

McKenzie's short academic career was compressed between

the two World Wars. Those were the years in which sociology was casting off its earlier preoccupation with social pathologies and reform issues and was emerging as a mature social science possessing a distinctive body of theory and set of problems. During the early part of that period there were indications of a transition in the making in several academic communities in the United States and in Europe. In none, however, was there such a lively ferment as that brewing at the University of Chicago. The so-called "Chicago school" of sociology soon rose to prominence and set a stamp upon the discipline that was to last for more than a generation. The genius of the Chicago group was expressed partly in its vigorous program of urban studies and partly in its theoretical contributions, notably human ecology. The urban studies and human ecology were two sides of the same coin. The new theoretical approach provided a framework for systematic empirical research, thus lending coherence and even some prospect of cumulative results to the series of studies that began to flow from the social science departments of the University. And, needless to say, the research findings tested and modified the proposition derived from the theory.

McKenzie was first a protégé and then a leader of the "Chicago school." His mentor R. E. Park and his colleague E. W. Burgess had, in 1921, put forward some notions of human ecology in a rather tentative fashion. But the highly imaginative and restless mind of Park was impatient with details and with the rigors of closely reasoned argument. Burgess, on the other hand, was drawn irresistibly to specific empirical problems. It thus fell to McKenzie, shortly after he finished his graduate studies, to write the first definitive statements of human ecology, which appear as the opening essays in this volume. They were not so regarded by their author, however; he looked upon them as preliminary statements put forth "in the absence of any precedent." Nevertheless, the ideas set forth in those early essays soon became implanted in sociological literature as immutable doctrine.

The appeal of an ecological point of view for McKenzie, and for Park as well, derived in considerable degree from the wide intellectual scope it opened to the student of society. In directing attention to the aggregate-environment relation, the new approach clearly overreached discipline boundaries and invited speculation concerning the unity of all life. Indeed, human ecology had its inception in sociology as a set of analogies drawn from studies of organization among lower forms of life by plant and animal ecologists. What was novel about the ecological analogies is that they posed comparisons between populations at different evolutionary levels rather than between a population and an individual as in the older organic analogy. In that respect they were on much safer ground. If those analogies appear to have been construed too literally on occasion, it may have been because the rawness and turbulence of life in rapidly growing American cities in the early part of the century seemed to strike a closer parallel to the struggle for existence in nature than was manifested in maturer cities of a later date. The quest for order often grasps at straws. But McKenzie was fully aware of the limitations of analogical reasoning, as indicated by his frequent reminders of the uniqueness of man among other forms of life. He found bio-ecological analogies useful sometimes for the purpose of stating a problem and sometimes as a means of dramatizing his presentations of findings. Still, the mere preference for analogies from that source pointed to an absorbing interest in the many evidences of continuity among the patterns of organization in lower and in higher levels of life. Furthermore, the fundamental interrelatedness of all living things was too important a fact to be treated lightly. How to reconcile that fact with the great versatility of man constituted a problem which lay always in the back of McKenzie's mind. Of one conclusion he could be certain: a sociological determinism was no more acceptable than was an environmental, a biological, or any other kind of determinism. The fact of institutional specialization might explain but did not justify the carving up of man into economic, political, social, and biological segments.

The emphasis upon the aggregate as the unit of observation formed a distinctive feature of human ecology. The implied hypothesis is that the cumulative effects of an aggregate of individuals pursuing their respective ends in a given environment and with a given technology produces a predictable pattern of relationships. This is not a denial of the purposiveness of individual behavior. Rather it is an assertion that purposiveness in the individual has no necessary relation to outcome in the aggregate. The variables and the data relevant in the study of the one, therefore, must be different from those employed in studies of the other. It was unfortunate that the interactions and the resulting patterns of organization to which this view called attention were initially characterized as "bio-social," for the adjective seemed to place human ecology beyond the pale of sociology. Actually, of course, the unintended consequences of human behavior are no more or less biological than are the intended consequences. On the other hand, the use of the word "natural" to describe human organization in the ecological view meant no more than it said, that is, that order could and did arise without a master plan or the guidance of a supreme intellect. But that competition was the sole or even the principal distributing and organizing agent, a then widely held theoretical position, was subsequently regarded by McKenzie as an oversimplification.

Environment was considered to be largely, though not exclusively, a matter of spaces and distances. If one starts with the assumption of an inescapable interdependence among men, as did McKenzie, the factor of accessibility is of uppermost importance. Physiography is experienced as a limiting or facilitating influence on the accessibility of man to man, resource distribution is measured in terms of accessibility, and even climate enters into determinations of accessibility. Clearly the reduction of environment to space is most readily defensible when a settlement unit such as the modern city is the object of analysis, for there almost all other features of the natural environment have been neutralized. Thus McKenzie first conceived human ecology as "a study of the spatial and temporal relations of human beings as affected by the selective, distributive and accommodative forces of the environment." While this simple, lucid statement inspired a great amount of empirical investigation, the effect it had in causing human ecology to be regarded as little more than a descriptive study of spatial distributions led its author to reappraise it as a misplacement of emphasis. Attention to spatial patterns, as McKenzie later recorded in his notes, should be subordinate and incidental to the analysis of sustenance relations.

The conception of environment as space also lends itself conveniently to the study of change. To the extent that environment may be transposed as accessibility, it becomes a function of the efficiency of transportation and communication instrumentalities. Thus the amount of territory that can be occupied and used by an aggregate is limited at any one time by the technical culture in its possession and is expanded over time by cumulative changes in its culture. No other fact gripped McKenzie's attention so fully as did this one. The conquest of distance with all its manifold consequences for human collective life held for him an almost romantic attraction. It led him into a lifelong concern with the processes and forms of social change as manifested in the changing scale of human organization. This interest, however, was never divorced from a concern with the morphology and functioning of territorially based systems of organization.

A focus upon the aggregate in an environmental context clearly placed human ecology in close kinship with geography, demography, economics, and other social sciences. But while each such discipline isolates a particular parameter of society for its special consideration, human ecology defines a problem that subsumes all the several parameters. That is to say, if organization is the means by which an aggregate resolves its environmental problem, one must deal with whatever is relevant to an understanding of organization. The emphasis falls upon the system as a whole instead of upon one or another of its various dimensions. This breadth of conception is one of the great virtues of human ecology and also the source of its major difficulties. A holistic as against a fragmentary view of man's collective life casts a much clearer light on the meaning of specific events and offers a closer approximation to realism. Perhaps that is why the ecological approach has been widely adopted in the social sciences, the health sciences, and other applied fields. The recent rise to popularity in sociology of a "macroscopic" view of social organziation is an affirmation of the ecological position. Yet the human mind is so given to analytical procedures that the wholeness of a thing often eludes it. Whatever may be the reason, operationalization of organization as a variable has not been accomplished, and many kinds of comparative studies have suffered thereby. Faced with that deficiency, McKenzie found it expedient to utilize whatever indicators of social organization were available. Those were found, more often than not, in economic data. A not surprising upshot was that human ecology was occasionally accused of being a thinly disguised economics. Such an accusation, to say the least, is a commentary on the difficulties inherent in a holistic point of view.

In McKenzie's treatment human ecology was, in a sense, a theory of limits. It argued that a population tends to develop its size and its organization up to the limits imposed by an environment and the technical culture at hand. Changes in the structure of the organization relax old limits and introduce new ones. The nature of the limits and the possibility of various accommodations to them constitute empirical questions. In contemplating the implications of this line of reasoning, one wishes that McKenzie had not been so sparing in his theoretical writing. But, as a matter of fact, he was not at ease with theory in the abstract. Theory had value for him in the degree to which it illuminated a body of data bearing on a problem. Accordingly, most of his general observations are found embedded in his research papers. One must often read between the lines in order to gather their full import.

His first empirical work, his doctoral dissertation in fact, was a pioneering study of the neighborhood, which proved to be a benchmark for much of the subsequent research on local life in a modern city. That study, the first two sections of which are included in this volume, was undoubtedly inspired by R. E. Park's earlier outline of a research program on the city entitled: "The City: Suggestions for the Investigation of Human Behavior in the Urban Environment." Unlike most of the later research on the neighborhood, McKenzie's study began with a description of the urban context, Columbus, Ohio, in which the smaller residential association occurred. In retrospect, the sociological theory he was able to bring to bear in his study seems more than a little flaccid, as indeed it was. That, of course, was precisely the circumstance that caused human ecology to be so favorably received when it appeared. But that event had not yet happened, though ecological intimations are numerous in the report of findings. An important contribution of the study was its imaginative demonstration of the uses of observational techniques in a field setting. At the time there were few precedents on which to draw. McKenzie found it necessary to improvise, and he did so in a highly successful manner. Although the methods he used have since been supplanted by improved techniques and the data are now old, the conclusions are as fresh and as pertinent as they would be had the study been done yesterday.

It is of interest to note that the report of the neighborhood study shows no traces of E. W. Burgess' later formulation of a general growth pattern of cities. That there were no foreshadowings of that ingenious hypothesis cannot be attributed to the fact that McKenzie, having already embarked upon his teaching career, wrote the dissertation in absentia. For the two men were close friends and colleagues on the faculty of Ohio State University. Apparently the idea had not yet occurred to Burgess, or, if it had, he kept it quietly to himself. There seems to be little doubt, however, that Burgess consulted the neighborhood study among other research reports prepared by students and colleagues in the course of crystallizing his thoughts on the development and form of the city.

Although his attention soon shifted to a larger scene, the local community never faded from McKenzie's interest. Knowledge of the urban center, in his judgment, was essential to an understanding of human organization in its regional and interregional dimensions. In his few discussions of local organization he identified a number of structural properties that were later investigated by different researchers. He noted, for example, the complementary processes of deconcentration of institutional operations and centralization of administration, the relationship of time-cost distance and the scale of organization, the effects of separation of home from work place, the differences in the ranges of daily circulations by different social classes, the hierarchical ordering of institutions, and the convergences of different institutions toward a common organization form. Some of these he mentioned in passing and left undeveloped. Others figured prominently in his later work.

One cannot read far into McKenzie's writings without being impressed by his profound interest in change. That interest was quite probably whetted by the year he was able to devote to foreign travel (1925–26). Most of that time was spent at the frontiers of empire, mainly in regions bordering the Pacific Ocean. There he observed at first hand the collisions of cultures, the minglings of races, the shifting settlement patterns, and the transformations of economies incidental to the penetrations of Western influences. The imprint of that experience was revealed in many ways. It introduced an unmistakable comparative coloration to his later work and, of course, enormously enriched his teaching. The seeming repetition, in changes at work in the Orient, of developments on earlier frontiers farther west added historic depth to his perspective. In that context he clarified the concept of dominance, which was destined to become an important analytic and descriptive tool of human ecology. Most significantly, however, McKenzie's observations abroad induced him to formulate his ideas about the process of change.

His thoughts on change revolved about two distinguishable yet complementary conceptions. One was a natural-history view of the form of change as developed by plant ecologists in their work on succession. The other was a cultural view, designated "expansion," in which was described the process of increase in scale of settlement organization. These two ideas had been joined by Burgess in his proposition concerning the growth of the city. In that proposal, city development is treated as an expansion of settlement from a center proceeding through alternating equilibrium and growth phases. There is thus laid down a set of concentric rings describing a declining intensity of land use with distance from the center. McKenzie was fully acquainted with the Burgess hypothesis. He, however, cultivated his ideas about growth or expansion in a series of regional studies. Presumably the broader basis for his theoretical statement was responsible for its taking on the aspect of a general growth model.

An enquiry into the nature of change invariably invokes the

question of how to account for stability. One solution to the apparent incompatibility of the two states is to regard them as alternating conditions. That tactic is most applicable where the data are sparse, the units under study are large and complex, and, further, where the agents of change are manifestly sequential in occurrence. These circumstances were usually present during the diffusion of an accumulating industrial technology over new areas of settlement and long-sheltered societies. McKenzie's study of "Ecological Succession in the Puget Sound Region" offers a neat example. There, eras of water, rail, and motor vehicle transportation were fairly widely spaced in time, so that a settlement pattern characteristic of each was able to emerge and approximate an equilibrium state before the onset of the next transportation regime. Roughly similar progressions were observable on more distant frontiers. Elsewhere, as in his discussion of "Movement and the Ability to Live," McKenzie describes mechanisms of stability maintenance in different kinds of societies. It is probable that the easy application of the concept of alternating stable and change states may have belonged to an historic period that was coming rapidly to a close in McKenzie's life time. He never disclosed the extent or nature of his commitment to a natural history or evolutionary theory of change. There is some reason to believe that he was content to use it simply as a convenient means of ordering a series of events for purposes of exposition. Of greater importance to him and to posterity was his concept of the process of expansion.

"Expansion" is a commonplace term that had long been used by economists, historians and other scholars to refer to the spread of ideas, the diffusion of practices, and the dispersions of peoples. McKenzie, however, gave it a formulation that incorporated many such phenomena into a general theory of growth. As he stated it, expansion involves the operation of centrifugal and centripetal processes through which a center develops its capability of sustaining reciprocal relations over a widening territory. Increases in scale presupposes involution of the organization at the center; for form must change as size is enlarged. The complex process is initiated by cultural inputs that either reduce the time and cost of movement or increase productivity, so that greater amounts of wealth may be devoted to the costs of overcoming the friction of space.

Here, then, was a conception of cumulative change or growth in which population, area, culture, and organization were contingent and interacting factors. It provided opportunity for the integration of a number of disparate theoretical elements. The theory is congenial, for example, with the hypothesis of city location put forth by C. H. Cooley and as modified by C. D. Harris and E. L. Ullman. Expansion, that is to say, proceeds most frequently from settlements strategically situated with reference to transportation and communication, whether that be at the intersections of interregional routes or at central places within regions. The accessibility of such sites makes available the substance of organization growth. By the same token, expansion offers a frame of reference in which cultural accumulation and the rise of civilization may be systematically treated. The locations that foster growth of a system have that effect because they are convenient places for the meetings of peoples from diverse backgrounds, the exchange of experiences, and the assembling of various techniques into new inventions. The developing organization supplies the structure required to contain a progressively more voluminous and elaborate culture. Many more particular hypotheses, such as that of Burgess, mentioned earlier, may be seen as special cases of the more general theory.

It is difficult to imagine a conceptualization more suited to a conviction of the fundamental interrelatedness of the factors of collective life. But while the theoretical structure reared upon that postulate had been nourished in the parochialism of the American city regarded as the prototype city, the concept of expansion forced human ecology into a much broader universe of accountability. It had to consider the impingement of contrasting civilizations upon one another and to extend the search for order into the internal processes of different cultures.

In his studies of expansion McKenzie turned first to the phenomenon in its interregional dimensions before bringing the problem to a focus within a region. That, whether by accident or design, was in accord with technological history. Improvements in the efficiency of long-distance, bulk-haul movements preceded by a substantial margin of time the gains made in short-distance transportation and communication. Interregional expansion proceeded from metropolitan centers, which threw out long tentacles of influence armed initially with the political powers of national states. Later the exercise of influence in frontier areas came to rely on the forces of economic and political persuasion. The more recent return to the use of political power, exerted through the manipulation of economic policy, had not begun in McKenzie's time, at least not with the refinements that were to appear after World War II.

His historical sense led him to recognize that the establishment of dominance over frontier zones could not be more than a temporary phase. The reorganizations that followed the invasion by economic and cultural influences from highly developed centers set processes of maturation afoot which eventually brought formerly subordinate areas into rivalry with dominant centers. One of the means by which this occurred, to which McKenzie gave much attention, was the formation of interethnic and interracial divisions of labor at resource sites, plantations, and trading posts. In such acculturative settings alien groups tended to move from lower to higher occupations and ultimately to enter into competition for control of the occupational structure. The detachment with which he analyzed the occupational capillarity, including the frictions and the efforts at exclusion it generated, barely conceals a very real sympathy for the underprivileged alien worker struggling for a foothold in a new environment. McKenzie thought he saw, in the sequences of events that took place at the frontiers of expansion, recurrences of the phylogeny of modern society. That hypothesis, obviously not original with him, has yet to be disposed of in comparative studies of modernization in new nations.

Just as expansion develops on a broad scale with the improvement of long-distance transportation facilities, it occurs also within regions and localities as the means of short-distance transportation and communication are improved and perfected. In the latter instance it becomes possible for agglomerations of settlement to spread over enlarging areas without loss of contact among the components and for a localized division of labor to become increasingly ramified while keeping pace with the deconcentration of population. This new kind of settlement organization, the metropolitan community, tends to supercede the city as the important urban unit. Although recognition of the metropolitan area had begun to appear in the data classifications of the United States Bureau of the Census as early as 1910, McKenzie was the first scholar to examine the process of metropolitan development systematically and in detail. His study, prepared in the early 1930's for the President's Committee on Recent Social Trends, was far more prophetic than he could have realized. The course of change that he observed was modified somewhat by the economic depression of the 1930's and again by materials scarcities during World War II years, but afterward it exploded into a massive deconcentration of urban population and institutions affecting every part of the country. This finally produced, in the 1950's, a belated awakening to the fact that metropolitan development represents one of the most important social trends of the twentieth century. Many of the attendant problems, which now are matters of general consternation, had been anticipated in McKenzie's early work. His monograph on *The Metropolitan Community* still stands as a landmark in the literature on that subject.

Research in metropolitan trends and patterns occupied the major part of McKenzie's time from the publication of his monograph until his death. The energies he bent in that direction, however, were channeled almost exclusively into the teaching of graduate students. Soon after joining the faculty of the University of Michigan, in 1930, as the first chairman of that institution's Department of Sociology, he organized an interdepartmental research seminar on the metropolitan community. Professorial colleagues in business administration, economics, geography and political science collaborated with him in making the seminar an unusually effective educational experience for graduate students and faculty alike. The Metropolitan Community Seminar continues to this day as a viable component of graduate instruction in the social sciences at Michigan.

One other concern vied with McKenzie's interest in metropolitan problems during his later years. That was a desire to organize his accumulated thoughts and experience in a comprehensive treatise on human ecology. His ideas on that subject had altered and matured greatly since his earlier writings. Indeed, they had reached out to such a breadth that their exposition would have constituted a life's work. But McKenzie had little time left, and the use of what remained to him was wasted by a recurring and deepening illness. The task was not completed. Although his writing was severely curtailed, he managed to communicate enough of his revised and extended thoughts to his students to remind them of the vitality and promise of the ecological point of view in social science.

In conclusion, a word must be said about the man as a teacher. He was not at his best before a large class. Even so, a student could not sit long in any of his crowded undergraduate courses without becoming aware of McKenzie's dedication to learning and of his respect for a seminal idea. The range and depth of his scholarship, however, were most fully revealed in a small group of students mature enough to share his thinking. His seminar discussions sparkled with wisdom, adroit use of his knowledge, and wry wit. But he regarded the seminar primarily as a forum for working scholars. His principle of higher education was that one learns by doing, as he himself had learned. Thus McKenzie urged his students into the field at the earliest opportunity to investigate problems through direct experience with appropriate data. Not always was the problem, so pursued, clearly conceived by the student. If he floundered, as many did, the student could expect hours in consultation with the teacher and a gentle encouragement to try again. On the other hand, an original thought or a perceptive observation was rewarded with enthusiastic interest and a demonstration of pride in the student's achievement. Invariably the student, the unsuccessful as well as the successful, found himself drawn into an intellectual partnership with the teacher. In consequence, McKenzie's colloquies with his coterie of students had an aura of excitement, of enterprise, and of common purpose.

Amos H. Hawley

I. Human Ecology

1

THE ECOLOGICAL APPROACH
TO THE STUDY OF
THE HUMAN COMMUNITY

1924

THE YOUNG sciences of plant and animal ecology have become fairly well established. Their respective fields are apparently quite well defined, and a set of concepts for analysis is becoming rather generally accepted. The subject of human ecology, however, is still practically an unsurveyed field, that is, so far as a systematic and scientific approach is concerned. To be sure, hosts of studies have been made which touch the field of human ecology in one or another of its varied aspects, but there has developed no science of human ecology which is comparable in precision of observation or in method of analysis with the recent sciences of plant and animal ecology.

I. *The Relation of Human Ecology to Plant and Animal Ecology*

Ecology has been defined as "that phase of biology that considers plants and animals as they exist in nature, and studies their interdependence, and the relation of each kind and individual to its environment."[1] This definition is not sufficiently comprehensive to include all the elements that logically fall within the range of human ecology. In the absence of any precedent let us tenta-

---

Reprinted from *The American Journal of Sociology*, vol. 30, no. 3, November, 1924.

[1]   *Encyclopedia Americana*, New York (1923), p. 555.

tively define human ecology as a study of the spatial and temporal[2] relations of human beings as affected by the selective, distributive, and accommodative forces of the environment. Human ecology is fundamentally interested in the effect of *position*,[3] in both time and space, upon human institutions and human behavior. "Society is made up of individuals spatially separated, territorially distributed, and capable of independent locomotion."[4] These spatial relationships of human beings are the products of competition and selection, and are continuously in process of change as new factors enter to disturb the competitive relations or to facilitate mobility. Human institutions and human nature itself become accommodated to certain spatial relationships of human beings. As these spatial relationships change, the physical basis of social relations is altered, thereby producing social and political problems.

A great deal has been written about the biological, economic, and social aspects of competition and selection, but little attention has been given to the distributive and spatial aspects of these processes. The plant ecologist is aware of the effect of the struggle for space, food, and light upon the nature of a plant formation, but the sociologist has failed to recognize that the same processes of competition and accommodation are at work determining the size and ecological organization of the human community.

The essential difference between the plant and animal organism is that the animal has the power of locomotion which enables it to gather nutriment from a wider environment, but, in addition to the power to move in space, the human animal has the ability to contrive and adapt the environment to his needs. In a word, the human community differs from the plant community in the two

2   As indicated later on in this paper, ecological formations tend to develop in cyclic fashion. A period of time within which a given ecological formation develops and culminates is the time period for that particular formation. The length of these time periods may be ultimately measured and predicted, hence the inclusion of the temporal element in the definition.
3   The word "position" is used to describe the place relation of a given community to other communities, also the location of the individual or institution within the community itself.
4   R. E. Park and E. W. Burgess, *Introduction to the Science of Sociology*, p. 509.

dominant characteristics of mobility and purpose, that is, in the power to select a habitat and in the ability to control or modify the conditions of the habitat. On first consideration this might seem to indicate that human ecology could have nothing in common with plant ecology, where the processes of association and adjustment result from natural unmodifiable reactions; but closer examination and investigation make it obvious that human communities are not so much the products of artifact or design as many hero-worshippers suppose.[5]

The human community has its inception in the traits of human nature and the needs of human beings. Man is a gregarious animal: he cannot live alone; he is relatively weak and needs not only the company of other human associates but shelter and protection from the elements as well. Brunhes says there are three essentials to the inception of the human community: the house, the road, and water.[6] Food may be transported more easily than shelter or water; the latter two therefore constitute, even under the most nomadic conditions, the essential elements in giving a location and a spatial fixity to human relations.[7] This is exemplified under our present regime of automobile tourist life, where water and shelter become the determining factors in the location of the camp.

The size and stability of the human community is, however, a function of the food supply and of the role played in the wider ecological process of production and distribution of commodities. When man makes his living from hunting or fishing, the community is small and of but temporary duration; when agriculture becomes the chief source of sustenance, the community is still small but assumes a more permanent character; when trade and commerce develop, larger communities arise at points of break in conveyance, that is, at the mouths of rivers, junctions of streams,

[5]   Although the actions of individuals may be designed and controlled, the total effect of individual action is neither designed nor anticipated.
[6]   *Human Geography*, p. 52.
[7]   Brunhes points out by a series of maps the very intimate relation between the distribution of human habitations and the water systems of different countries. He also demonstrates the relation of the modern industrial community to the regions of coal deposits.

at waterfalls, and shallows where streams are forded. As new forms of transportation arise, new points of concentration occur and old points become accentuated or reduced. Again, as goods for trade are made in communities, still other points of concentration come into existence, determined largely by sources of power and raw material.[8]

II. *Ecological Classification of Communities*

From the standpoint of ecology, communities may be divided into four general types: first, the primary service community, such as the agricultural town, the fishing, mining, or lumbering community, which serves as the first step in the distributive process of the outgoing basic commodity and as the last stage in the distributive process of the product finished for consumption. The size of such communities depends entirely upon the nature and form of utilization of the extractive industry concerned, together with the extent of the surrounding trade area. The community responds in size to any element that affects the productivity of the economic base or the extent of the area from which it draws its sustenance. But, in any event, so long as such a community does not assume any other function in the larger ecological process, it cannot grow in population beyond a few thousand inhabitants.

The next type of community is the one that fulfils the secondary function in the distributive process of commodities. It collects the basic materials from the surrounding primary communities and distributes them in the wider markets of the world. On the other hand, it redistributes the products coming from other parts of the world to the primary service communities for final consumption. This is commonly called the commercial community; it may, however, combine other functions as well. The size of this type of com-

[8] The close relation existing between the coal and iron areas and the location of modern industrial communities has frequently been pointed out. L. C. A. Knowles says: "Apart from special and exceptional circumstances industry in Europe and the United States tends to grow up within easy railway access to the great coal areas and on these areas the population is massed in towns" (*The Industrial and Commercial Revolutions in Great Britain during the Nineteenth Century*, p. 24).

munity depends upon the extent of its distributive functions. It may vary from a small wholesale town in the center of an agricultural plain to that of a great port city whose hinterland extends halfway across the continent. Growth depends upon the comparative advantages of the site location.

The third type of community is the industrial town. It serves as the locus for the manufacturing of commodities. In addition it may combine the functions of the primary service and the commercial types. It may have its local trade area and it may also be the distributing center for the surrounding hinterland. The type is characterized merely by the relative dominance of industry over the other forms of service. There is practically no limit to the size to which an industrial community may develop. Growth is dependent upon the scope and market organization of the particular industries which happen to be located within its boundaries. Industrial communities are of two general types: first, those that have diversified and multiple industries organized on a local sale of products, and, second, those that are dominated by one or two highly developed industries organized on a national or world-sale of products.

The fourth type of community is one which is lacking in a specific economic base. It draws its economic sustenance from other parts of the world, and may serve no function in the production or distribution of commodities. Such communities are exemplified in our recreational resorts, political and educational centers, communities of defense, penal or charitable colonies. From the standpoint of growth or decline such communities are not subject to the same laws that govern the development of towns that play a part in the larger productive and distributive processes.[9] They are much more subject to the vicissitudes of human fancies and decrees than are the basic types of human communities. Of course, any community may and usually does have accretions added to its population as a result of such service. It

[9]   To be sure, if the interests in question are commercialized, the growth of the community is subject to the same laws of competition as the other types of communities, with the exception that change is likely to be more rapid and fanciful.

may, for instance, be the seat of a university, of a state prison, or it may be a recreational resort for at least certain seasons of the year.

III. *Determining Ecological Factors in the Growth or Decline of Community*

The human community tends to develop in cyclic fashion. Under a given state of natural resources and in a given condition of the arts the community tends to increase in size and structure until it reaches the point of population adjustment to the economic base. In an agricultural community, under present conditions of production and transportation, the point of maximum population seldom exceeds 5,000.[10] The point of maximum development may be termed the point of culmination or climax, to use the term of the plant ecologist.[11] The community tends to remain in this condition of balance between population and resources until some new element enters to disturb the *status quo*, such as the introduction of a new system of communication, a new type of industry, or a different form of utilization of the existing economic base. Whatever the innovation may be that disturbs the equilibrium of the community, there is a tendency toward a new cycle of adjustment. This may act in either a positive or negative manner. It may serve as a *release* to the community, making for another cycle of growth and differentiation, or it may have a retractive influence, necessitating emigration and readjustment to a more circumscribed base.

In earlier conditions of life, population was kept down to the community balance by variations in the death rate, or, as in the case of Greek cities, the surplus population emigrated in groups to establish new colonies—offshoots of the mother-city. Under modern conditions of communication and transportation, population adjustment is maintained by a ceaseless process of individual migrations. As a result of the dynamic conditions prevailing

---

[10]   See H. P. Douglass, *The Little Town*, p. 44.
[11]   F. E. Clements, *Plant Succession*, p. 3. Carr-Saunders refers to the point of population adjustment to resources as the "optimum."

throughout the civilized world during the last fifty years, many communities have passed through swift successive cycles of growth or decline, the determining factors being changes in forms and routes of transportation and communication and the rise of new industries.

Some advantage in transportation is the most fundamental and most important of the causes determining the location of a distributing center. It may almost be said to be the only cause for the formation of such centers. For some reason or reasons a particular place is more conveniently and cheaply reached by many people than any surrounding point; and, as a result, they naturally exchange commodities there. The country store is located at the crossing of roads. There also is the village. In a mountain country the market town is at the junction of two, or, still better, of three valleys. Another favorite location is the end of a mountain pass, or a gap that is a thoroughfare between two valleys. If rivers are difficult to cross, settlements will spring up at the safest ferries or fords. In a level plain, a town will be near its center, and a focus of roads or railroads in such a plain, fertile and populous, will almost surely make a city.[12]

It is the railroad and the steamship that determine where a new business shall be developed, quite as often as the government policy. The grant of special rates and privileges to shippers is nowadays the most efficient kind of protection.

It is this quickening and cheapening of transportation that has given such stimulus in the present day to the growth of large cities. It enables them to draw cheap food from a far larger territory and it causes business to locate where the widest business connection is to be had, rather than where the goods or raw materials are most easily produced. And the perfection of the means of communication, the post-office and the telegraph, intensifies the same result.[13]

The entire net increase of the population of 1870 to 1890 in Illinois, Wisconsin, Iowa, and Minnesota was in cities and towns possessing competitive rates, while those having non-competitive rates decreased in population, and in Iowa it is the general belief that the

[12]   J. Russell Smith, *Industrial and Commercial Geography* (1913), p. 841.
[13]   A. T. Hadley, "Economic Results of Improvement in Means of Transportation," quoted in Marshall, *Business Administration*, p. 35.

absence of large cities is due to the earlier policy of the railways giving Chicago discriminating rates.[14]

The advent of the trolley line and more recently of the automobile has produced still further disturbing elements in the growth of human communities. Their effect has been chiefly to modify the life of the small town or village, causing the decline of some and the sudden growth of others. The introduction of these two forms of transportation, more particularly of the automobile, has been the most potent force in our recent American history in affecting redistribution of our population and in the disorganization of our rural and small-town institutions, which grew up on the basis of a horse-and-vehicle type of mobility.[15]

The evolution of new types of industry is another feature that becomes a determining factor in the redistribution of the country's population. As we review our census reports we see the emergence each decade of one or more important industries; first, the textile industry causing concentrations of population in the eastern states, then the development of the iron and steel industry with its center of operations gradually shifting farther and farther west, and more recently the advent of the automobile and oil industries making for enormous concentration of population in certain states of the Union, also the motion-picture industry with its concentrated center in southern California. The emergence of a new industry has a far-reaching effect in disturbing the *status quo* of communal life. Competition soon forces the new industry to concentrate its productive enterprises in one or two communities; these communities then serve as great magnets drawing to themselves the appropriate population elements from communities far and near.

IV. *The Effect of Ecological Changes on the Social Organization of Community*

Population migrations resulting from such sudden pulls as are the outcomes of unusual forms of release in community

14   L. C. A. Knowles, *The Industrial and Commercial Revolutions in Great Britain during the Nineteenth Century* (1921), p. 216.
15   See Gillette, *Rural Sociology* (1922), pp. 472–73.

growth may cause an expansion in the community's development far beyond the natural culmination point of its cyclic development, resulting in a crisis situation, a sudden relapse, disorganization, or even panic. So-called "boom towns" are towns that have experienced herd movements of population beyond the natural point of culmination.

On the other hand, a community which has reached the point of culmination and which has experienced no form of release is likely to settle into a condition of stagnation. Its natural surplus of population is forced to emigrate. This type of emigration tends to occasion folk-depletion in the parent community. The younger and more enterprising population elements respond most sensitively to the absence of opportunities in their home town. This is particularly true when the community has but a single economic base, such as agriculture, lumbering, mining. Reformers try in vain to induce the young people to remain on the farms or in their native villages, little realizing that they are working in opposition to the general principles of the ecological order.

Again, when a community starts to decline in population due to a weakening of the economic base, disorganization and social unrest follow.[16] Competition becomes keener within the community, and the weaker elements either are forced into a lower economic level or are compelled to withdraw from the community entirely. There are, of course, periodic and temporary fluctuations in the economic balance, due either to circumstances which affect the entire economic order or to the vicissitudes of the particular industry from which the community draws its sustenance. These temporary fluctuations, however, while important from the standpoint of social well-being, do not comprise the basic determinants of community development.

The introduction of an innovating element into the adjustment of a community may be designated as the initial stage of an invasion which may make for a complete change in the structure and organization of the community. The introduction of a new mode of transportation, for instance, may transform the economic organiza-

[16]   For a good statistical summary of the decline in village population in the United States from 1900 to 1920, see Gillette, *Rural Sociology*, p. 465.

tion of a community and make for a change in population type.

Thus the Harlem Railroad transformed Quaker Hill from a community of diversified farming, producing, manufacturing, selling, consuming, sufficient unto itself, into a locality of specialized farming. Its market had been Poughkeepsie, twenty-eight miles away, over high hills and indifferent roads. Its metropolis became New York, sixty-two miles away by rail and four to eight miles by wagon-road.

With the railroad's coming, the isolated homogeneous community scattered. The sons of the Quakers emigrated. Laborers from Ireland and other European lands, even negroes from Virginia, took their places. New Yorkers became residents on the Hill, which became the farthest terminus of suburban travel.[17]

The establishment of a new industry, especially if it displaces the previous economic base, may also make for a more or less complete change of population without greatly modifying the size of the community. This condition is exemplified in many of the small towns of the state of Washington which have changed from lumbering to agriculture or from one type of agriculture to another. In many cases few of the previous inhabitants remained after the invasion of the new economic base.

As a community increases in size, however, it becomes better able to accommodate itself to invasions and to sudden changes in number of inhabitants. The city tends to become the reservoir into which the surplus population drains from the smaller communities round about.

V. *Ecological Processes Determining the Internal Structure of Community*

In the process of community growth there is a development from the simple to the complex, from the general to the specialized; first to increasing centralization and later to a decentralization process. In the small town or village the primary universal needs are satisfied by a few general stores and a few simple institutions

[17]   Warren H. Wilson, "Quaker Hill," quoted in Sims, *Rural Community*, p. 214.

such as church, school, and home. As the community increases in size specialization takes place both in the type of service provided and in the location of the place of service. The sequence of development may be somewhat as follows: first the grocery store, sometimes carrying a few of the more staple dry goods, then the restaurant, poolroom, barber shop, drug store, dry-goods store, and later bank, haberdashery, millinery, and other specialized lines of service.[18]

The axial or skeletal structure of a community is determined by the course of the first routes of travel and traffic.[19] Houses and shops are constructed near the road, usually parallel with it. The road may be a trail, public highway, railroad, river, or ocean harbor, but, in any case, the community usually starts in parallel relation to the first main highway. With the accumulation of population and utilities the community takes form, first along one side of the highway and later on both sides. The point of junction or crossing of two main highways, as a rule, serves as the initial center of the community.

As the community grows there is not merely a multiplication of houses and roads but a process of differentiation and segregation takes place as well. Residences and institutions spread out in centrifugal fashion from the central point of the community, while business concentrates more and more around the spot of highest land values. Each cyclic increase of population is accompanied by greater differentiation in both service and location. There is a struggle among utilities for the vantage-points of position. This makes for increasing value of land and increasing height of buildings at the geographic center of the community. As competition for advantageous sites becomes keener with the growth of population, the first and economically weaker types of utilities are forced out to less accessible and lower-priced areas. By the time

[18]   In actual count of some thirty-odd communities in and around Seattle this was about the sequence of development.
[19]   The axial or skeletal structure of civilization, Mediterranean, Atlantic, Pacific, is the ocean around which it grows up. See Ramsay Traquair, "The Commonwealth of the Atlantic," *Atlantic Monthly*, May, 1924.

the community has reached a population of about ten or twelve thousand, a fairly well-differentiated structure is attained. The drugstore, the department store, and the hotel holding the sites of central part is a clearly defined business area with the bank, the highest land value. Industries and factories usually comprise independent formations within the city, grouping around railroad tracks and routes of water traffic. Residence sections become established, segregated into two or more types, depending upon the economic and racial composition of the population.

The structural growth of community takes place in successional sequence not unlike the successional stages in the development of the plant formation. Certain specialized forms of utilities and uses do not appear in the human community until a certain stage of development has been attained, just as the beech or pine forest is preceded by successional dominance of other plant species. And just as, in plant communities, successions are the products of invasion, so also in the human community the formation, segregations, and associations that appear constitute the outcome of a series of invasions.[20]

There are many kinds of intra-community invasions, but in general they may be grouped into two main classes: those resulting in change in use of land, and those which introduce merely change in type of occupant. By the former is meant change from one general use to another, such as of a residential area into a business area or of a business into an industrial district. The latter embraces all changes of type within a particular use area, such as the changes which constantly take place in the racial and economic complexion of residence neighborhoods, or of the type of service utility within a business section. Invasions produce successional stages of different qualitative significance, that is, the economic character of the district may rise or fall as the result of certain types of invasion. This qualitative aspect is reflected in the fluctuations of land or rental values.

The conditions which initiate invasions are legion. The following are some of the more important: (1) changes in forms and

[20]   Compare F. E. Clements, *Plants Succession*, p. 6.

routes of transportation;[21] (2) obsolescence resulting from physical deterioration or from changes in use or fashion; (3) the erection of important public or private structures, buildings, bridges, institutions, which have either attractive or repellent significance; (4) the introduction of new types of industry, or even a change in the organization of existing industries; (5) changes in the economic base which make for redistribution of income, thus necessitating change of residence; (6) real estate promotion creating sudden demands for special location sites, etc.

Invasions may be classified according to stage of development into (a) initial stage, (b) secondary or developmental stage, (c) climax. The initial stage of an invasion has to do with the point of entry, the resistance or inducement offered the invader by the prior inhabitants of the area, the effect upon land values and rentals. The invasion, of course, may be into an unoccupied territory or into territory with various degrees of occupancy. The resistance to invasion depends upon the type of the invader together with the degree of solidarity of the present occupants. The undesirable invader, whether in population type or in use form, usually makes entry (that is, within an area already completely occupied) at the point of greatest mobility. It is a common observation that foreign races and other undesirable invaders, with few exceptions, take up residence near the business center of the community or at other points of high mobility and low resistance. Once established they gradually push their way out along business or transportation thoroughfares to the periphery of the community.

The commencement of an invasion tends to be reflected in changes in land value. If the invasion is one of change in use, the value of the land generally advances and the value of the building declines. This condition furnishes the basis for disorganization. The normal improvements and repairs are, as a rule, omitted, and the owner is placed under the economic urge of renting his prop-

21   For good discussion of the effect of new forms of transportation upon communal structure see McMichael and Bingham, *City Growth and Values* (1923), chap. 4; also Grupp, *Economics of Motor Transportation* (1924), chap. 2.

erty to parasitic and transitory services which may be economically strong but socially disreputable, and is therefore able and obliged to pay higher rentals than the legitimate utilities can afford. It is a well-known fact that the vices under the surveillance of the police usually segregate in such transitional areas.[22]

During the course of development of an invasion into a new area, either of use or type, there takes place a process of displacement and selection determined by the character of the invader and of the area invaded. The early stages are usually marked by keenness of competition, which frequently manifests itself in outward clashes. Business failures are common in such areas and the rules of competition are violated. As the process continues, competition forces associational groupings. Utilities making similar or complementary demands of the area tend to group in close proximity to one another, giving rise to subformations with definite service functions. Such associations as amusement areas, retail districts, market sections, financial sections, and automobile rows are examples of this tendency.

The climax stage is reached in the invasion process once the dominant type of ecological organization emerges which is able to withstand the intrusions of other forms of invasion. For example, in the development of a residential district, when it is not controlled in advance by building restrictions, the early stages of growth are usually marked by wide variations in the type and value of buildings constructed. But, in the process of development, a uniform cost type of structure tends to dominate, gradually eliminating all other types that vary widely from the norm, so that it is customary to find a considerable degree of economic homogeneity in all established residential districts. The same process operates in areas devoted to business uses, competition segregates utilities of similar economic strength into areas of corresponding land values, and at the same time forces into close proximity those particular forms of service which profit from mutual association

[22]   By actual count in the city of Seattle over 80 per cent of the disorderly houses recorded in police records are obsolete buildings located near the downtown business section where land values are high and new uses are in process of establishment.

such as financial establishments or automobile display-rooms. Once a dominant use becomes established within an area, competition becomes less ruthless among the associational units, rules of control emerge, and invasion of a different use is for a time obstructed.

The general effect of the continuous processes of invasions and accommodations is to give to the developed community well-defined areas, each having its own peculiar selective and cultural characteristics. Such units of communal life may be termed "natural areas,"[23] or formations, to use the term of the plant ecologist. In any case, these areas of selection and function may comprise many subformations or associations which become part of the organic structure of the district or of the community as a whole. It has been suggested that these natural areas or formations may be defined in terms of land values,[24] the point of highest land value representing the center or head of the formation (not necessarily the geographic center but the economic or cultural center), while the points of lowest land value represent the periphery of the formation or boundary line between two adjacent formations.

Each formation or ecological organization within a community serves as a selective or magnetic force attracting to itself appropriate population elements and repelling incongruous units, thus making for biological and cultural subdivisions of a city's population. Everyone knows how racial and linguistic colonies develop in all of our large cities, but the age and sex segregations which take place are not quite so obvious to common perception. In the city of Seattle, which has in general a sex composition of 113 males to 100 females, the downtown district, comprising an area inscribed by a radius of half a mile or so, has from 300 to 500 males to every 100 females. But in the outlying districts of the city, except in one or two industrial sections, these ratios are reversed. Females predominate in numbers over males in all the residential neighborhoods and in the suburbs of the city. This same condition is true with regard to the age distribution of population. The school census shows an absolute decline in the number of children of

[23]   A term used by members of the Department of Sociology in the University of Chicago.
[24]   This has also been suggested by the Chicago group.

school age in the central districts of the city although the total population for this area has shown an increase for each decade. It is obvious, then, that the settler type of population, the married couples with children, withdraw from the center of the city while the more mobile and less responsible adults herd together in the hotel and apartment regions near the heart of the community.

This process of population-sifting produces not only increasing mobility with approach from the periphery to the center of the formation, but also different cultural areas representing different mores, attitudes, and degrees of civic interest. The neighborhoods in which the settler type of population resides, with their preponderance of women and children, serve as the custodians of the stabilizing and repressive mores. It is in the Seattle neighborhoods, especially those on the hill-tops, that the conservative, law-abiding, civic-minded population elements dwell. The downtown section and the valleys, which are usually industrial sites, are populated by a class of people who are not only more mobile but whose mores and attitudes, as tested by voting habits, are more vagrant and radical.

2

THE SCOPE OF HUMAN ECOLOGY

1926

IN THE STRUGGLE for existence in human groups social organization accommodates itself to the spatial and sustenance relationships existing among the occupants of any geographical area. All the more fixed aspects of human habitation, the buildings, roads, and centers of association, tend to become spatially distributed in accordance with forces operating in a particular area at a particular level of culture. In society physical structure and cultural characteristics are parts of one complex.

The spatial and sustenance relations in which human beings are organized are ever in process of change in response to the operation of a complex of environmental and cultural forces. It is the task of the human ecologist to study these processes of change in order to ascertain their principles of operation and the nature of the forces producing them.

It is perhaps necessary at the outset to indicate the relation of human ecology to the kindred sciences of geography and economics. It has been claimed that geography is human ecology.[1] There are doubtless many points in common between the two disciplines; but geography is concerned with place; ecology, with process. Location, as a geographical concept, signifies position on the earth's surface; location as an ecological concept signifies

---

Reprinted from *The American Journal of Sociology*, vol. 32, no. 1, part 2, July, 1926.

[1] H. H. Barrows, "Geography as Human Ecology," *Annals of the Association of American Geographers* 13 (March 1923): 1–14.

position in a spatial grouping of interacting human beings or of interrelated human institutions.

Research in economics and commercial geography on land value,[2] marketing, transportation, commerce, factory and business location frequently has ecological significance. The difference between economics and ecology lies mainly in the direction of attention. Business economics, the division of economics having most ecological significance, is usually approached from the point of view of the businessman who may want to know the best place to locate a factory or the best method of marketing a commodity. The ecologist studies the same economic problems, but in relation to the processes of human distribution. The chain-store system of marketing goods, for instance, might be studied by the economist as a system of retail marketing, whereas the ecologist might study it as an index of the process of decentralization.[3]

Ecological distribution.—By this term is meant the spatial distribution of human beings and human activities resulting from the interplay of forces which effect a more or less conscious, or at any rate dynamic and vital, relationship among the units comprising the aggregation. An ecological distribution should be distinguished from a fortuitous or accidental distribution, where spatial relationships are, or seem to be, largely a matter of chance rather than the resultant of competing forces. For example, the aggregation of people waiting for the door of a theater to open represents a fortuitous spatial distribution; but their distribution in the theater, according to the kind of tickets they present, is a temporary ecological distribution. Although less complex and exacting, this distribution is quite similar to that which takes place in the community at large under conditions of free competition and choice.

The spatial distribution of economic utilities, shops, factories,

[2]   Note such studies as R. M. Hurd, *Principles of City Land Values* (1905); C. C. Evers, *Commercial Problems in Buildings* (1914); E. M. Fisher, *The Principles of Real-Estate Practice* (1923); Ely and Morehouse, *Elements of Land Economics* (1924); F. S. Babcock, *The Appraisal of Real Estate* (1924).

[3]   Such a study is being made by E. H. Shideler, "The Retail Business Organization as an Index of Community Organization" (in manuscript).

offices, is the product of the operation of ecological forces quite as much as is the distribution of residence. The business man who attempts to locate his factory or place of business with scientific exactness seeks the position of maximum advantage: that is, he seeks a point of equilibrium among competing forces. For this reason the value of location is always relative, and changes as one or more of the cooperating forces gain or lose in relative significance. A community, then, is an ecological distribution of people and services in which the spatial location of each unit is determined by its relation to all other units. A network of interrelated communities is likewise an ecological distribution. In fact, civilization, with its vast galaxy of communities, each of which is more or less dependent upon some or all of the others, may be thought of as an ecological distribution or organization.[4]

Ecological unit.—Any ecological distribution—whether of residences, shops, offices, or industrial plants—which has a unitary character sufficient to differentiate it from surrounding distributions may be called an "ecological constellation." The metropolitan area, with its various districts of residence, business, and industry integrated about a common center usually called the city is an ecological constellation. Such groupings may vary in degree of ecological interdependence from the conurbations which are found in each of the strategic areas of commerce and industry to the larger national or international communal federations linked financially and industrially with a metropolitan center such as London or New York.

Mobility and fluidity.—An ecological organization is in process of constant change, the rate depending upon the dynamics of cultural, and particularly technical, advance. Mobility is a measure of this rate of change; it is represented in change of residence, change of employment, or change of location of any utility or service. Mobility must be distinguished from fluidity, which represents movement without change of ecological position. Modern means of transportation and communication have greatly increased the fluidity of both people and commodities. Increased fluidity,

4   Ecological distribution, as here used, is synonymous with ecological organization.

however, does not necessarily imply increased mobility. In fact, it produces the opposite effect by making residence relatively independent of the place of work; also by extending the territorial zone in which the individual may seek the satisfaction of his wishes.

Fluidity tends to vary inversely with mobility. Slums are the most mobile but least fluid sections of a city. Their inhabitants come and go in continuous succession, but, while domiciled within a given area, have a smaller range of movement than the residents of any of the higher economic districts. The unequal fluidity of different districts of the city and of different individuals within the same district is an important factor in the processes of segregation and centralization. Youth tends to be more fluid than old age or childhood, giving rise to characteristically different centers of interest and varying regions of experience for each age group.

Distance.—Ecological distance is a measure of fluidity. It is a time-cost concept rather than a unit of space. It is measured by minutes and cents rather than by yards and miles. By time-cost measurement the distance from A to B may be farther than from B to A, provided B is upgrade from A.

Communal growth and structure are largely functions of ecological distance as a time-cost concept.[5] This basis of distance determines the currents of travel and traffic, which in turn determine the areas of concentration and the locations of cities. Likewise, communal structure is a response to distance in the local movements of commodities and people. The uneven expansion of cities along the routes of rapid and cheap transportation is but an obvious result of the time-cost measurement of distance. American cities, unlike European cities, are seldom circular in shape, owing to the fact that they have usually grown up without systematic planning, and therefore their intramural transportation is frequently less uniformly developed than is the case in most European cities. American cities—and this is particularly true since the advent of the automobile—tend to spread out in starlike fashion along the lines of rapid communication. The maximum linear distance from the periphery to the center of the city is seldom over an hour's travel by the prevailing form of transportation.

5   See *Plans of New York and Environs*, maps and diagrams, p. 27.

Ecological factors.—The changing spatial relations of human beings are the result of the interplay of a number of different forces, some of which have general significance throughout the entire cultural area in which they operate; others have limited reference, applying merely to a specific region or location. For instance, the shaft elevator, introduced in the seventies, and steel construction, introduced in the nineties, and the more recent advent of the automobile have acted as general factors in affecting the concentration of population and organization of communities. On the other hand, geographic factors, such as rivers, hills, lakes, and swamps, may have either general or limited significance with regard to ecological distribution, depending upon the pecularities of local conditions. Certain factors, such as bridges, public buildings, cemeteries, parks, and other institutions or forces have only limited significance in attracting or repelling population.

Ecological factors may be classified under four general heads: (1) geographical, which includes climatic, topographic, and resource conditions; (2) economic, which comprises a wide range and variety of phenomena such as the nature and organization of local industries, occupational distribution, and standard of living of the population; (3) cultural and technical, which include, in addition to the prevailing condition of the arts, the moral attitudes and taboos that are effective in the distribution of population and services; (4) political and administrative measures, such as tariff, taxation, immigration laws, and rules governing public utilities.

Ecological factors are either positive or negative; they either attract or repel. It is part of the task of the ecologist to measure the dispersive and integrative influence of typical communal institutions upon different elements of the population. Such knowledge would be of great value in city-planning, as it would enable the community to control the direction of its growth and structure. Effort must always be made to isolate the determining or limiting factors in a specific ecological situation.

Ecological processes.—By ecological process is meant the tendency in time toward special forms of spatial and sustenance groupings of the units comprising an ecological distribution. There are five major ecological processes: concentration, centralization, segregation, invasion, succession. Each of these has an opposite or negative aspect, and each includes one or more subsidiary processes.

Regional concentration.—This is the tendency of an increasing number of persons to settle in a given area or region. Density is a a measure of population concentration in a given area at a given time. World-population density maps indicate in a general way the significance of geographical factors in the distribution of human beings. While formerly the limits of concentration were defined by the conditions of local food supply, modern industrialism has created new regions of concentration, the limits of which are defined not by the local food supply but by the strategic significance of location with reference to commerce and industry.

The townward tendency is operating in every civilized country. As in other countries so in Japan the dominant characteristic of the new industrialism is the trend of population from the country to the city. . . . In the case of Tokyo, the capital, population during the last twenty-five years has increased from 857,780 to 2,500,000, while Osaka, the greatest industrial center of the Empire, during the same period has grown from 500,000 to over 1,500,000; Nagoya, from 200,000 to 450,000, Yokohama has increased fourfold, and Kobe, fivefold. The five greatest industrial centers above mentioned have thus increased 325 per cent, or 300 per cent more than the nation as a whole. . . . Great areas which ten years ago were taken up with rice fields or marshes are now reclaimed and covered with factories or labor tenements, and property values at the same time have gone up more than 1,000 per cent. . . . These cities may be justly taken as focal points to reveal the metamorphosis of Japan from a feudal to an agricultural country, and now to the age of steam, electricity, and steel.[6]

The territorial concentration of population resulting from industrialism and modern forms of transportation and communication is more dynamic and unpredicatable[7] than were the older concentrations controlled by factors of the local environment. Modern territorial concentration is never the result of natural population increase alone. It always represents the shifting of population from

[6]   *Present-Day Impressions of Japan* (1919), p. 539.
[7]   The census bureau has not recently published estimates of population increase for such dynamic cities as Los Angeles, Detroit, Seattle.

one territory to another. Practically all food-producing areas of countries which have come under the influence of modern machine industry have decreased in population during the last few decades.[8]

The limits of regional concentration of population in a world-economy of large-scale industry are determined by the relative competitive strength which the particular region possesses over other regions in the production and distribution of commodities. The degree of concentration attained by any locality is therefore a measure of its resource and location advantages as compared with those of its competitors. This strength is shown in the struggle for hinterland, raw materials, and markets, and depends upon the conditions of transportation and communication.[9]

Regional specialization—Regional specialization in production is the natural outcome of competition under prevailing conditions of transportation and communication. Territorial specialization has two points of special significance for the human ecologist. In the first place it produces an economic interdependence between different regions and communities which changes the sustenance relations not only of the individuals within the community but also of the different communities to one another. In the second place it makes for regional selection of population by age, sex, race, and nationality in conformity with the occupational requirements of the particular form of specialized production.[10]

[8]   None of our leading food-producing states during the decade 1910–20 showed a percentage increase in population equal to the increase for the country as a whole.

A recent study shows that three-fourths of Iowa's counties had from 20 to 30 per cent fewer people living on farms in 1920 than in 1885. Moreover, the farm population for the state as a whole decreased from 1,160,000 to 1,420,000 (*Wallaces' Farmer*, March 29).

[9]   The literature of economic geography is largely devoted to discussion of the factors determining strategic points of commerce and industry.

[10]   Few American cities at the present time have normal age and sex distribution of the population. The percentage of persons in the age group fifteen to forty-five is usually much higher for cities than for rural districts or for the country as a whole. Furthermore, industrial specialization tends to create single-sex cities. Textile cities such as Lowell, Paterson, New Bedford, have a predominance of women, while heavy-industry cities, such as Pittsburgh, Akron, Seattle, have a predominance of men.

Dispersion.—The obverse of concentration is dispersion. Concentration in one region usually implies dispersion in another. Steam transportation, by increasing the fluidity of commodities, ushered in a new epoch in regional concentration; motor and electric transportation, by increasing the fluidity of people, is now producing a new era in dispersion. Whatever retards the movement of commodities limits concentration, and whatever facilitates the movement of people makes for dispersion. The forces at work during the past few years have been favorable to dispersion. High freight-rates, high taxes, and labor costs are forcing many industries to disperse or relocate. On the other hand, the automobile and rapid-transit lines are permitting the concentrated urban populations to spread out over adjacent territory.

Centralization.—Centralization as an ecological process should be distinguished from concentration, which is mere regional aggregation. Centralization is an effect of the tendency of human beings to come together at definite locations for the satisfaction of specific common interests, such as work, play, business, education. The satisfaction of each specific interest may be found in a different region. Centralization, therefore, is a temporary form of concentration, an alternate operation of centripetal and centrifugal forces. Centralization implies an area of participation with center and circumference. It is the process of community formation. The fact that people come together at specific locations for the satisfaction of common interests affords a territorial basis for group consciousness and social control. Every communal unit, the village, town, city, and metropolis, is a function of the process of centralization.

The focal point of centralization in the modern community is the retail shopping center. The market place, at which buyers and sellers meet, has always had a potent centralizing or community-making significance. Since economic contacts are more abstract and impersonal than other kinds of contacts, the trade center has more general attractive significance, and therefore more community-making influence, than the school, the church, the theater, or any other type of interest center. It is retail shopping that creates the "Main Street" of the little town and the city of the metropolitan community.

The distance from the center to the periphery of any unit of centralization depends upon the degree of specialization which the center has attained and on the conditions of transportation and communication. In regions or districts where human energy is the chief motor power the units of centralization are seldom more than a few miles in radius, as is illustrated by the village communities of the Orient. In the agricultural town of America, prior to the advent of the automobile, Warren H. Wilson found that the "team-haul"[11] (the distance that a team could travel to the center and return on the same day) defined the outer limits of the trade area.

Focal points of centralization are invariably in competition with other points for the attention and patronage of the inhabitants of the surrounding area. Thus the present conditions of centralization always represent but a temporary stage of unstable equilibrium within a zone of competing centers. The degree of centralization at any particular center is, therefore, a measure of its relative drawing-power under existing cultural and economic conditions. The introduction of a new form of transportation, such as the automobile, completely disturbs the ecological equilibrium and makes for a reaccommodation on a new scale of distance.

Centralization under any given conditions of transit and concentration takes place in cumulative fashion, increasing with its own momentum until it reaches the point of equilibrium or saturation. Then, unless relief is afforded by the introduction of new avenues of transit, a retrograde movement commences, giving rise to new units of centralization or new developments of old units. In this way new communities are born within the metropolitan area.

Centralization may take place in two ways: first, by an addition to the number and variety of interests at a common location, as, for instance, when the rural trade center becomes also the locus of the school, church, post-office, and dance hall; second, by an increase in the number of persons finding satisfaction of a single interest at the same location.

Specialization and centralization.—As the regional concentration and fluidity of the population increases, territorial specialization of interest satisfaction follows. The urban area becomes studded with centers of various sizes and degrees of specializa-

[11]   *The American Town.*

tion, which is a magnet drawing to itself the appropriate age, sex, cultural, and economic groups. Time specialization takes place as well as place specialization. At different hours of the day and night the waves of selective centralization ebb and flow. As a New York bohemian facetiously remarked, the commuter's train carries to the city in the early morning the workers, an hour or so later the clerkers, and about midday the shirkers. A similar cycle is repeated by the night population of amusement-seekers.

Types of centers.—Communal points of centralization may be classified according to (1) size and importance as indicated by land values and concentration; (2) the dominant interest producing the centralization, such as work, business, amusement; (3) the distance or area of the zone of participation.

Every community has its main center called the main street, the town, or the city, which is a constellation of specialized centers. The larger the community, the more specialized are the divisions of its center and the wider the zone of patronage. Civilization is a product of centralization. The evolution of economic organization from village and town to metropolitan economy is but the extension and specialization of centralization of each of the dominant interests of life.[12]

Location and movement of centers.—Centralization is a function of transportation and communication. Centers are located where lines of traffic meet or intersect, and vary in importance, other things equal, with the number and variety of converging lines of transit. The "city" is the point of convergence of all the main avenues of transportation and communication, both local and intercommunal.

Most centers are responsive to the trends of distribution and segregation of the local population. The main retail shopping center, which is usually the point of highest land value, tends to move in the direction of the higher economic residential areas, but is held fairly close to the median center of population.[13] Local busi-

[12]   See N. S. B. Gras, *An Introduction to Economic History.*
[13]   The point of highest land value in the business center of Seattle has moved during the last fifty years in the same direction and at the same rate as the median center of population.

ness centers are more mobile; they respond quite accurately to local trends of segregation and fluidity. Financial centers are less responsive to the currents of travel. Being centers of wide participation, they tend to become of great physical value, and therefore acquire great stability.[14] Work centers are controlled by forces which frequently transcend the bounds of community; those of the basic manufacturing type tend to move out to the fringe of the community, thus making for decentralization.

Leisure-time centers, not associated with trade centers, are comparatively unstable, as is indicated by the dynamic changes in land values.[15] Conditions of concentration and fluidity become determining factors in their distribution. The motion-picture theater, operating on the chain-store principle, is causing new centers to be established far from the downtown center, and new white-light areas are arising in different sections of the city.[16]

Decentralization and recentralization.—These are but phases of the centralization process. New units of centralization are constantly appearing and established units constantly changing in significance.[17] By decentralization is meant the tendency for zone areas of centralization to decrease in size, which of course implies a multiplication of centers, each of relatively less importance. In this sense decentralization is taking place in all metropolitan areas with reference to some interests, while at the same time more extreme centralization is occurring in connection with other interests. In studying the process of centralization, therefore, it is important to find what particular aspects of life are being organized on the basis of smaller centers, what on the larger centers, and what seem to be the factors involved.

General observation leads one to believe that the centralization

---

[14]   Note the location and great stability of Wall Street.

[15]   See Felix Isman, *Real Estate* (1924).

[16]   This is well illustrated by the present tendency in Chicago. During the last few months three motion-picture theaters of the "superdreadnaught" type have been erected far out from the loop at pivotal intersections of transportation. Each represents an expenditure of from two and one half to three million dollars and has a seating capacity of about five thousand.

[17]   Note John T. Faris, *The Romance of Forgotten Towns* (1925).

of any interest varies directly with the element of choice involved in the satisfaction of the interest. Standardization of commodities, both in quality and in price, minimizes the element of choice, with the result that all primary standardized services tend to become more and more highly centralized.[18]

Segregation.—Segregation is used here with reference to the concentration of population types within a community. Every area of segregation is the result of the operation of a combination of forces of selection. There is usually, however, one attribute of selection that is more dominant than the others, and which becomes the determining factor of the particular segregation. Economic segregation is the most primary and general form. It results from economic competition and determines the basic units of the ecological distribution. Other attributes of segregation, such as language, race, or culture, function within the spheres of appropriate economic levels.

Economic segregation decreases in degree of homogeneity as we ascend the economic scale; the lower the economic level of an area, the more uniform the economic status of the inhabitants, because the narrower the range of choice. But as we ascend the economic scale each level affords wider choice, and therefore more cultural homogeneity.

The slum is the area of minimum choice. It is the product of compulsion rather than design. The slum, therefore, represents a homogeneous collection as far as economic competency is concerned, but a most heterogeneous aggregation in all other respects. Being an area of minimum choice, the slum serves as the reservoir for the economic wastes of the city. It also becomes the hiding-place for many services which are forbidden by the mores but which cater to the wishes of residents scattered throughout the community.

[18]   A study of the shopping habits of about two thousand families of a middle-class residential district in Seattle showed that about 90 per cent bought their groceries in the neighborhood; 70 per cent, their drugs; 50 per cent, their hardware and a smaller percentage, their furniture and clothes. In leisure-time activities, a much higher percentage attended local, rather than downtown, churches, but the opposite was true of the attendance at the moving-picture theater.

Invasion.—Invasion is a process of group displacement; it implies the encroachment of one area of segregation upon another, usually an adjoining area. The term "invasion," in the historic sense, implies the displacement of a higher by a lower cultural group. While this is perhaps the more common process in the local community, it is not, however, the only form of invasion. Frequently a higher economic group drives out the lower-income inhabitants, thus enacting a new cycle of the succession.

Invasion should be distinguished from atomatization; the latter is a consequence of individual displacement without consciousness of displacement or change in cultural level.

Succession.—In human and plant communities change seems to take place in cyclic fashion. Regions within a city pass through different stages of use and occupancy in a regularity of manner which may eventually be predictable and expressible in mathematical terms. The process of obsolescence and physical deterioration of buildings makes for a change in type of occupancy which operates in a downward tendency in rentals, selecting lower and lower income levels of population, until a new cycle is commenced, either by a complete change in use of the territory, such as a change from residence to business or by a new development of the old use, the change, say, from an apartment to a hotel-form of dwelling.

The thing that characterizes a succession is a complete change in population type between the first and last stages, or a complete change in use. While there is not the intimate connection between the different stages in a human succession that is found between the stages in a plant succession, nevertheless there is an economic continuity which makes the cycles in a human succession quite as pronounced and as inevitable as those in the plant succession. Real-estate investigators are beginning to plot the stages in use succession by mathematical formulas.

The entire community may pass through a series of successions, due to mutations of its economic base affecting its relative importance in the larger ecological constellation. The population type usually changes with the changing of the economic base, as, for instance, when an agricultural community changes to a mining or a manufacturing community.

Structure.—Ecological processes always operate within a more or less rigid structural base. The relative spatial fixity of the road and the establishment furnishes the base in which the ecological processes function. The fact that the movements of men and commodities follow narrow channels of rather fixed spatial significance gives a structural foundation to human spatial relations which is absent in the case of plant and animal communities.

The history of civilization shows a gradually increasing flexibility of the structural skeleton in which ecological processes operate. Prior to the advent of the railroad the movements of people and commodities were largely controlled by the course of the water systems: river, lakes, and seas. The coming of the railroads in the early part of the nineteenth century marked the first great release with regard to population distribution. New regions of concentration immediately arose, while old regions either declined or commenced a new cycle of growth. The advent of motor transportation and the good-roads movement affords a freedom to human distribution which is unique in history, making for a redistribution of people and institutions on a much more flexible base than was ever known before.

3

DEMOGRAPHY, HUMAN GEOGRAPHY, AND HUMAN ECOLOGY

1934

THE HUMAN community, in its material or physical aspects, includes three basic factors: population, geographic habitat, and material culture. For purposes of scientific inquiry, these three physically distinct but functionally interdependent classes of phenomena may be treated separately or as interrelated entities. The community may be considered abstractly as a population aggregate composed of individual persons having nothing in common save the fact that they occupy a limited geographical territory. The different human elements may be counted, classified according to common traits, and dealt with in a purely statistical and mathematical way. The same population group may be studied in its relation to the territory it occupies; that is, as a human agglomeration in process of adjustment to a specific physical environment. Again, it may be studied as an organic unit in which the symbiotic relations of the diverse human and cultural elements are the chief objects of attention. Thus considered, the population aggregate represents a functional association of human activities; in other words, a community.

For each of these three approaches to the study of a human community, a special discipline has arisen. The study of the human community as a population aggregate, pure and simple, has acquired the title of demography;[1] the study of the community from

---

Reprinted from *The Fields and Methods of Sociology*, ed. L. L. Bernard (New York: Ray Lang & Richard Smith, 1934), chap. 4.

[1] Term first used by Achille Guillard in his *Éléments de statistique humaine ou démographie comparée* (Paris, 1855).

the viewpoint of the relation between the population group and the physical habitat is the special function of geography; while the study of the community as a symbiotic unity has recently come to be known as human ecology.

Obviously, then, demography, geography, and human ecology are closely related branches of knowledge. They use much the same fundamental data, but differ in focus of attention and method of investigation. A brief survey of the trend in interest and research may help to disclose the essential differences and also the interrelations of these three disciplines.

Demography

Demography may be described in general terms as the study of population aggregates. Wolfe defines it more specifically as the "numerical analysis of the state and movement of human population, inclusive of census enumeration and registration of vital processes and of whatever quantitative statistical analysis can be made of the state and movement of population on the basis of fundamental census and registration data."[2] Demography, therefore, appears to have as its unique field the study of the vital processes of population aggregates. Its initial task is the taking of periodic inventories of population groups and the registration of vital processes. It then proceeds to classify and analyze its fundamental data and to ascertain the movements, vital and spatial, of the population group through time. Its method is statistical and mathematical, and its findings are basic to every other branch of social science.

The progress of demography as a science depends, therefore, upon the efficiency of census enumeration and vital registration; that is, upon the accuracy, extent, and comparability of the fundamental data. The relative backwardness of demographic science and of social science in general is due largely to the fact that census enumeration and vital registration of sufficient accuracy and regularity for statistical and mathematical analysis is of quite recent

[2] Wolfe, A. B., "Demography," *Encyclopedia of the Social Sciences*, 5:85–86.

origin. While a few countries have census and vital registration data of a fair degree of scientific value extending back for a hundred years or more, the practice of national bookkeeping has been developed for the most part within the last fifty years. Even today only about two-thirds of the population of the earth is enumerated at regular intervals. Moreover, vital registration in many countries, including the United States, has lagged far behind census enumeration.

In recent years, however, considerable advance has been made in both census and vital-registration procedure. Demographic data have increased in extent and reliability in most parts of the civilized world. The development in census enumeration has been particularly rapid in the United States. Each federal census since the middle of the nineteenth century has furnished the demographer and student of social science with an increasing volume of statistical information about the population of the nation. According to W. M. Steuart, Director of the Census, the 1930 census of the United States "will comprise more than 30 volumes containing something like 40,000 pages of printed matter, mostly statistical tables. This represents great expansion over the preceding census (1920) when the number of volumes was 11 and the number of printed pages about 14,000."[3] To be sure, a vast amount of this census material does not relate directly to population, but it furnishes the demographer with an almost unlimited range of data bearing directly or indirectly upon his subject.

The general widening of the range of statistical information relating to population has naturally increased the scope of demographic inquiry and has led to many specialized fields of investigation. The increasing efficiency of vital-registration and morbidity data has given rise to a division of demography in which the subject of attention is the health and vitality of the population. It has also furnished material for many specialized studies of vital processes. Improvement in statistics relating to international migration has opened a field of investigation pertaining to the geographic shifts of population. But this field of demographic inquiry has as yet progressed little beyond the descriptive stage; consisting

[3]   Letter to the author, October 21, 1932.

largely of the collection of data and the determination of the direction of migration.

Another specialized field of demography, but one which the demographer, for one reason or another, has been somewhat loath to enter, deals with the quality of population. So far, the demographer has limited his task to the description and statistical analysis of differential birthrates of various income and occupational classes of the population. The subject of eugenics has been left for the most part to the student of genetics and the social reformer.

The present stage of demographic inquiry represents the convergence of two somewhat different historic lines of approach to the study of population aggregates. First, the problem approach for which Malthus (1776–1834) set the stage; and second, the statistical and mathematical approach, the most notable early exponent of which was Quetelet (1798–1874), the Belgian astronomer and statistician who was a contemporary of Malthus. While the problem and statistical approaches to demography have never been completely separated, the main objects of attention down almost to the present day have been notably different. The one has emphasized the economic aspects of population growth; the other has stressed the description and analysis of vital tendencies. The former has led to the conceptualization of demography in terms of social problems, such as unemployment, poverty, standard of living, war; and has given rise to a number of subjective concepts —overpopulation, underpopulation, population optimum—which are not amenable to statistical treatment. The problem approach has given demography a peculiarly static connotation and has introduced much heated controversy into demographic investigation. Titles of some recent books reflect the emotional character of this approach: *Mankind at the Crossroads; Standing Room Only; The Shadow of the World's Future; The Menace of Color; Danger Spots in World Population.*

The statistical and mathematical approach on the other hand —the true demographic approach—has focused attention for the most part on the biosocial movements of population groups. Its concepts are objective and serve as tools in research. It is in this branch of demography that scientific progress has been made. The general tendency is for the broad population theorist, the person who inherited the Malthusian tradition, to become more of a demographer and less of a philosopher. Most of the recent texts on population abridge the space devoted to a discussion of general theories and stress the analysis of demographic data. This shift of emphasis is of course associated with the rapid increase in the available statistical data on population. Indeed the range of statistical information has become so extensive that the demographer is tempted to pursue his analysis of population into almost every aspect of social relations. Thus a recent textbook on population includes in its table of contents such subheadings as: "The High Cost of Manufacturing in Large Cities"; "Possibilities of Decentralizing Industry"; "Recreation"; "Music and Drama." This merely indicates that the demographer, like many of his colleagues in the other social-science disciplines, is no longer disposed to confine his attention to what is recognized as the core of his subject, but feels at liberty to carry his analyses into a wide zone of marginal territory.

Human Geography

While there has been rapid advance in demographic science along statistical and mathematical lines—that is, in the definition of terms, refinement of rates, computation of relationships, and the analysis of biosocial tendencies—surprisingly little progress has been made in the geographic phases of the subject. Statistical areas are almost as unscientifically determined today as they were half a century ago. The political unit—nation, state, county, city, or smaller civil division—still constitutes the statistical basis of census enumeration and vital registration. The reason for this is obvious. The purpose of a census is primarily political rather than scientific. It is to provide information for governmental and administrative action rather than for advancement of scientific knowledge.

The national unit in general furnishes an adequate statistical basis for ordinary demographic analysis. Its boundaries are sufficiently stable, and it usually has enough communal and cultural unity to warrant its use as a statistical area for analytic, comparative, and historical demography. The national unit serves the purposes of the descriptive and analytic demographer better than those of the populationist who is interested in computing ratios between numbers and bushels. With the growth of commerce and the general trend toward the economic interdependence of nations, the population theorist has been compelled more and more to compute his population-food ratios on a world rather than a national basis. He is still limited, however, due to the inadequacy of his data, largely to the field of speculation and prophecy. His hypotheses, though interesting, are not scientifically demonstrable.

It is with respect to the fractional units into which the nation is divided that the demographer, particularly the American demographer, has made the least progress. The limitations of the smaller statistical areas as units of demographic inquiry are self-evident. States and counties are purely arbitrary statistical areas with little or no direct relation to the natural grouping of population. The corporate areas of towns and cities coincide more closely with the actual facts of population patterning, but they are too unstable in boundaries to serve as adequate units for statistical purposes. This applies also to the subareas into which the large cities are divided for census enumeration. The development of the census tract, or small constant unit area, marks the first real advance that has been made in many years in the spatial aspects of demography in this country; however, this procedure is still limited to a few large cities.

Although demographers have paid little attention to the improvement of the spatial aspect of their subject, they attempt to show tendencies in demographic patterning as well as movements in vital processes. They measure and compare densities, and classify populations according to degree of nucleation, that is, according to urban-rural proportions. Such computations and comparisons are far from having the scientific validity that characterize the analysis of biosocial processes. It is impossible adequately to compare densities on the basis of present statistical areas. It is equally difficult to compare urbanization tendencies by the present unscientific procedure in territorial classification. This applies not merely to historical comparison within the country itself but more particularly to comparisons between countries. There is no uniform definition as yet, among the various countries, of the urban-rural concept. The minimum size of the population aggregate used in different countries as a criterion of urbanization ranges from 500 to 20,000.[4]

Demography and Human Geography

There is a close relation between demography and human geography. The demographer starts with population as his subject of inquiry and carries his investigation into the relation between population aggregates and the territory they occupy. The Malthusian populationist in particular is compelled to consider the geographical aspects of his problem. In order to compute his population-food ratios he must pay almost as much attention to the conditions of the habitat as to the vital tendencies of the inhabitants. The human geographer, on the other hand, focuses his attention upon the physical environment, and carries his analysis through to population and cultural considerations. Accordingly, the human geographer almost invariably becomes a populationist also. His interest, however, centers chiefly on the visual aspects of human settlement rather than on the statistical analysis of biosocial processes. The systematic geographer, who deals in a general way with the human world, traces the changing pattern of population distribution over the surface of the earth, interpreting it in terms of geographical and cultural factors. He classifies his geographical regions according to the influence they exert upon human activity. In recent years the geographer, at least the regional geographer, has tended to narrow his field of investigation to definite regions. His unit of study is the natural geographic region, in other words, "a district of more than local order of magnitude for which statements respecting forms in the natural or cultural landscapes apply throughout."[5] Beginning as he does with

[4]   Steuart, W. M., "Urbanization," *Encyclopaedia Brittanica* (14th ed.), 22:893–94.

[5]   Finch, V. C., "The Influence of Geology and Physiography upon the Industry, Commerce, and Life of a People as Described by Carl Ortwin Sauer and Others," *Methods in Social Science*, ed. Stuart A. Rice (1931), p. 238.

the unified physical region, he attempts to trace and measure the relations that exist between the conditions of the physical landscape and the superimposed cultural features. In this respect, the regional geographer is concerned with all the visual phenomena of his area, including the cultural activities as well as the population. To the extent that the census provides him with the details of population distribution, it serves as one of his sources of information. The geographer, however, does not rely entirely upon the demographer for his population data. By field investigation, he locates his agglomerations and studies in detail the relations of the human phenomena to the local geographical setting.

Human Ecology

Human ecology differs from demography and human geography in that the main object of attention is neither the population aggregate nor the physical-cultural habitat but rather the relations of man to man. The human ecologist, obtaining his point of view and some of his concepts from the plant and animal ecologists, concerns himself with the nexus of sustenance and place relations of the individuals and institutions which give the community its characteristic form and organization. Basic to the ecological idea is the concept of competition. The underlying assumption is that the fact of a struggle is associated with the function of order.[6] Competition among human beings involves struggle for position—that is, for a sustenance niche and a spatial location in which the individual or institution may survive and function.

The unit of ecological study is the communal organism, which is at once an aggregation of individual persons, a geographical and cultural habitat, and an interrelated and interdependent biosocial unity. The community thus conceived has many things in common with the plant and animal community. Its component units are bound together by the interdependence which arises out of specialization and division of labor. Its numbers are regulated in aggregate, and in each particular niche or occupation by com-

[6]   See Hamilton, Walton H., "Competition," *Encyclopedia of the Social Sciences*, 4:141–47.

petition. The characteristic form or spatial pattern of the community—the typical arrangement of population and institutions—is likewise conceived to be a function of competition and competitive-cooperation. The relations of the associational units in the human as in the plant and animal community are dynamic, ever changing in response to environmental factors and ever tending toward an equilibrium or balance. Equilibrium in the modern human community is largely a function of mobility.

The basic difference between human ecology and the ecologies of the lower organisms lies in the fact that man is capable of a higher level of behavior in his adaption process. As a cultural animal man creates, within limitations, his own habitat. Symbiotic relations in human society represent adjustments to a cultural as well as to a bio-geographic setting. And the fact that culture, or the superorganic, tends toward uniformity within the area of common dissemination of traits furnishes the basis for the similarity of spatial and symbiotic patterns found in widely separated human communities. The human ecologist attempts to discover, classify, and explain these typical features of human association. In this respect he differs from the geographer, who is concerned more with what is unique or different in the various areas of human habitation.

Research of a distinctly ecological character is limited and fragmentary. To be sure, there is a vast body of material scattered throughout the literature of social science that has ecological significance. But as yet no attempt has been made to systematize and interpret it from an ecological standpoint. The work done thus far pertaining most directly to the ecology of the community tends to fall into two different fields of attention: (1) studies of the spatial distribution of biosocial phenomena within the urban area, and (2) studies pertaining to the determination of the natural—as opposed to the political—boundaries of the local communal organism. The first group of studies originated in social surveys conducted for purely practical purposes, but there has been a gradual development of research in this field motivated by theoretical rather than by practical considerations. Such studies[7] as *The*

[7]   See bibliography.

Ghetto, The Gang, The Hobo, The Gold Coast and the Slum, dealing with segments of life in the city of Chicago, belong in this
latter category. Investigations of this type, however, are not confined to the purely ecological aspects of the situation. They usually
include data bearing on social behavior.

In 1923 E. W. Burgess sought to systematize the results of
studies made by graduate students in the city of Chicago, and to
interpret them in terms of a general, and what he considered to be
a typical, pattern of urban expansion. He developed the hypothesis
that a city grows in a characteristic fashion through the operation
of centrifugal and centripetal forces. By a series of concentric
circles radiating from the main business center of the city, he
gave graphic representation to what he conceived to be the "ideal"
pattern of urban expansion.[8]

On the basis of Burgess' hypothesis that urban expansion takes
place in a wavelike fashion from the center outward, giving rise
to cultural gradients overtly distinguished by types of dwellings
and human occupants, Shaw proceeded to compute juvenile delinquency rates in Chicago by concentric zones from the center of
the city to its periphery. His figure indicated a pronounced tendency for the rates to decline with each successive zone outward.[9]
He subsequently applied the same technique to a study of juvenile
delinquency in a number of other American cities and found a
similar gradient pattern of distribution.[10]

Meanwhile, R. C. White made a more extensive application of
Shaw's idea in a study of adult criminals and their offenses in the
city of Indianapolis.[11] Finding that adult crime in that city tended
to conform to the gradient pattern of distribution which Shaw
found for juvenile delinquency in Chicago, White developed the investigation further by correlating his criminal statistics with other

[8]   Burgess, E. W., "The Growth of the City: An Introduction to a
Research Project," *Pub. Amer. Sociol. Society*, 18:85–97 (1923).
[9]   Shaw, Clifford R., *Delinquency Areas* (1929).
[10]   Shaw, Clifford R., and McKay, Henry D., *Report on the Causes of
Crime*, vol. 2 (Washington: National Commission on Law Observance and
Enforcement, 1931).
[11]   White, R. Clyde, "The Relation of Felonies to Environmental Factors in Indianapolis," *Social Forces* 10 (May, 1932):498–509.

bio-social and economic phenomena, such as family welfare cases, general mortality rates, and percentage of land used for business purposes. He found a high degree of correlation among the phenomena, each series showing a gradient pattern directly or inversely correlated with the crime rate. This type of research indicates the value of the ecological approach to the study of urban social conditions and throws new light on the general processes involved in communal expansion.

The second type of ecological study, and one which has engaged the attention not merely of the ecologist but also of the community planner and business executive, is the attempt to delimit what might be termed the "natural" as opposed to the "administrative" boundaries of the communal unit. Interest in this subject originated with the rural sociologists. Some twenty years ago, C. J. Galpin issued a small bulletin entitled *A Method of Making a Social Survey of a Rural Community*,[12] in which he outlined a technique for determining the boundary of the actual as opposed to the legal village community. A few years later he amplified his technique in his classic little study, *The Social Anatomy of a Rural Community*.[13]

Galpin's idea, and more particularly his method, inaugurated a new era in rural social research. From general discussions of social conditions, students of rural life have turned their attention to more detailed studies of local relations within the village communal area. This new approach is basic to the rapid development of rural sociology in recent years.

Interest in delimiting the zones of city influence is of still more recent origin. In fact, most of the objective attempts to delimit the margins of the city community have been made within the last decade, and were motivated largely by practical rather than scientific considerations. The problem has two aspects. The first pertains to the determination of the margins of the local urban area, that is, the area inscribed by the daily shuttling of population

---

12   *Circular of Information*, no. 29 (University of Wisconsin Experiment Station, Madison, Wisconsin, 1912).
13   *Research Bull.*, no. 34 (University of Wisconsin Experiment Station, Madison, Wisconsin, May, 1915).

between residence and place of employment. This area tends to become an urban unit from the point of view of land utilization and the common use of municipal services. It is therefore considered as the logical territory for city planning and census purposes,[14] and is usually described in terms of population density and municipal functions. Ecologically it may be defined as the area in which local division of labor takes place in a direct and personal manner.

The second aspect of the problem, and one which has received much attention in recent years, is the delineation of the city's local marketing territory, that is, the surrounding area dominated by the city's business activities. Obviously the extent of this territory varies for different kinds of economic service. With the development of motor transportation, particularly the use of the motor truck in local shipments, the trade area has become the geographical unit of operation for an increasing number of business functions.

The first systematic attempt to divide the entire area of the nation into city-trading territories was made by the United States Bureau of Foreign and Domestic Commerce. In an atlas[15] published in 1927, the Bureau outlined the wholesale grocery trading territory tributary to each of the important warehouse centers in the United States. The boundaries of these trade areas were determined by actual merchandising practice as ascertained through correspondence with leading firms. Since then, this same government agency has made a number of commercial surveys of selected regions.[16] In these later studies, city trade areas are outlined by more careful field investigation. While the procedure adopted by the Bureau is more or less arbitrary, the work has served to stimulate general interest in the regional community concept. Most of

[14]   See Fifteenth Census of the United States, 1930, *Metropolitan Districts* (1932), pp. 5–6.
[15]   *Atlas of Wholesale Grocery Territories*, Domestic Commerce Series, no. 7 (U. S. Department of Commerce, 1927).
[16]   *Commercial Survey of the Pacific Southwest, Distribution of Dry Goods in the Gulf Southwest, Commercial Survey of the Pacific Northwest*, Domestic Commerce Series, nos. 37, 43, 51 (U. S. Department of Commerce, 1930, 1931, 1932).

the large cities of the nation have in recent years prepared maps of the territory which they consider as belonging to them by virtue of proximity and local communal dominance. Likewise newspapers and other advertising agencies catering to large distributors supply maps and statistical information regarding the scope and merit of the territory accessible to the leading key cities of the nation. While the bulk of this work has no scientific value, its very appearance indicates the rising consciousness of the community as an economic or functional entity rather than a political entity.

Interest in determining the geographic scope of the large city community is no longer limited to the man of affairs. The theoretical student has now taken up the subject. Park and Newcomb have approached it from the standpoint of newspaper circulation. Proceeding on the assumption that the territory dominated by the daily papers distributed from a given center is not only economically but also socially and perhaps culturally tributary to that city, Park and Newcomb have conducted intensive studies of newspaper circulation in the area surrounding Chicago and certain other mid-western cities. Their studies are designed to show not merely the territory dominated by the central metropolis but also the pattern of integration of the entire constellation of centers which make up the regional complex.[17]

The regional community, as defined in terms of function, offers a virgin field for ecological research. This complex type of communal organism, emerging in response to motor transportation, represents an institutional readjustment to a new scale of local distance. The functional or ecological region differs from the geographic region in that it is a product of contact and division of labor rather than of unity in physical environment. Structurally the ecological region is axial in form. The basic elements of its spatial pattern are centers, routes, and rims. It is composed of a constellation of centers, the interrelationship of which may be described as that of dominance and subordination. Every region

---

[17]   Park, Robert E., "Urbanization as Measured by Newspaper Circulation," *American Journal of Sociology* 25 (July, 1929): 60–79. This is part of an extended, but as yet unpublished, study made by Park and Newcomb of newspaper circulation in midwestern territory.

is organized around a main center composed of institutions and services which cater to the region as a whole and which integrate it with other regions. The subcenters are seldom complete in their institutional or service structure; they depend upon the main center for the more specialized and integrating functions.

Preliminary investigation and research relating to the regional community has been confined for the most part to attempts to define its area and to give statistical expression to its economic and human resources. While some progress has been made in this regard, no satisfactory technique has yet been devised for determining its various zones of influence or describing its *modus operandi*. Ecological research in this new field of practical and scientific interest requires for its development better statistical data than are available at the present time. In order to trace the important details of population patterning, the statistical areas of census enumeration must be smaller in size and more constant in boundary. It is highly desirable that the census tract, as at present applied to the incorporated areas of certain of our large cities, should be extended to include a much wider reach of regional territory.

Inasmuch as ecological research must take account of the movements of products and people and the spatial shifts of institutions and services, its progress depends upon the development of statistical data from which indices of these processes may be established.

In conclusion I should like to suggest the advisability of establishing a central statistical bureau in each large regional community in the United States. This bureau would collect and organize all official statisitcs relating to the region and would attempt to standardize and centralize unofficial statistics which have general value for the measurement of change in the internal organization of the community. It is obvious that the regional community has become the basic economic and social unit in American civilization, and, in fact, throughout the modern world. An understanding of the factors in its expansion and ecological organization can be obtained only by a more efficient procedure of social accounting.

Bibliography

Demography

Carr-Saunders, A. M., *The Population Problem*, 1922.

Dublin, Louis I. and Lotka, Alfred J., "On the True Rate of Natural Increase," *Journal of the American Statistical Association* 20 (1925): 305–39.

Field, James A., *Essays on Population*, ed. Helen Fisher Hohman, 1930.

Jerome, Harry, *Migration and Business Cycles*, 1926.

Koren, John, ed., *The History of Statistics*, 1918.

Kuczynski, R. R., *The Balance of Births and Deaths*, 2 vols., 1928–31.

———. *Fertility and Reproduction; Methods of Measuring the Balance of Births and Deaths*, 1932.

Newsholme, Arthur, *The Elements of Vital Statistics*, new ed., 1924.

Pearl, Raymond, *The Biology of Population Growth*, rev. ed., 1930.

Sanger, Margaret, ed., *Proceedings of the World Population Conference*, 1927.

Thompson, Warren S., *Population Problems*, 1930.

Whipple, G. C., *Vital Statistics: an Introduction to the Science of Demography*, 2d ed., 1923.

Willcox, Walter F., ed., *International Migrations*, 2 vols., 1929–31.

———. "Census," *Encyclopedia of the Social Sciences*, 3:295–300 (1930).

Human Geography

Barrows, H. H., "Geography as Human Ecology," *Annals Association of American Geographers* 13 (1923): 1–14.

Brunches, Jean, *Human Geography*, tr. T. R. LeCompte, 1920.

Colby, C. C., "The California Raisin Industry: A Study in Geographic Interpretation," *Annals Assn. Amer. Geographers* 14 (1924): 49–108.

Huntington, Ellsworth, *The Human Habitat*, 1927.

Ogilvie, A. G., *Great Britain: Essays in Regional Geography*, 1928.

Platt, R. S., "A Detail of Regional Geography," *Annals Assn. Amer. Geographers* 18 (1928): 81–126.

Ratzel, Friedrich, *Anthropogeographie*, 2 vols., 2nd ed., 1899–1912.

Sauer, C. O., "Geography of the Pennyroyal," *Kentucky Geological Survey*, 6th ser., 22 (1927).

Vidal de la Blanche, Paul, *Principles of Human Geography*, tr. Millicent T. Bingham, 1926.

Visher, S. S., "Social Geography," *Social Forces* 10 (Mar., 1932): 351–54.

Human Ecology

Anderson, Nels, *The Hobo*, 1923.

Baker, James, "Symbiosis: Prolegomenon to the Study of Ecology," *Science Progress* 25 (Jan., 1931) : 435–48.

Brocard, Lucien, "Regional Economy and Economic Regionalism," tr. F. Cyril James, *Annals of the American Academy of Political and Social Science* 112 (1932) : 81–92.

Burgess, E. W., ed., *The Urban Community*, 1925.

Child, C. M., *The Physiological Foundations of Behavior*, 1924.

Clements, F. E., *Plant Succession*, 1916.

Douglas, H. Paul, *The Surburban Trend*, 1925.

Durkheim, Emile, *De la division du travail social*, 1893.

Elton, Charles, *Animal Ecology*, 1927.

Gras, N. S. B., *An Introduction to Economic History*, 1922.

Hurd, Richard M., *Principles of City Land Values*, 1905.

McKenzie, R. D., *The Neighborhood: A Study of Local Life in the City of Columbus, Ohio*, 1923.

———. *The Metropolitan Community*, 1933.

Mantoux, Paul, *The Industrial Revolution in the Eighteenth Century*, tr. Marjorie Vernon, 1927.

Maunier, René, *L'origine et la fonction économique des villes*, 1910.

Park, R. E., Burgess, E. W., and McKenzie, R. D., *The City*, 1925.

Regional Survey of New York and its Environs, 8 vols., 1927–31.

Smith, Sir Hubert Llewellyn, director, *The New Survey of London Life and Labor*, 2 vols., 1930–32.

Thrasher, Frederick M., *The Gang*, 1927.

Wirth, Louis, *The Ghetto*, 1928.

Zorbaugh, Harvey W., *The Gold Coast and the Slum*, 1929.

II. The Local Community

4

THE NEIGHBORHOOD: A STUDY OF LOCAL LIFE IN THE CITY OF COLUMBUS, OHIO

1921

I. *City Structure*

COLUMBUS IS a city of about 210,000 inhabitants, according to the latest census. There are forty-three other cities in the United States which, from the point of view of population, fall in the same class.[1] Of these cities eleven are in the New England states, eight in the Middle Atlantic, seven in the East North Central, two in the West North Central, two in the Mountain, and five in the Pacific states.

Inasmuch as the modern city is largely an industrial institution it is important to know the nature of a city's leading industries. Eighteen of the cities in question have for their main industry the production of iron and steel products, eight have textiles and clothing, four lumber, three boots and shoes, three baking and confectionery, two publishing and printing, two preserving and canning, one rubber goods, one furniture, one jewelry, and one cotton-seed oil.[2]

Reprinted from *The American Journal of Sociology*, vol. 27, September, 1921, and November, 1921.

1   The estimated population of Columbus for 1916 was 209,722. It belongs to the third group of American cities, those having a population of 100,000 to 300,000. There was a total of forty-four cities in this group in 1916. *General Statistics of Cities* (1916).

2   This classification was made from the *Census of Manufactures*, vol. I (1914) and is based on census returns (1910). Undoubtedly in several instances the leading industry of 1910 is not the leading industry of today. The industry employing the greatest total number of employees was taken as the leading industry.

These cities may again be classified according to the relative importance of their leading industries. Nine of the forty-four cities of this group are characterized by the national importance of their major industries.[3] For example, Patterson, New Jersey, Fall River, Lowell, and Lawrence, located in Massachusetts, belong to the textile and clothing group and have their industries organized on a nation-wide sale of products. Similarly, Akron with its rubber goods, Grand Rapids with its furniture, Youngstown with its iron and steel products, represent the type of city with a single dominant industry organized on a national scale. The majority of the cities in this group, however, are not characterized by a single outstanding industry but possess numerous small industries of approximately the same size, the larger part of their business being limited to local trading areas. Cities with this type of industrial life may be called diversified cities.[4] Columbus belongs in this latter class.[5] It has three relatively important types of industry; foundry and machine-shop products; the construction of cars, locomotives, and heavy machinery, and the manufacture of boots and shoes.

Most of our great cities are circular or star shaped unless directly modified by geographical peculiarities. This structure is due to the inherent nature of city development when uncontrolled by conscious design. "Whatever the type of city, growth consists of movement away from the point of origin, and is of two kinds; central, or in all directions, and axial, or along the water courses, railroads, and turnpikes which form the framework of cities."[6]

[3]   Cities in which the major industry employed more than twice as many workers as the industry next in order, and more than the total listed for the classification "all other industries," I have classified here as "single-industry cities."

[4]   See C. A. Beard, *American City Government* (1912), pp. 26–29, for a classification of types of American municipalities.

[5]   Columbus, like almost every other city of its size, manufactures articles which are sold throughout the entire country, also in foreign lands, but Columbus is not dominated by any particular industry, nor does it have the habit of advertising in any of the national journals such as the *Post*, *Literary Digest*, etc.

[6]   Richard M. Hurd, *Principles of City Land Values (Record and Guide, 1903)*. Adapted as a reading in Marshall, Wright, and Field, *Materials for the Study of Elementary Economics* (1913), p. 620.

Columbus is shaped like a Greek cross. Its two leading thoroughfares, Broad and High streets, intersect at right angles near the junction of the Scioto and Olentangy rivers. High Street, the business backbone of the city, runs north and south for a distance of about nine miles within the corporation limits. Broad Street, on the other hand, runs east and west, or nearly so, and forms the arm of the cross. This street comprises part of the old Lincoln Highway. Topography has had something to do in determining the rough outlines of the city's structure. The junction of the two rivers just mentioned furnishes the basis for the crosslike appearance of the city. Expansion has followed the lines of least resistance along the south side of the Scioto River and the east bank of the Olentangy.

The distribution of business, industry, and population within the confines of any large city is determined by the operation of economic forces which tend to produce certain similarities of structure with respect to all big cities.

Generally speaking, the utility of land in the city falls into three classes: business utility, industrial utility, and residential utility. The areas devoted to these purposes are separated by more or less definite lines and are themselves subdivided according to the specific nature or class of use for each purpose. Business area for instance lies generally at the focus of local transportation routes or in other words at the point of intersection of the strongest lines of local travel. This point is very often at the geographical center of the city which can be reached from all sections of the city with equal facility. The industrial area on the other hand has no one definite location, as has the business area. Depending largely on railroad facilities, it soon becomes scattered throughout all sections of the city, forcing its way from all directions in wedges almost to the business heart. There is generally no control and no concentration other than that offered by the railroad lines. To residential purposes is devoted the rest of the land in the city. This is generally of three classes: fine residential area; general residential area; and tenement area. The first of these preempts those sections of the city which have the greatest number of pleasing and natural advantages. The second, in general, lies along the thoroughfares and highways which have the best transportation facilities and also along such railroads as provide suburban transportation. The third class, the tenement areas, are generally found in the industrial regions and in the pockets or areas that lie between railroad lines and close to the center.[7]

The central business section of Columbus, as indicated on Map I, is located near the geographical center of the city. It comprises an area of about half a mile in length and three blocks in width, the central part of which is the junction of the two streets already mentioned. This is the corner of the State House grounds, also the site of the city's leading hotel. One does not *feel* that he is "down town" until he reaches this corner.[8]

Immediately surrounding the central business section of most cities is to be found a more or less distinguished area, comprising wholesale establishments, low class hotels and apartment houses, second-hand stores, and cheap places of amusement. This region is usually inhabited by a migratory class of people, such as day laborers, immigrants, and negroes. It also tends to become the rendezvous of the vicious and criminal classes.

The factors distributing values over the city's area by attracting or repulsing various utilities, are, in the case of residences, absence of nuisances, good approach, favorable transportation facilities, moderate elevation, and parks; in the case of retail shops, passing street traffic, with a tendency toward proximity to their customer's residences; in the case of retail wholesalers and light manufacturing, proximity to the retail stores which are their customers; in the case of heavy wholesaling or manufacturing, proximity to transportation; and

[7]   E. H. Bennett, "Planning for Distribution of Industries," *Annals of the American Academy of Political and Social Science* (January, 1914), pp. 217–18.

[8]   Referring to the defects of the round city, John P. Fox, Secretary of the Transit Committee, City Club of New York, writes, "The round city, as found in America, tends to have a congested business center, with high buildings, high land values, high rents, congested streets and similar faults. It tends to require riding to and from work, especially if one wishes to live anywhere near the country. It requires too many radiating streets to reach surrounding territory, using more land than necessary. It makes it impossible to build one adequate rapid transit line to serve all the central district and the residence sections. It buries most people in its midst too far from the country, the latter being reached only by riding, which many poor people cannot afford to do" ("Relation between Transit and Housing," *Annals of the American Academy*, January, 1914, p. 160).

in the case of public or semi-public buildings, for historical reasons, proximity to the old business center; the land that is finally left being filled in with mingled cheap utilities, parasites of the stronger utilities, which give a low earning power to land otherwise valueless.[9]

Such a disintegrated area is quite conspicuous in the city of Columbus. Surrounding the main business section on all sides for a distance of from one to a dozen blocks there is a black and grimy area unfit for human habitation. Here cheap boarding houses and questionable hotels are wedged in between large warehouses and wholesale establishments. This region is very largely given over to colored people and poor whites.[10] Prior to the suppression of segregated vice in the city a considerable part of this section was occupied by keepers of immoral resorts. The eastern part of this district contained, in the early days, the homes of many of the wealthiest residents of the city. However, with the expansion of business and the development of modern means of transit, the well-to-do moved farther east along Broad Street, leaving their now obsolete homes to be used as places of business or to be subdivided into cheap apartments for the poor.

Most of our cities, due to their rapid growth, have districts that are going through a transition from resident districts to factory and business districts. Rents from dwellings are decreasing, while land value is greatly increasing. The owners of many of these homes, foreseeing the opportunity to sell the land for business purposes in one year or ten years, will not repair or improve their houses, because they argue it would be a waste to put more money in the houses that will in themselves bring no return when selling the land.[11]

The primary industries of most cities tend to be located near the outskirts of the city's corporation, along water fronts and railroad tracks. Smaller industries, especially those employing women

---

9   Richard M. Hurd, *op. cit.*, p. 620.
10   In his study of 4,500 employees in factories located in Norwood and Oakley, suburbs of Cincinnati, Graham Romney Taylor found that "nearly half, or 44.68 per cent, live in thickly populated parts of downtown Cincinnati, five miles from their work" (*Satellite Cities*, p. 97).
11   Mildred Chadsey, "The Old House as a Social Problem," *Annals of the American Academy*, January, 1914, p. 87.

and unskilled labor, seek low-priced areas near street-car lines and so may be located in almost any part of the city. Around the primary industries independent communities develop which have a life of their own distinct from the rest of the city, such, for example, as the stockyard district of Chicago. Subcommunities of another type, due to the difference of population selection, form around any important center, such as a university, park, school, or other public institution.

Transfer points, owing to concentration of daily streams of people and consequent opportunity to shops, are strategic points in a city's area, creating business subcenters, whose prospects of increasing values are limited only by the number and quality of the people likely to utilize them. As examples, note the marked effect of transfers in New York at Broadway and 34th Street, Madison Avenue and 59th Street, Lexington Avenue and 59th Street; also in New Haven at Chapel and Church streets; in Denver at 15th and Lawrence streets; and many transfer points in the outlying districts of Chicago.[12]

Columbus has three significant industrial communities. One is located in the twelfth ward and contains the plants of the Jeffrey Manufacturing Company, which employs about 4,000 men, and the High Malleable Company, which employs about 700 men. The second industrial area lies along the Scioto River, extending from First Avenue down to the center of the city. In this district are the plants of the Lamneck Furnace Company, the Nye and Sons Stove Company, and the Hulse Furniture Company. The third industrial section is found in the south end of Columbus. Here are the large steel industries of the city, including the Buckeye Steel Casting Company, the Columbus Branch of the American Rolling Mill Company, the Seagraves Manufacturing Company, and others. In addition to these manufacturing areas the shops of the different railroads form other industrial communities. The Hocking Valley Shops are located in a bend of the Scioto River in the western part of Ward 2, making this section of the ward much less stable than the remaining German part of it, which lies east of High Street. Similarly the large Pennsylvania Shops, located a short distance northeast of the United States barracks, account for the mixed foreign and negro section found there.

[12]   Richard M. Hurd, *op. cit.*, p. 622.

Each of these industrial areas has a more or less distinctive community life of its own. The residents of these communities are very largely people who work in the nearby industries. While their economic status is that of the day-laboring class, still their population elements comprise a mixture of practically all racial and national stocks. There is a distinct tendency, as may be seen by Map I, for the different racial and linguistic groups to form little colonies within these industrial communities. This is especially noticeable with respect to the industrial area surrounding the South Columbus Steel Works. This is a motley district, practically every street represents a different racial or national aggregation.

The population of any city is distributed according to economic status into residential areas of various rental or real estate values. Family income tends to segregate the population of a city into different economic districts much the same as the price of tickets at a theater divides the audience into several different strata of economic and social distinction.

The main consideration in the individual selection of a residence location is the desire to live among one's friends or among those whom one desires to have for friends; for which reason there will be as many residence neighborhoods in the city as there are social strata.[13]

In order to bring into relief the various levels of economic distribution of the population of Columbus a measure of comparative economic status was sought. It was finally decided to take the average per elector tax returns on household furniture as a standard of rating. Household furniture returns are listed from the home address rather than from the down-town office, and, therefore, furnish a territorial distribution of this sort of property. The returns were calculated by wards and the totals divided by the number of registered electors for the same year in each ward.[14]

The measure of economic status here adopted is not without its

13   *Ibid.*, p. 621.
14   The ward totals were divided by the number of registered electors rather than by the number of householders, inasmuch as each householder is allowed one hundred dollars tax exemption on furniture, and, therefore, in the lower economic regions only a small percentage of the families made returns at all.

shortcomings. In the first place the ward is not a homogeneous economic area. It frequently includes the extremes of wealth and poverty. This is true, for example, with respect to the sixth ward, the eastern end of which contains some of the most luxuriant homes in the city, while the western corner represents a broken-down colored section. But, on the whole, the classification of wards, as determined by this form of measurement, corresponds almost precisely with the common-sense rating as based on general observation. Map I indicates the results of this study.

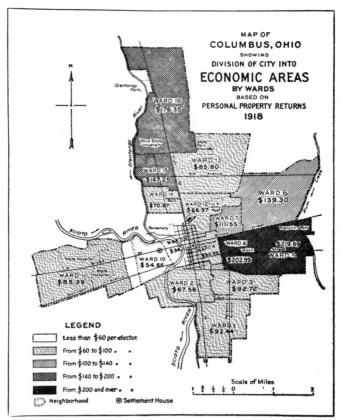

MAP I

The first impression gained from an examination of this map will be the striking difference in economic status of the various wards in the city. Wards 4 and 5 with their economic status of $202 and $219 respectively, stand in bold contrast to Wards 9 and 10 whose per elector status is less than one quarter as great. The latter wards are also the most mobile sections of the city. Wards 15 and 16 comprise the university district and represent the middle class type of home. The relatively low rating of Ward 11 is due to the presence of a large negro colony located near its southern border, also to a disintegrated neighborhood lying north of the State Hospital for the Insane. On the other hand, Ward 1 is probably rated a bit too high. This is a foreign locality surrounding the South Columbus Steel Works and our measure of economic status applies merely to citizens.

Racial and national sentiments tend to subgroup the population of the different economic areas of a city into more intimate social divisions. "Every great city has its racial colonies, like the Chinatowns of San Francisco and New York, the Little Sicily of Chicago, and various other less pronounced types."[15] Columbus has several such racial and national colonies, each with a more or less distinct social life of its own.

The colored population[16] is, in general, distributed around the periphery of the main business section, along the river flood plains, near the railroad tracks, and around the industrial plants. Most of Ward 9 is inhabited by colored people. During the past few years the colored families, especially the new arrivals from the South, have been pushing their way out into Ward 14, driving the Italians, who previously occupied this territory, still farther north. The northern boundary line of Ward 9, Goodale Street, is now

15   Robert E. Park, "The City: Suggestions for the Investigation of Human Behavior in the City Environment," *American Journal of Sociology* 20:582.
16   In 1910 Columbus had a colored population of 12,739, which, when compared with the total population of the city, constituted at that time a higher percentage of negroes than was to be found in any other city in the state. Moreover, this number has been greatly augmented by the influx of negroes from the South during the past few years.

almost entirely inhabited by negroes. The river end of this street, together with the immediately surrounding territory, was originally known as "Fly Town," receiving this name on account of the migratory tendencies of workers employed in the nearby factories, also on account of the lawlessness of the place. In this section the Godman Guild Social Settlement House is located.

The largest colored community in the city lies just east of the central business district. This community includes practically all of Ward 7 with the exception of a few streets on which are located some of the best residences in the city. It also extends into the southwestern corner of Ward 6, the eastern half of Ward 8, and the western part of Ward 4. The central part of this colored community lies north of Long Street between Seventeenth Street and Taylor Avenue. This region is indisputably surrendered to negroes. It is a city of black within the larger community. Here are found colored policemen, colored hotels, stores, churches, poolrooms, picture theaters, as well as separate colored schools. The colored people have their own local organization called "The Negro Republican League."

Of the minor negro colonies . . . attention should be called to the one in the extreme south end of the city, adjoining the steel plants; to the colored neighborhood in the eleventh ward, reference to which will be made later; to the colored district surrounding the Jeffrey Manufacturing Plant in Ward 12; and to the smaller colored localities adjoining the university campus.

Columbus has one large Jewish colony, lying a few blocks east of the southern end of the main business section of the city. This district is bounded on the north by Rich Street, on the east by Parsons Avenue, on the south by Livingston Avenue, and on the west by Grant Street. In this quadrangle, comprising about twelve city blocks, there is located the Jewish Schonthal Community House, Temple Israel, the Agudas, Achim Synagogue, Tiffereth Israel Synagogue, the Beth Jacob Synagogue, the Ahavath Sholen Synagogue, and the Jewish Progress Club. The area described, however, is not inhabited entirely by Hebrews. The population is a mixture of colored and Jewish people. This is the home of the

Orthodox Jews of Columbus.[17] The so-called "Reformed" Jews, which include, as a rule, the Jews of German nationality, are dispersed along the eastern section of the city in the better residential district between Broad Street and Bryden Road.

The renowned German section[18] of the city extends along South High Street from Livingston Avenue as far south as Washington Park, bounded on the east by Parson Avenue, and on the west by the Hocking Valley tracts. It comprises an area of about a square mile and falls, for the most part, within the second ward. Many of the most prominent of the old German families reside along High Street south of Livingston Avenue. Practically all of these families own their homes and many of them have resided here for over thirty years. The whole community, just outlined, is fundamentally German. The dwellings represent the typical German village structure, built close up to the sidewalk, with garden space and chicken house in the rear. Many of the alleys are lined with small residences. Frequently the owner of a fine home will have a small building on the rear of his lot occupied by a tenant family. The shops, churches, and other public places of this district are owned and operated by Germans, and the German language is used almost exclusively.

II. *Mobility*

"The city is the spectroscope of society; it analyzes and sifts the population, separating and classifying the diverse elements."[19]

17   This is the historic Jewish neighborhood of Columbus and is noted for the solidarity of its local life. Graham Taylor says, "The family-like fellowships persistently growing out of and around the Jewish synagogue, which is the most ancient type of the neighborhood still surviving, perpetuate the spirit of neighborliness and give it more or less flexible, but long accepted, forms of development" (*Religion in Social Action* [1913], p. 149.
18   According to the 1910 Census, Columbus had 5,722 foreign-born Germans, which was the largest single foreign-born nationality in the city (*Thirteenth Census of United States*, 3:428).
19   A. F. Weber, *The Growth of Cities in the Nineteenth Century* (1899), p. 442.

Mobility of population may be considered under three heads: change of residence from one community to another, change of residence from one neighborhood to another within the community, and mobility without change of residence.[20] The official sources of information on these subjects are very inadequate. The census reports furnish data concerning nationality and interstate migrations,[21] but aside from that we know nothing about the movements of people from one community to another,[22] much less the movements that take place within the community itself.

That the mobility of modern life is intimately connected with many of our social problems there is general consensus of opinion. Assuming that a reasonable amount of mobility is both inevitable and desirable, nevertheless, it is unquestionably true that the excessive population movements of modern times are fraught with many serious consequences.

Perhaps the most obvious effect of the mobility of the population within a city is the striking instability of local life. Neighborhoods are in a constant process of change; some improving, others deteriorating. Changes in incomes and rents are almost immediately registered in change of family domicile. Strengthened economic status usually implies the movement of a family from a poorer to a better neighborhood, while weakened economic status means that the family must retire to a cheaper and less desirable

[20]   Robert E. Park says, "Mobility in an individual or in a population is measured, not merely by change of location, but rather by the number and variety of the stimulations to which the individual or the population responds. Mobility depends, not merely upon transportation, but upon communication" (*American Journal of Sociology* 20:589).

[21]   The 1910 Census records the percentage of the population of each state born within the state. This gives a general impression of the relative mobility of the different states. The percentage of people born within the state in which they were counted varies from 94.7 for North Carolina to 21.8 for Wyoming. Ohio is above the average in stability with a percentage of native born of 74.4 (*Thirteenth Census of United States*, 1:712).

[22]   See Bucher's *Industrial Evolution* (Wickett translation), chap. 10, for an interesting study of internal migrations of population in Germany. He shows that of the population of Prussia in 1880, 57.6 per cent were born in the municipality where enumerated (p. 354), and for Bavaria (1871) 61.2 per cent (p. 355).

district.[23] So in every city we have two general types of neighborhood; the one whose inhabitants have located there on the
basis of personal choice, and the other whose inhabitants have
located there as a result of economic compulsion. The former, as
we shall see later, contains the possibilities for the development of
neighborhood sentiment and organization, while the latter lacks
the necessary elements for reconstruction.

Rapid community turnover also plays havoc with local standards and neighborhood mores. It is impossible to have an efficient
local opinion in a neighborhood where the people are in constant
move. It has repeatedly been affirmed by students of society that
the decay of local standards is a pertinent cause of moral laxness
and disorderliness.

We are dependent for moral health upon intimate association with
a group of some sort, usually consisting of our family, neighbors, and
other friends. It is the interchange of ideas and feelings with this
group, and a constant sense of its opinions that makes standards to
right and wrong seem real to us. . . . When we move to town, or go to
another country, or get into a different social class, or adopt ideas that
alienate us from our former associates, it is not at all certain that we
shall form new relations equally intimate and cogent with the old.
A common result, therefore, is a partial moral isolation and atrophy
of moral sense. If the causes of change are at all general we may have
great populations made up largely of such displaced units, a kind of
"anarchy of spirits" among whom there is no ethos or settled system
of moral life at all, only a confused outbreak of impulses, better or
worse.[24]

The flux of modern life also intensifies all problems connected
with government, national, state, or local. The fact that we have
a residence qualification for voting leaves an increasingly large
number every year of disfranchised citizens. This too applies espe-

---

23   "A study of five hundred families who, in 1913, moved from one
home to another has clearly shown that in 63 per cent of the cases poorer
accommodations were secured because of a recent change in the family income which caused a necessary change in the amount of rent that could
be spared" (Carol Aronovici, *Housing and the Problem* [1920], p. 20).
24   C. H. Cooley, *Social Process*, pp. 180–81.

cially to a class, the migrant laborer, which has no other means of participation in social control.

Our distinguished critic, James Bryce, drew attention years ago to the relation between mobility and government.

In no state of the union is the bulk of the population so fixed in its residence as everywhere in Europe; in many it is almost nomadic. Except in some of the stagnant districts of the South, nobody feels rooted to the soil. Here today and gone tomorrow, he cannot readily contract habits of trustful dependence on his neighbors. Community of interest or of belief in such a cause as temperance, or protection for native industry, unites him for a time with others similarly minded, but congenial spirits seldom live long enough together to form a school or type of local opinion which develops strength and becomes a proselytizing force. Perhaps this tends to prevent the growth of variety of opinion. When a man arises with some power of original thought in politics, he is feeble if isolated, and is depressed by his insignificance, whereas if he grows up in a favorable soil with sympathetic minds around him, whom he can in prolonged intercourse permeate with his ideas, he learns to speak with confidence and soars on the wings of his disciples. One who considers the variety of conditions under which men live in America may certainly find ground for surprise that there should be so few independent schools of opinion.[25]

Students of municipal government are constantly calling attention to the difficulty of creating interest in municipal affairs among people who are in constant move.[26] Stability of residence as a rule implies home ownership, which in turn gives rise to local sentiment and interest in neighborhood surroundings. In a region where the population is continually shifting there is little opportunity for the development of neighborhood sentiment, and as a result, local concerns are usually left to take care of themselves. It is hard to develop interest in neighborhood affairs among fam-

[25]   *American Commonwealth*, 2 (1907) : 289–90.
[26]   Hart (*Actual Government*, pp. 210–11) points out that the American habit of moving is an important cause of bad city government. Goodwin in his *Municipal Government*, p. 26, also emphasizes the relation of population movement to the problem of local government.

ilies who are the while conscious of the temporary nature of their domicile within the district.

The problems which the mobility of population presents to political reformers are likewise common to social workers in other fields. Organizations dealing with delinquency and dependency are hampered in their efforts by the frequent movements of their "cases."[27] Similarly the church, trade union, and other voluntary forms of association lose in their efficiency through the rapid turn-over of their local membership lists.[28]

In considering the general causes of the present mobility of population it is important to view the subject from both its psychological and its social aspects. Thomas and Znaniecki have grouped the dominant individual wishes or desires into four general classes: "the desire for recognition or status; the desire for safety or security; the desire for power; the desire for new experiences."[29] It is of course obvious that the relative strength of these different desires varies in different individuals and at different ages in the

[27]   In a study of 324 newly "closed" cases in the records of the Social Welfare League of Seattle, it was found that the average length of time the families were under the jurisdiction of the organization was five months; and the average number of changes of residence during that period was 2.2. Moreover, 45.8 per cent of the cases were closed because the family had moved away from the city.

[28]   In a study made of 2,049 resignations from the Seattle Chamber of Commerce (June, 1917, to December, 1920), Mr. Suen Chen, a student in sociology, discovered that 764 or 37.3 per cent of those resigning had been members of the organization less than one year; 787 or 38.3 per cent had been members more than one year but less than two years; 328 or 16.1 per cent had been members more than two years but less than three years; while the remaining 170 or 8.1 per cent had been members three years or more. Moreover, 604 or 29.4 per cent of the total number resigning gave as their reason for leaving the organization change of residence to another community.

The present membership of the Seattle Chamber of Commerce (December, 1920) is 3,034; of this number 634 or 20.9 per cent have been members for one year or less; 1,197 or 39.4 per cent have been members for two years or less; and 1,517 or half the total number have been members for three years or less.

[29]   *The Polish Peasant in Europe and America* (1918), 1:73.

same individual. E. L. Thorndike says, "old age, femaleness, and physical weakness" seem to favor "the long familiar physical and social environment," while "adolescence, maleness, and energy"[30] seem to be combined with the roaming disposition.

Of the four types of desires just mentioned, the desires for security and recognition find their chief satisfactions in the solidarity and intimacy of the small local group; while the desires for power and new experience attain their fullest fruition in a wider social milieu. The rigoristic codes of the small stable community have never afforded adequate satisfaction to the human impulses of the more energetic members of the group. The solidarity of the primitive neighborhood group was undoubtedly, to a greater extent, the product of a hostile external environment rather than the result of spontaneous human impulses. As Struckenberg says, "Frequently the inherent qualities of men have less power to unite than the desire to antagonize what is averse to them. . . . Prejudice, hatred, and opposition are powerful factors in association."[31]

Adam Smith contrasts the strong clan-feeling which still in the eighteenth century prevailed among the Scotch Highlanders with the little regard felt for remote relatives by the English, and observes that in countries where the authority of the law is not sufficiently strong to give security to every member of the State the different branches of the same family choose to live in the neighborhood of one another, their association being frequently necessary for their common defence: whereas in a country like England, where the authority of the law was well established, "the descendants of the same family, having no such motive for keeping together, naturally separate and disperse, as interest or inclination may direct.[32]

On the social side it is scarcely necessary to draw attention to the leading causes of intercommunity migration. The sudden change from a predominantly agricultural to a predominantly industrial society has occasioned a mobility of life unknown before. As long as the soil furnished the chief basis of economic income man was obliged to live a comparatively stable life in a fixed and

---

[30]   *Original Nature of Man* (1913), 1:56.
[31]   *Sociology, the Science of Human Society*, 1:86.
[32]   E. Westermarck, *Moral Ideas* (1908), 2:223.

definite locality. With the development of the modern capitalistic regime, the presence of the individual is no longer necessary to insure the productivity and security of his property. He may now, if he chooses, invest his savings in interest-bearing securities which require neither his personal presence nor his attention to insure an income. He is thus left free to live, if he so desires, a nomad life.[33] Of course all classes in society are not equally free to move about. The middle-class tradesman and many of the professional groups are more or less tied to definite localities by the very nature of their work. On the other hand, the well-to-do and the day-laborer are free to move almost at will.

Our modern factory system is the chief cause of the present migratory tendencies of the wage-earning class. In an open labor market with employers competing with one another in their demands for labor, the wage earner is fast becoming a sort of tourist who spends but a short period in each community during his trip around the country.

Seasonal or intermittent occupations, temporary jobs, commercial depressions, occasional unemployment, and a general sense of the lack of permanency in the tenure of their industrial positions, pull settled families up by the roots and seldom leave them long enough in one place to take root again. Our manual workers are more and more transient. Many among them are forced to become tramping families.[34]

Moreover, change of residence from one section to another within the community is quite as disturbing to neighborhood association as its movement from one community to another. In order to get an idea of the comparative mobility of the population of the various local areas in Columbus, a study was made of the changes in the lists of the registered electors during the period of one year. The records of each year's registration are listed by precincts by the city's Board of Elections. The 1917 list of names was compared with the 1918 list, and the percentage of names per precinct of the

33   See Bodkin, *Problems of Modern Democracy*, pp. 180 ff., for a brief discussion of this subject.
34   Graham Taylor, *Religion in Social Action* (1913), pp. 143–44.

1917 list that reappeared in the 1918 list was taken as a measure of the relative stability of the precinct. For example, if a certain precinct had 100 registered electors for 1917 and only 75 of these names reappeared in the 1918 list, the percentage stability of that precinct would be rated as 75. The city is divided into 262 precincts, each of which comprises about two or three blocks. The average registered electorate per precinct was, in 1918, 175. From this small geographical unit it is possible to get a rather intimate knowledge of the extent of local mobility of population.

Taking the city as a whole, only 58.6 per cent of the registered electors of 1917 re-registered in 1918. In other words, of the qualified voters of 1917, almost one-half failed to requalify to vote in their old precincts in 1918. The percentage of registration of electors varies greatly, of course, in the different sections of the city, precincts ranging from 31.0 per cent to 77.8 per cent. The most mobile precinct is located in Ward 9 near the Scioto River, while the most stable precinct lies in the center of the old German neighborhood in the northern corner of Ward I.

. . . Failure to re-register is not definite proof that the elector has migrated from the confines of his precinct. He may merely have omitted to perform this privilege of citizenship. On the other hand, movements of non-citizens are not recorded in this study. But, despite these limitations, I believe the method here employed furnishes an approximately true picture of the comparative population movements of different sections of the city.

It is quite evident . . . that the down-town section, including the main business area and its immediately surrounding territory, is by far the most mobile part of the city. But this is to be expected, considering the nature of this section. As we have already seen, most of the people living near the business center are of the boarding-house and cheap hotel class. The more stable parts of the city are to be found, for the most part, in the better residential districts, in the eastern, northern, and western extremities of the city. The large German neighborhoor, lying immediately south of the main business section, practically all falls in the class of highest stability, while the industrial area, located farther south in Ward I, comprises one of the most mobile sections of Columbus.

The correlation between stability and economic status is quite interesting. . . . Taking the ward averages for stability and comparing them with the ward averages for economic status, we get the result shown in Table I.

TABLE I

RELATION BETWEEN WARD STABILITY AND ECONOMIC STATUS

Ward	Average Re-registration per Ward (per cent)	Average Economic Status per Ward
9	43.7	$ 34.11
8	44.4	80.55
12	50.6	66.97
15	53.7	147.25
13	57.7	85.80
14	57.7	70.87
1	60.4	92.44
10	60.6	54.66
7	60.6	111.55
6	61.9	139.30
2	62.9	67.56
16	63.1	176.35
11	64.1	85.39
4	65.3	202.99
5	65.5	219.89
3	66.0	92.72

This table shows, in general, that stability varies directly with economic status. For example, Ward 9, which has the lowest economic status of all the wards in the city, has also the lowest re-registration of electors, which means the lowest stability. On the other hand, Wards 4, 5, and 16 fall considerably above the average in stability, and rank high in economic status. Wards 2 and 3 appear to be exceptions; they have high stability and low economic status. But as we have already seen, these wards contain the large stable German neighborhood, the residents of which, while home owners and relatively prosperous, maintain a lower standard of living than the average American of similar economic status.

Let us now examine the relation between mobility, dependency, and juvenile delinquency. The two spot maps (IV and V) show the geographical distribution of the official cases of dependency and juvenile delinquency for a one-year period, May, 1918, to May, 1919. As might be expected, the majority of the dependency cases are segregated in the low economic areas surrounding the central business district. The colored cases form conspicuous groups near the railroad tracks and the river, also in the eastern part of the city near Franklin Park.

The most striking feature concerning the geographical distribution of juvenile delinquency is the rather even dispersion of cases throughout the entire city. Single streets or individual family groups rather than neighborhoods seem to form the nuclei for wayward children. There is, apparently, but slight correlation between the segregation of dependency and that of delinquency.

It will be observed [from Table II] that Wards 8, 9, and 12, which comprise the central part of the city, and which rank highest in mobility, also rank high in extent of both dependency and delinquency; while Wards 4, 5, 15, and 16 rank high in stability and have relatively little dependency or delinquency. However, the relation between mobility and dependency is much more conspicuous than the relation between mobility and delinquency. For example, Wards 13 and 14 have almost average stability but rank highest for the whole city in their percentages of juvenile delinquency. These two wards happen to include industrial areas and have comparatively large colored and immigrant populations.

While our method of measuring mobility does not indicate whether the movements of families are from one community to another or from one neighborhood to another within the community, still a few sample cases seem to show the latter type of movement predominates. For instance, in Ward 9, out of the total 743 registered electors for 1917 whose names reappeared in the 1918 list, 141, or an average of 19.1 per cent, were listed with different street adresses within the confines of their respective precincts.

TABLE II

WARD VARIATIONS IN STABILITY, DEPENDENCY, AND JUVENILE DELINQUENCY

WARD	NUMBER OF* REGISTERED VOTERS FOR 1918	STABILITY†	CASES OF DEPENDENCY‡		CASES OF DELINQUENCY	
			No.	Percentage	No.	Percentage
9............	1757	43.7	82	4.67	27	1.54
8............	2225	44.4	75	3.37	26	1.17
12............	2062	50.6	94	4.56	25	1.21
15............	2661	53.7	23	.86	12	.45
13............	3062	57.7	51	1.67	49	1.60
14............	2344	57.7	58	2.47	39	1.66
1............	2950	60.4	58	1.79	45	1.53
10............	2477	60.6	82	3.31	35	1.41
7............	2721	60.6	44	1.62	23	.85
6............	2995	61.9	65	2.17	32	1.07
2............	2496	62.9	57	2.28	32	1.28
16............	4540	63.1	24	.51	18	.39
11............	3171	64.1	53	1.67	28	.88
4............	2884	65.3	56	1.94	19	.66
5............	3477	65.5	26	.74	12	.35
3............	3635	66.0	45	1.24	34	.94
Total........	45,457	....	893	....	456	....
Average for city	....	58.6	....	1.97	....	1.00

* The number of registered electors furnishes our only clue to the ward populations of the city, as the ward boundaries have been modified since the 1910 census was taken.

† The term "stability" implies here, as formerly, the percentage of the 1917 electors who re-registered in the same precincts in 1918.

‡ The cases of dependency and delinquency here recorded are known in the organizations concerned as "official cases," that is, they are the more permanent and serious cases with which the organizations have to deal.

When it is recalled that the precinct in Columbus comprises a very small area of but on or two city blocks, it is obvious that quite a considerable amount of mobility is from house to house within the same neighborhood. Another sounding was taken in Ward 16, an area of higher economic status. All the families in a single block were canvassed. Of the fifty-one families visited, eleven had been on the street less than one year, thirty-two less than five years, and the remainder from five to ten years. Forty-one families had moved to the street from some other section of Columbus, and of this number, twenty-eight had moved to the street from the immediately surrounding neighborhood.

Again, there is a type of mobility that is not indicated by

change of residence, but which is almost as significant from the standpoint of neighborhood life. This is measured by the ability of the individual, due to modern methods of communication, to utilize the larger social environment afforded by the community as a whole. The automobile, street car, telephone, and press, together with increased leisure time, have all contributed greatly to the breakdown of neighborhood ties. Moreover, the disintegrating effects of these modern means of communication are not confined to the city alone. They have equal significance with reference to life in the country. To quote Cooley:

In our own life the intimacy of the neighborhood has been broken up by the growth of an intricate mesh of wider contacts which leaves us strangers to people who live in the same house. And even in the country the same principle is at work, though less obviously, diminishing our economic and spiritual community with our neighbors.[35]

Warren Wilson says:

In those states in which the trolley system has been extended into the country, for instance Ohio and Indiana, the process of weakening the country population has been hastened. Sunday becomes for country people a day for visiting the town and in great numbers they gather at the interurban stations. The city and town on Sunday is filled with careless, hurrying groups of visitors, sight-seers and callers, who have no such fixed interest as that expressed in church-going or in substantial social processes. For the time being interurban trolley lines have dissipated the life of the country communities.

Referring to the use of the telephone and rural free delivery Wilson continues:

The old acquaintance and the intimate social relations of the country community have not been helped by the telephone; and along with the presence of aliens in the community, one quarter or one half or three quarters of the population, the telephone has had the effect of lowering the standards of intimacy and separating the households in the country from one another. The Rural Free Delivery has put the country people into the general world economy and for the time being has loosened the bonds of community life.[36]

[35]   *Social Organization* (1912), p. 26.
[36]   *The Evolution of the Country Community*, p. 128.

It is an obvious fact that in isolated rural communities or backward city neighborhoods where the telephone has not become an instrument of common usage and where poverty restricts the use of secondary means of transportation, or where linguistic barriers prevent communication with the outside world, in such neighborhoods are to be found the best examples of the old neighborly forms of association. I shall, however, reserve for a later chapter the discussion of the influences of secondary means of communication upon social life in a city neighborhood.

III. *The Neighborhood*

The general effect of the continuous sifting and sorting of a city's population, as we have seen in the foregoing chapters, is to produce a patchwork of local areas differentiated from one another by cultural, racial, or linguistic peculiarities. In common parlance such areas are usually designated as localities, districts, colonies, or neighborhoods. Since the neighborhood is one of our oldest social institutions and since it is again coming into the focus of attention of writers on urban questions,[37] let us briefly examine its applicability to local life in the city environment.

Probably no other term is used so loosely or with such changing content as the term neighborhood, and very few concepts are more difficult to define. The word neighborhood has two general connotations: physical proximity to a given object of attention, and intimacy of association among people living in close proximity to one another. On the flat plains of the agricultural states there are no objective marks by means of which the stranger can distinguish one rural neighborhood from another, yet almost any individual approached can give a very definite answer as to what constitutes his neighborhood; it simply embraces the area round about his home in which reside those families with whom he has intimate and direct personal relations.

In the city, on the other hand, there are very distinct objective differences between the various residential areas, but little or no personal acquaintance or group association among the families of

[37]   See e.g., such recent books as M. P. Follett's *The New State* (1918), and John Daniel's *America via the Neighborhood* (1920).

any particular area. It is on account of these peculiarities of city life that we find so many different usages of the term neighborhood. Some writers are accustomed to use the word as implying mere physical proximity to a certain institution or topographical feature.[38] Others refer to the neighborhood as a cultural area,[39] sufficiently differentiated from the surrounding territory to be considered as a unit, while others again use the word in its traditional sense as implying intimacy of association[40] and personal acquaintance.

The concept neighborhood has come down to us from a distant past and therefore has connotations which scarcely fit the facts when applied to a patch of life in a modern large city. As far back

[38]   Stuckenberg, *Sociology* (1903), 1:81.

[39]   Park defines the neighborhood, "The City: Suggestions for the Investigation of Human Behavior in the City Environment" (*American Journal of Sociology* 20:579), as "a locality with sentiments, traditions, and a history of its own."

[40]   Cooley lists the neighborhood as an example of a "primary group" (see *Social Organization*, chap. 3) and he defines a "primary group" elsewhere (*Amer. Jour. of Sociol.* 25:327) as "an *intimate* group, the intimacy covering a considerable period and resulting in a habitual sympathy, the mind of each being filled with a sense of the mind of the others, so that the group as a whole is the chief sphere of the social self for each individual in it of emulation, ambition, resentment, loyalty, etc." Kellogg in a rather vague way says, "the neighborhood is an intermediate group between the family and the city, among those communal organizations in which people *live* as distinct from purposeful organizations in which they *work* (*Charities and Correction* [1909], p. 176). Taylor (*Religion in Social Action*, p. 166) states that "the neighborhood is to be regarded as an extension of the home and the church, and is identified closely with both." Wood refers to the neighborhood (*Amer. Jour. of Sociol.* 19:580), as "the most satisfactory and illuminating form of the social extension of personality, of the interlacing and comprehensive complex of the interplay of personalities; the social unit which can by its clear definition of outline, its inner organic completeness, its hair-trigger reactions, be fairly considered as functioning like a social mind." Sanderson (*Publications of the American Sociological Society* 14:86–87) distinguishes between the community and the neighborhood as follows: "the community is the smallest geographical unit of organized association of the chief human activities; . . . the neighborhood is the smallest association group of families, with regard to place; it has no organization of activities."

as we have record, human society seems to have been composed of a vast number of small, intimate groups more or less definitely attached to fixed localities.

W. G. Sumner says (*Folkways*, p. 12), "The concept of 'primitive society' which we ought to form is that of small groups scattered over a territory." Most of the native peoples of the present day live in small neighborhood groups knit together by notions of kinship, common custom, and local feeling. The Dyaks of Borneo live in small villages, "each of which is inhabited by a dozen families and sometimes by several hundred persons, peacefully living together" (P. Kropotkin, *Mutual Aid* [1907], p. 110). "The Arunta of Central Australia are distributed in a large number of small local groups, each of which occupies a given area of country and has its own headman . . . and the members of each group are bound together by a strong 'local feeling' " (Edward Westermarck, *Moral Ideas*, vol. 2 [1908]: 199). L. T. Hobhouse relates that "the Yahgans . . . live in small groups of three or four families, without any regular clan organization, though with fairly well established customs to which the feeling of the community lends support, a support which is frequently vindicated by force of arms. . . . The Veddahs consist of a mere handful of scattered families living sometimes in trees, in the rainy season often in caves, though they are capable of making primitive huts. They are hunters, and each Veddah, with his wife and family, keeps his hunting ground for the most part scrupulously to himself" (*Morals in Evolution* [1906], part 1, pp. 43–47). Referring to the Yakuts of Siberia, Sumner says (quoted by Thomas, *Social Origins*, p. 83), "The largest number of settlements contain four or five huts, with twenty or thirty souls." Similar examples might be added indefinitely.

The group forming habit of human beings is, of course, a biological inheritance from our prehuman ancestors. As Shaler says (*The Neighbor*, pp. 52–53), "the tribal habit of man is not an invention made by him. It evidently was inherited from his ancestors of the lower life, for among all Quadrumana clearly to be reckoned his collateral but near organic and psychic kinsmen, this social habit prevails. The creatures usually dwell in groups which are evidently held together by a sympathetic bond, and are in more or less hostile relations to other groups of the same or diverse species, so that we may regard the tribal motive as even more affirmed than it could have been by human experience."

As long as primitive groups lived in a more or less migratory fashion, the conception of common kinship, whether fictitious or real, seems to have been the dominant bond of union. But with the development of more stable modes of life within definite territorial locations the bond of kinship gradually becomes replaced by the bond of neighborhood. Maine says (*Early History of Institutions* [1875], p. 72), "I think, upon trustworthy evidence, that, from the moment when a tribal community settles down finally upon a definite space of land, the Land begins to be the basis of society in place of Kinship."

The universality of the village community form of social organization has been well attested by Maine, Gomme, and others. Outside of the large cities the village community comprises the leading mode of social life for the peoples of all eastern countries. Moreover the present Russian mir, the Polish zadruga, and the Swiss canton, all present many of the characteristics of their eastern prototypes. Furthermore, to quote W. G. Sumner (*The Challenge of Facts and Other Essays*, p. 314), "the picture presented by the settlements in this country until the beginning of the eighteenth century was that of little groups of farmers scattered along the coast and rivers, forming towns under the loosest possible organization." These early villages, of course, formed the nuclei of our well-known New England town system.

Even with the development of city life the small neighborhood units tend to persist within the larger corporations. "The ancient city of Teheran . . . was divided into twelve districts, almost totally isolated from one another and permanently at variance with one another" (R. M. MacIver, *Community*, p. 251). The same tendency is seen in Rome, whose seven hills formed seven distinct neighborhoods. De Coulanges in *The Ancient City* shows that the Greek city was but a federation of local groups, each of which had its own religious and civil independence, and acted as a unit resenting interference on the part of the larger community. Of course similar tendencies toward local autonomy may be witnessed constantly in our own cities at the present time. Our cities grow by the inclusion of "satellite communities," and frequently such communities refuse to become absorbed in the larger corporations, and usually after surrendering their political autonomy retain for years a strong local consciousness and social independence.

In its traditional application the term neighborhood stood for rather definite group sentiments, which were the products of the intimate personal relations among the members of the small isolated communities of which society was formerly composed. The primary face-to-face associations of the traditional neighborhood group formed a universal nursery for what Cooley calls "the primary ideals," such as loyalty, truth, service, and kindness.[41]

Small homogeneous societies, such as the Russian mir, the Polish zadruga, or the isolated rural village, furnish our best examples of primary groups, that is of groups with a single set of definitions of life to which all the members adhere with an emotional unanimity. The ideas pertaining to group welfare have dominance over individual wishes, consequently there is a minimum amount of individuality when compared with life in a modern city. The solidarity of the traditional neighborhood is of the spontaneous, unreflective type.[42] It is the result of common human nature responding to common stimuli. The relation between individuals of the group is that of equality. Referring to the early village life in this country, Sumner says (*op. cit.*, p. 296), "It is plain that equality is the prevailing characteristic of this society; its members are equal in fortune, in education, in descent (at least after a generation or two), in mode of life, in social standing, in range of ideas, in political importance, and in everything else which is social and nobody made them so." Wood, in recounting the personal traits of our modern professional neighbor, the city boss, expresses a similar idea (American Journal of Sociology 19:580), "The local boss, however autocratic he may be in the larger sphere of the city with the power which he gets from the neighborhood, must always be in and of the local people: and he is always very careful not to

---

41   *Social Organization*, chap. 4.
42   See James Mark Baldwin, *The Individual and Society* (1911), chap. 2.

try to deceive the local people so far as their distinctively local interests are concerned. It is hard to fool a neighborhood about its own neighborhood affairs." It is this insistence upon social equality among neighbors that deters the development of latent leadership in our rural communities.[43]

The solidarity of the traditional neighborhood included physical as well as social objects. The old swimming pool, the familiar hills and trees, the architecture and location of buildings, all function as sentimental attachments of the neighborhood. The individual becomes so closely identified with all these objects of early and intimate contact that they tend to form a part of the "extended self." Dr. W. I. Thomas,[44] in discussing the efforts of Germany to Prussianize Poland, says, "If the primary group is distinguished by face-to-face and sentimental relations I think it is correct to say that the land of the peasant was included in his group. And this land sentiment is the most important factor in the failure up to date of the plans of the colonization commission." Attachment for locality is even today a significant force in the segregation of a city's population.

Loyalty, self-sacrifice, and service are the natural products of the intimate personal neighborhood groups. As Tufts says, kindness suggests kinness, and applied originally to members of the "we-group" only.[45] Kropotkin, in his *Mutual Aid*, furnishes us with a vast array of evidence concerning the reciprocal kindness of members of primitive communities. Sumner describes (quoted by Thomas, *Social Origins*, p. 79) the neighborly relations of the Yakuts of northern Siberia: "If one man's cow calves earlier than those of others, custom requires that he shall share cream and milk with those neighbors who at that time have none." Cooley says (*Social Organization*, p. 38), "one is never more human, and, as a rule, never happier, than when he is sacrificing his narrow and merely private interest to the higher call of the congenial group." In his book *The American Town* (1906), page 32, J. M.

---

[43] See an article by G. Walter Fiske, *Publications of Amer. Sociol. Society* 11:59.

[44] *Amer. Jour. of Sociol.* 19:632.

[45] Cf. Tufts, *Our Democracy, Its Origins and Its Task*, chap. 3.

Williams describes the typical relationship between neighbors as follows: "A man must stand ready to help his neighbor as well as himself. Thus, when two woodsmen were working independently in adjoining wood-lots, each would impulsively run to the help of the other as he struggled to 'skid' a log upon a bob-sled. 'I'll help you and you help me in return' represents the complete relation. . . . To be 'close-fisted' as to fail of generosity in time of a neighbor's need was bad enough, but to fail to return, when needed, help generously extended, was meanness too abject for expression."

Of course social friction and petty jealousies are as much the products of neighborhood association as are self-sacrifice and mutual aid. As E. C. Hayes[46] says, "While instinctive cohesion is stronger in small groups, so also is personal friction greater, and the members of a small group much in spatial proximity must have more in common, in order to render their union permanent and strong, than is required to bind together larger populations."

In order to get an expression of the common-sense conception of the neighborhood within the city, I had the students in my classes at Ohio State University who were residents of Columbus, write answers to the following questions: "Draw a map of that part of your city which you consider to be your neighborhood. Indicate on the map the location of your home, and state the number of years you have lived there. Give your reasons for bounding your neighborhood as you do." The following statements are typical of the fifty-seven replies analyzed:

(1) These are the streets I traverse oftenest. (2) On these streets live the people with whom I am acquainted and associate. (3) When we get in this part of town we feel that we are getting near home. (4) I consider this my neighborhood because it includes the houses nearest my home and because I know most of the families in this vicinity very intimately. (5) These are the streets that I used to play in and I still know most of the families residing here. (6) To my mind the word neighborhood includes the people right around my house; it is the vicinity very near. (7) We speak of anything happening within a square of our home as being in our neighborhood but we do not know half of the people who live there. We have lived on this street

[46] *Introduction to Sociology*, p. 76.

six years. (8) I used to play with the children from most of these families (that is, families within an area of about a block and a half on the same street) ; my small brother made me acquainted with others. I have lived here nine years. (9) Neighborhood to me means the people living in the same block we live in, those across the alley in the rear, and those living in the block across the street. (10) I consider the cross streets as the boundary of our neighborhood, the streets being so wide, especially where I live, that we do not recognize the people on the other side. I have lived here fourteen years. (11) I consider that this constitutes our neighborhood (an area of a couple of blocks) because these are the families that we come in contact with most frequently on the street car and at community gatherings. (12) I consider these particular streets my neighborhood because generally they are the only surrounding scene and the only people with whom we come in daily contact. (13) I have no particular reason for using this boundary as the boundary of our neighborhood except that it is the block in which we live, the families here are not of the sociable type; I have lived here for four years. (14) I should say that my immediate neighborhood consists of the two southeast and southwest blocks; while the block at the northwest is also my neighborhood it is not my immediate neighborhood because we do not associate with these people and the spirit of the two factions is different. I have lived in this section for six years. (15) I consider my immediate neighborhood around the square S. to M. avenues since that is where I have lived the last five years. I think this is my neighborhood because we meet these people oftener and feel that we know them better.

From a consideration of these statements and from an examination of the maps which accompanied them, it is clear to me that the conception which the average city dweller holds of his own neighborhood is that of a very small area within the immediate vicinity of his home, the limits of which seem to be determined by the extent of his personal observations and daily contacts.

But in referring to neighborhoods in general in Columbus, much larger areas seem to be implied, spatial proximity to some central focus of attention being the determining feature. For example, it is local custom to speak of "Indianola," "Glen Echo," "The Hilltop," "West Side," etc., as various neighborhoods within the city, although each of these areas embraces many streets and contains thousands of people. What then is the city neighborhood? For certain administrative purposes it is important to consider these larger geographical expressions as units of neighborhood interest, while for other purposes, where intensity of social opinion counts, the smaller nuclei of common life may prove more effective units.

The segregation of the population within a city along racial, economic, social, and vocational lines, tends to give to different local areas at least an external coloring which enables one to draw more or less definite lines of demarkation between them. In the course of time these different areas acquire a sort of homogeneity and a historical continuity which develops a rudimentary sense of self-consciousness. This self-consciousness is usually enhanced if the area acquires a name designating its chief feature of attention, such as Niggertown, Flytown, Little Italy, etc. Such areas are, as a rule, in constant process of change, but since their selective influences attract about the same class of people from year to year their external aspects maintain a somewhat regular form. While districts of this sort vary greatly in size and in social solidarity, and while they may possess but few of the characteristics of the traditional neighborhood, nevertheless they possess sufficient significance from the standpoint of social selection, and have sufficient importance in community organization to warrant some such characterization as the term neighborhood.

If we consider the neighborhood then in this more general sense as representing a patch of common life within the larger community, which is sufficiently differentiated from the city as a whole to be thought of as a unit, we have several different types of neighborhoods represented in Columbus. Taking as our criterion for the classification of these neighborhoods the chief element in population selection, we have three grades of economic neighborhoods,[47] that is, areas representing three fairly distinct economic

[47]   Consult Map II, "Economic Areas in Columbus," for the locations of these different economic neighborhoods. It will be observed that, with but one exception, the south side, the economic status of the wards increases as one goes from the center out toward the periphery of the city. In fact the most exclusive neighborhoods all lie beyond the corporation limits. On the east side the suburban village of Bexley is the restricted area for the city's social elite. For many years Columbus has vainly sought to have

divisions. These may be grouped as poor, middle class, and wealthy residential districts.

On the other hand, we have distinct racial and national groups where the chief elements in population selection are consciousness of kind, common language, and traditions. These are represented in Columbus by the large negro neighborhood on East Long Street, by the mixed Hebrew and colored neighborhood immediately east of the central part of the city, and by the homogeneous German neighborhood on South High Street.

In the third place we have the industrial neighborhood, in which reside the employees of a large industry, as, for example, the "South Side Neighborhood" surrounding the Columbus Steel Works, the chief factor in social selection being convenience to place of employment. Such neighborhoods usually represent a mixture of racial and national groups.

Again we may classify neighborhoods according to the status of their historical development into nascent, self-conscious, and disintegrating neighborhoods.[48] Like all other social groups, city neighborhoods are ever in a process of change. Fluctuations in rental and land values, due to the vacillation of city life, produce continuous movements of population from one section of the city to another, thus changing the economic and racial complexion

---

this village enter the corporation, but up to date the villagers have preferred their local autonomy to the anonymity of city life. On the uplands, just beyond the western extremity of the city, are three other exclusive residential villages, Grand View Heights, Marble Cliff, and Upper Arlington. These villages are all of comparatively recent origin and the real estate restrictions limit the population to the wealthy home-owning class. Local consciousness is quite pronounced in all three and several experiments in community enterprises have been introduced, such as the local paper, the community church, the community kitchen, etc.

Another new residential section of the more exclusive type is fast developing just beyond the northern limits of the city. Many new additions have been opened up in this vicinity during the past few years, and the Highlands east of the Olentangy River are rapidly becoming adorned with beautiful homes and picturesque gardens.

[48]   See Robert E. Park, *op. cit.*, p. 581.

of neighborhoods within a comparatively short space of time.[49]

The city neighborhood differs considerably from its traditional prototype in that it represents a much more selected social group. Economic, racial, and cultural forces, by distributing the population into different residential sections, give to the city neighborhood an external appearance of homogeneity that is not frequently found in small villages or rural neighborhoods—a homogeneity, however, as we shall see later, which is more apparent than real. Racial prejudice, national clannishness, and class conflict, all function as social forces to give the city neighborhood what self-consciousness or solidarity it may possess.

IV. *Experiments in Neighborhood Organization*

The city of Columbus offers a number of rather unusual examples of the spontaneous development of local sentiment. In addition to the local improvement associations which have been organized in each of the larger local divisions of the city for the purpose of directing the general business interests, several streets have formed organizations to promote the interests of the residents on a single street or city block. Some of these organizations have interesting histories, and as experiments in the development of local sentiment are worthy of consideration. As far as can be ascertained these local organizations are all confined to the northern and western sections of the city, regions which are comparatively new, and for the most part occupied by homeowners.

Oakland Avenue Flower and Garden Club.[50]—Oakland Avenue is located near the center of the sixteenth ward, a few blocks

[49] This is especially true with respect to immigrant neighborhoods. The economic progress of the immigrant is faster, as a rule, than that of the slum-dwelling American; consequently more immigrants than Americans graduate from the poorer neighborhoods. The district surrounding the Godman Guild Settlement House of Columbus has, according to the Settlement head, changed its immigrant population several times during the past decade.

[50] See Map I for the locations of each of the neighborhoods described in this chapter.

north of the university campus. The part of the street that is organized extends from High Street on the west to Indianola Avenue on the east—a distance of about a quarter of a mile. The street is now thirteen years old, having been held in reserve by a real estate firm while the surrounding area was built up. A number of property restrictions have given a physical uniformity to the street and at the same time made for a selection of population. There is a building restriction ranging from $2,500 to $3,000 (prewar prices) as a minimum cost per residence. The lots are wide, and the homes are required to be built thirty feet back from the curb line, thus leaving a uniformly wide space for lawns and shrubs. Double dwellings and apartment houses are forbidden, also places of business.

The street became formally organized in the spring of 1912, the year of the Columbus Centennial. During that spring the Columbus Flower and Garden Club was formed in order to promote general interest in city beautification. A prize was offered for the best-kept street in the city. Under the capable direction of one of the leading residents of the street, the "Oakland Flower and Garden Club" was organized. Meetings of the residents were held in the Northwood School, located at the foot of the street, with the result that an enthusiastic program for street beautification was adopted. Large granite boulders were erected at both ends of the street, giving it an individuality and prominence apart from the general neighborhood. Uniformity in design of lawn decoration was adopted with the result that, at the end of the year, the citizens of the street celebrated the jubilee of being the proud winners of the civic prize for the most beautiful street in the city. Meanwhile a local paper, the *Oakland Avenue News*, was periodically published and distributed to all the families on the street.

The enthusiasm engendered by this successful start has never quite died out although it has diminished in intensity and has required careful fanning on the part of a few indomitable spirits whose interest in the success of the undertaking has remained unabated. Although a comparatively stable street, the extent of change of residence has been one of the chief causes of the fluctuating interest in the organization. Of the eighty-five families whose names were listed in the street directory published in the *Oakland Avenue News* for September, 1913, thirty-eight had moved from the street before June, 1918—a period of five years.

The organization, designed primarily to promote street beautification, subsequently gave rise to many local activities of a social and neighborly nature, among which may be mentioned the admirable practice of sending floral tributes to neighbors in case of sickness, or death; social picnics in which all families on the street participate, ladies' clubs, and a renowned bowling team, composed of male residents of the street.

Northwood Avenue Flower and Garden Club.—Northwood Avenue, which lies next to, and runs parallel with, the street just described, supports a similar organization. In fact I might have described the two streets together, were it not for the strong neighborly rivalry and unitary group character of each. Northwood has a physical basis for group life precisely similar to that of Oakland Avenue. It formed a part of the same real estate division and, therefore, was subjected to the same street restrictions. Its street organization was motivated by the same cause as that of Oakland Avenue but did not start off under quite such propitious circumstances. It took the Northwood residents a bit longer to get into teamlike action, but, once started, their organization has retained its health and vitality even better than that of its rival.

In the spring of 1917, with the assistance of some of my students, I made a brief study of the Northwood organization in order to get some clues respecting the nature of its group life. Every home on the street was visited with a brief questionnaire. I shall succinctly summarize here the results of our findings at that time. Questionnaires were filled out by fifty-one families. Of these, eleven had been living on the street less than one year, thirty-two less than five years, and the remainder from five to ten years. All but three of the male heads of households were native-born Americans, and thirty-seven of the fifty-one male heads were born in the state of Ohio, six of whom were born in Columbus.

In reply to the question, "Why did you select this street as a place of residence?" fourteen said that it was on account of the attractive features of the street; another fourteen said it was because the house suited them; twenty could give no particular reason for their decision; while three maintained that their selection was due to the presence of friends and relatives on the street. Moreover, thirty-two families stated that they knew nothing of the street organization, prior to taking up residence there, while the remaining nineteen families were familiar with the social activities of the street and were more or less attracted to it on that account.

With respect to intimacy and personal acquaintance, nine families stated that they did not have even a speaking acquaintance with any other family on the street; thirty-five families reported that they had a speaking acquaintance with more than ten families on the street; while seven reported that they had a speaking acquaintance with more than thirty families. Six families stated that they were related, either by blood or marriage, to one or more families on the street.

Of the male heads of households, twelve reported no affiliation with community clubs or fraternal orders of any sort; twenty-three were members of but one fraternal organization; while sixteen belonged to two or more clubs. As regards religious affiliations, eleven different sects were represented, including membership or attendance at twenty-four different churches. Moreover, the leading bread winners were distributed among twenty-eight different forms of occupation, and of these only nine reported drawing any clientage from the immediate neighborhood.

An effort was made to sound the attitudes of the different householders toward their street organization and its leading functions. Of the fifty-one families, twenty stated that they had never attended any of the street's meetings; thirty-nine considered the organization definitely worth supporting; of these, twenty considered its main value to be the promotion of friendship and neighborly feeling, while the remaining nineteen valued it chiefly from the standpoint of its effect upon property values. Twelve families did not consider the organization worthy of support. Concerning the street practice of sending flowers to neighbors in the event of sickness or death, twenty-nine families reported having received such floral tributes, and all but four indicated positive appreciation of the custom and thought it should be continued.

Turning now to a consideration of the street paper, the *Northwood Avenue Bulletin,* this little paper has been published at irregular intervals ever since 1912. It is an unusually attractive little sheet containing many interesting views of the street and supplying information with respect to gardening and other matters of family interest. It also carries a page headed "Neighborhood Happenings," under which are listed news items pertaining to the people of the street. This paper represents the idea of one or two enthusiastic promoters and has been published at a loss to the few people most intimately concerned. An effort was made to ascertain the attitudes of the householders toward this paper, with the interesting result that forty-two of the fifty-one families were strong in their approval of it and considered that its publication should be continued.

Although a few of the families residing on this street at the time the above survey was made were opposed to any attempts to start "this small town stuff" in the city, still all but five maintained that it would cause them considerable regret to have to leave the street. Many families who stated that they had not the time to participate actively in the work of the street organization nevertheless endorsed the movement as being distinctly meritorious.

Ninth Avenue neighborhood.—Another interesting example of local manifestation of neighborhood sentiment and one which has been brought to the attention of the citizens of Columbus for the past decade or so is that of the residents of West Ninth Avenue. This little street, only two short blocks in length, is located close to the southwest corner of the university campus, in Ward 15. The Neil Avenue street-car line forms the eastern boundary of the neighborhood, and the university farm borders it on the west.

Unlike the streets just described, the Ninth Avenue neighborhood supports no formal organization or street paper, but for years past the residents of the street have shown evidence of a distinct group feeling, which reaches its highest culmination every year in a Fourth of July celebration. At this time the street is roped off from city traffic, and all the residents of the block participate in a general street picnic, followed in the evening by a display of fireworks, which has become a tradition in the local life of the community. The street is much shorter than either of the others described, making it unnecessary to develop secondary means of communication, such as the local newspaper.

In physical appearance the street differs considerably from the surrounding area. In the first place it is built up with a distinctly superior type of residence from that found in the neighboring locality, the assessed value of the homes ranging from $4,000 to $15,000. The lawns are spacious and uniformly deep, lending a unitary character to the street.

In our brief study of this street we found that its group life depended very largely upon the energetic activities of a single family. The head of this household and his wife make a hobby of fostering neighborhood sentiment among the residents of the street. The meetings that are held to plan entertainments, etc., are usually conducted at this man's residence.

In addition to the club life that prevails among the residents of this street, such as picnics for the children, social activities of the women, and quoit games among the men, various other forms of collective action for local purposes have taken place. For instance, the street has persistently acted as a unit to keep its western vista over the university farm free from obstruction. It has also had several experiments in corporate action in fighting the intrusion of objectionable structures within its limits.

Glenmawr Avenue Improvement Association.—This little neighborhood is located in an attractive spot near the northern end of the sixteenth ward. The nature of this community and the purpose of its organization are well described in the following words of its secretary:

There is a park thirty-five feet wide and about one thousand feet long in the center of Glenmawr Avenue, and when the street was improved this space was left by the city with no improvements whatever, not even grass. It was necessary for the property owners to improve the condition of this park, and, therefore, the organization was formed with a view to beautifying the park and establishing a standard in the carrying forward of any improvements on the street, such as placing shade trees, constructing sidewalks, placing steps from the street to the yard, etc. Present membership, sixty-eight families. Any property owner on Glenmawr Avenue or any families renting property located on that street are eligible to become members.

The organization was able to have an ordinance passed through council permitting the placing of the sidewalks within two feet of the curb rather than five feet as is ordinarily required, which avoided the cutting off of the lawns thus reducing the front yard space.

The park, which was simply a bare space of ground, has been made level, fertilized, and a good standard of grass obtained. Seventy shade trees have been placed along the edge of the park and between these shrubbery has been placed. At the ends of the park, flower beds with perennial flowers are maintained and gravel walks placed at intervals across the park to avoid persons having to cross from one side of the street to the other walking on the grass.

An ordinance was passed last fall by the Council of the City of Columbus, at the suggestion of the Association, requiring the installation of five cobble-stone pillars, on which cluster lights will be installed through the center of the park. The grass in the park is taken care of by the residents without expense.

This Association also endeavors to have at their business meetings social entertainments for the residents of the street only, and by so doing have created a friendly feeling among the residents that could not otherwise have existed.

The money necessary to carry on the improvements that have been made in the park is obtained by assessment of the various residents of the street, the amount being collected without any hardship, and there is always money in the treasury to carry on improvements that might be authorized.[51]

The foregoing organization was formed in the spring of 1914, its meetings are held monthly at the home of one of the residents of the street. It serves an area of about two city blocks.

The Hilltop neighborhood.—The Hilltop is more than a neighborhood; it is a city within a city. It is a community of about 15,000 people, topographically separated from the city proper. It is an area complete in itself, having its own schools, churches, stores, shops, parks, fire-hall, social clubs, local newspaper, and improvement association, which is really equivalent to a chamber of commerce.

[51]   Letter received from the secretary, January, 1920.

The Hilltop . . . lies in the extreme western end of the city, about four miles west of the state's Capitol. As the name implies, the Hilltop is a promontory rising considerably above the "flats" which separate it from the heart of the city. The division now comprises an area of several square miles and includes within its confines the State Hospital for the Insane.

Comparatively speaking, the Hilltop is a new section of Columbus. Its chief development as a residential area has taken place during the past fifteen years, but once available for settlement its attractive topographical features made it an eldorado for the better class of home-seekers, with the result that it is now a city of new homes clustered around the few historic residences which graced the landscape in days gone by. Moreover, it is a region of considerably historic importance. Camp Chase of Civil War renown was located here, also the Confederate Cemetery, which lies in the southwestern part of the district.

Barring a small Italian neighborhood, located on McKinley Avenue at the rear of the Hospital for the Insane, and a larger colored colony located in the south along Sullivant Avenue, the Hilltop is primarily inhabited by white American stock, the majority of whom are home-owners of the more prosperous class. An astonishingly large number of the leading public men of the city have their homes in this region, which fact doubtless accounts, in good measure at least, for the public spirit displayed among the residents of the Hilltop.

The negro neighborhood, just referred to, is the "fly in the ointment" with respect to the community pride of the people of the Hilltop. This colored section, covering an area of about six blocks, with a population of approximately 600 people, is not a recent development. A number of the colored families have resided in this spot for over thirty years, but a fresh influx of colored settlers arrived immediately after the Springfield riots a decade or so ago. A real estate dealer, devoid of "social vision" and "greedy for gain," sold his property to these people with the result that they are now fixtures in the community. Aside, however, from the acute social problems arising out of their presence in the schools, the colored people live to themselves and do not come in contact with the general social life of the community. The colored neighborhood has its own churches, stores, and motion-picture house, and the Camp Chase street-car line is used almost exclusively for transportation to and from the city. This colored neighborhood is one of the most orderly and progressive negro localities in the city. According to the estimate of one of the oldest colored residents, 7 per cent of the families own their homes; and it is a matter of local pride that "no one has been sent to the penitentiary from this district during the past twenty-five years."

The local consciousness of the residents of the Hilltop has manifested itself in many ways. In the first place a local paper called the *Hilltop News* is published weekly and read by more than "eight thousand Hilltoppers every week." This sheet is the "official organ of the Hilltop business men" and carries advertising and news items of local interest. It also serves as the official spokesman for the Hilltop Improvement Association, an organization of Hilltop residents designed to promote the welfare of the "Hilltop, its people and their homes."

The Hilltop Improvement Association was organized in 1911 for the purpose just stated. It was promoted by a number of the most enterprising citizens of the community including one of the city's most prominent councilmen. No local organization of the city has been more active in the promotion of local interests, or has achieved more for the territory served, than the Hilltop Improvement Association. Its field of activities has included negotiations with the city council for the procuring of local satisfactions, such as a recreation building, street-car accommodation, city deliveries, etc. It has also stimulated local pride in the care of property and in the repulsion of undesirable commercial encroachments, and at the same time has done much to engender a feeling of neighborliness and sociability among the people.

The community consciousness among the people of the Hilltop is due largely to the peculiar topographical features of the district, which give it a unitary character quite distinct from the rest of the city. Moreover its conflict with the city proper in regard to flood protection measures relative to the flood area which separates it from the down-town district, has resulted in the development of the "we feeling" as contrasted with the rest of the city. In addition to this, the boosting attitude has been maintained by the comparatively large number of enterprising public citizens who have their homes in this district. These home-owners appreciate the significance of local community pride and consciously attempt to stimulate it in their locality.

Conclusions.—From a study of these and other experiments in neighborhood organization, I venture the following conclusions concerning neighborhood work in general. First, that neighborhood sentiment is most easily engendered where the physical basis of life affords a unitary character sufficient to differentiate the neighborhood from the larger community.

Second, neighborhood sentiment thrives best where there is a homogeneity and stability of population accompanied by a high percentage of home ownership.[52] Third, other things being equal, the difficulty of maintaining local interest in local projects varies directly with the extent of territory covered and the number of families included. There is considerable evidence to show that a street more than two blocks in length tends to divide itself into subgroups, especially when two different street-car lines are used by the residents in communication with the down-town district. Fourth, it may be stipulated that interest in the most obviously beneficial local enterprises, even under the most favorable conditions, is not as spontaneous and natural as many of our promoters of neighborhood enterprises seem to assume. In each experiment in neighborhood organization cited above, the interest in local affairs has been more or less artificially sustained by the "hard work" of a few energetics promoters.

Nevertheless, the value of such street organization cannot be doubted. No one who has visited any of the streets which have

[52]   According to our general test of stability for Columbus, i.e., the percentage of the 1917 electors who re-registered in their respective precincts in 1918, the organized neighborhoods just described rank comparatively high in stability. The average re-registration for the entire city was 58.6 per cent and for the most stable precinct 77.8 per cent. The precinct in which Oakland and Northwood avenues are located had a re-registration of 75.5 per cent, the Ninth Avenue precinct a re-registration of 69.1 per cent, and the Glennmawr precinct 64.9 per cent.

been described would question the superior merits of corporate action over the haphazard ways of traditional individualism. Aside from the social benefits accruing from local collective action, the effect on real estate values is in itself an important consideration, and one which real estate companies are beginning to appreciate.[53]

[53]   I have been informed by several residents of the streets in question that they have been offered valuable concessions by real estate companies to promote similar organizations in new residential divisions which are now being put on the market.

5

SPATIAL DISTANCE AND COMMUNITY ORGANIZATION PATTERN

1927

Transportation

COMMUNITY ORGANIZATION inevitably becomes accommodated to space and time factors. The local community is spatially organized with reference to the daily movements of population, which in turn are limited by the prevailing forms of communication and transportation. In other words, the local distribution of homes and interest centers falls within a plane the maximum area of which cannot be greater than the physical distance which can be daily traversed using the current mode of transportation.

The slower the form of transport the smaller the range of the community. Prior to the introduction of mechanical agencies of transportation and communication, local communities—villages, towns and cities—encompassed relatively small areas. The human-energy-transport communities of Japan and China are exceedingly compact and undifferentiated. The ox and cart villages of India embrace wider zones. Fields and wells are located farther from the home than is the case in those parts of China and Japan where human energy is the only method of movement. The horse and vehicle communities of Europe and America have much wider zones of participation than the slower transit communities of the East. But even the horse and buggy community cannot embrace a zone of more than 10 or 12 miles in diameter and most of the movement takes place within a much smaller area.

Reprinted from *Social Forces*, vol. 5, June, 1927.

Fluidity

The great revolution in communal area and structure came when mechanical agencies of communication and transportation displaced the earlier animal forms. This revolution in movement is so recent that we are unaware of its real significance. Much of our thinking is still colored by the horse and buggy tradition of distance. Of course the stage coach days of Europe and America are little more than a lifetime removed. The first United States Census published in 1790 gives a vivid picture of the primitive conditions of fluidity which existed at the time that our political institutions were formed.

But the greater part of the world is at present in even a more primitive stage of fluidity. The most striking difference between America and Asia is in regard to movement. Excluding a few of the larger cities, life in Asia is stagnant, immobile.[1] Peasants may be seen toiling in the fields, or trudging along the dusty roads and narrow paths which intersect the rice fields and tie the villages together. But there is no constant and rapid movement on highways such as one sees in this country. Rural Europe is but a shade more fluid. Although it possesses, in most parts, a well developed system of highways, still the automobile has scarcely begun to traverse them. One may travel for weeks through Europe without seeing more than a dozen automobiles on the highways beyond the immediate suburbs of the larger cities.

The situation, however, is different in the cities. The great urban centers throughout the world are much alike in matters of transportation. Kobe, Shanghai, Bombay and Cairo have almost as efficient forms of intramural transit as Berlin, Paris, London, New York. Modern fluidity in the Old World is an urban monopoly. Just outside the confines of the city, the peasant carries on his daily activities in much the same fashion as his forebears did

[1]   "Of the 42,794,155 persons enumerated in Madras, 42,584,293 were born in the Presidency. . . . 99 per cent of the population were born in the division in which they were enumerated" (Census of India, 1921, 13:46).

generations ago. The railway has placed him in a new economy; he buys and sells in a wider market; his daily movements, however, have changed but little.

The steam railway with its fixed right-of-way and definite train schedule has had little effect upon life in the small community. It has altered intercommunal relations but it has not materially changed the spatial distribution of homes and service centers in the smaller communities. This is especially true with reference to village and town life in the Old World. Coming as it did to Asia and Europe when the country was already settled, the railway effected little change on village and rural institutions. The villages of the East have scarcely any connection with the railroad systems. If the track happens by accident to run through a village there is usually no provision for stopping. The only service rendered by the new form of transportation is the killing of the villager's chickens or the blowing of the thatch from the roofs of his buildings.

The great revolution in local fluidity came not with the railway and telegraph but with the local forms of transportation and communication, the electric tram, the telephone, and, more especially, the automobile. And as I have already intimated, these agencies of local fluidity are still largely confined to this part of the world, that is, as far as rural life is concerned.

The automobile, supplemented by the telephone and now by the radio, has instituted a new spatial regime in this country. The extent to which it has speeded up our life is difficult to estimate. The census of motor car registration shows that there is now an automobile to every six persons for the country as a whole. The ratio for different states varies from three in California to fourteen in Alabama.[2] Assuming that each car is driven from eight to ten thousand miles per year, it is safe to say that the average rural American travels as many miles in one year as the average Indian villager does in a lifetime.

The automobile has not only increased fluidity, it has also increased flexibility. Movement is no longer directed along a few fixed channels as in the case of the steam or electric train. It has

[2]   *Facts and Figures of the Automobile Industry*, National Automobile C. of C., 1926.

become as diversified as the street and road system. This greater fluidity and flexibility made possible by the automobile is the cause of profound changes in local spatial distribution. It has affected the country even more than the city because there it has replaced the horse while in the city it has merely supplemented the street car. In other words, the automobile, by providing every village and almost every farmstead with rapid transportation, has converted the entire country into an urban pattern of home and service center distribution.

Specialization and Centralization

The first effect of increased fluidity is a redistribution of homes and interest centers. The new agency of transportation serves as a release and effects a new spatial distribution of local institutions in conformity with the degree of elasticity provided. Some centers move farther from the home, while others remain as before or may come even closer to the home. A redistribution of interest centers took place in the city with the advent of electric street cars. The old diversified centers which characterized the prestreet-car city underwent a rapid transformation as soon as the electric railway connected them with the city's center. The more specialized services, both retail and professional, segregated in the down-town section. On the other hand, the primary and general services as a rule shifted to new subcenters located at important intersections of the intramural system. The degree of specialization of services found in any subcenter varies with the size and importance of the center.

In general it may be said that the more specialized the service the more centralized it becomes, that is, the wider its zone of patronage. On the contrary, the more standardized the service with respect to frequency of use, quality and price, the more decentralized it becomes or the narrower its zone of patronage.[3] The city

3   From a study of shopping habits of 1250 families in the University District, Seattle, it was found that 90 per cent bought their groceries from local dealers, 51 per cent their hardware, 35 per cent their furniture, and 24 per cent their clothes (*University District Herald*, March 5, 1925).

therefore represents a series of trade zones the diameters of which are a measure of the degree of specialization and centralization of the various interest centers under given conditions of density and fluidity.

The automobile has had opposite effects with respect to city and country. Congestion has increased distance to the center of the city and therefore has occasioned decentralization of many service centers which under the street car regime were located in the heart of the city. On the other hand, motor transportation, through its greater flexibility than the street car, has decreased distances in the less congested parts of the city and therefore produced new subcenters located farther apart than the street car subcenters and possessing more specialized service centers.[4] Moreover, as distance from the home to the periphery is shorter than that from the home to the center of the city, the motor car as been the cause of diverting a considerable number of the leisure time centers from the heart of the city to points located outside the corporation limits. This tendency is particularly marked in the Pacific Northwest, where the cities are surrounded by a marginal unsettled region now made accessible by a network of hard surfaced roads.[5]

The effect of the automobile on rural life has been quite the opposite. That is, the motor car has released many of the interest centers of the open country, villages, and small towns, and centralized them in the more important centers. In this way the automobile is changing the life of the rural community in much the same way as the street car changed the life of the old primary subcenters of the city.

[4]   The history of the motion picture theater is interesting in this regard. It started as a widely distributed neighborhood institution, then moved to the center of the city to compete with the regular theater, again it is coming back to the neighborhood but on a larger scale than before and located farther apart on sites convenient to motor traffic. See *Annals of the American Academy*, September, 1926, pp. 99–100.

[5]   Country Clubs and Road Houses have multiplied during the last five years along the highways connecting the Puget Sound Cities. The pleasure ride is part of the entertainment, so institutions too close to the city are at a disadvantage with those farther out.

The county seat, which exemplifies the typical large town surrounded by smaller places, is becoming the city center of specialized services and amusements for the surrounding rural and village population. The automobile has effected even greater changes in rural than in urban life. First, because it furnished greater mastery of distance on the open country highways than in the congested city streets and second, because a higher percentage of the rural people own automobiles.[6]

Of course, the increased fluidity furnished by the automobile has not been of uniform influence throughout. Certain elements of the population are more fluid than others. There are no substantiating data, but it is probable that the curve of fluidity bears some relation to age, marital condition, and economic status. This unequal fluidity is the cause of considerable disorganization of the primary institutions,[7] a disorganization which is more obvious in the country than in the city because the revolution in overcoming distance there has been more profound.

The maximum zone of patronage or degree of centralization possible for any service center is, in the last analysis, determined by the time-cost factor in overcoming distance. The old team-haul community was defined by the distance a team ordinarily traveled in a day from the home to the center and return—a distance of about ten miles. The automobile zone of patronage cannot be measured by the same unit of time because habits of time consumption seem to have changed since the coming of this speedier form of transit. Instead of the day, the hour, or at most the two hour drive seems to mark the limit of distance that a person will ordinarily go to an interest center. This time of course is greatly increased on special occasions, holidays, and weekends, but the communal structure gets its dominant shape from the shorter daily movements.

[6]   "Sixty-four per cent of all registered cars in United States are in cities and towns of 25,000 and less" (*Nation's Business*, November, 1926).

[7]   Zimmerman and Taylor's discovery that many of the village groups of Wake County, N. C., have lost their primary group characteristics since the coming of the automobile, could doubtlessly be duplicated in many other parts of the country (Rural Organization, N. C. Agricultural Experiment Station, Raleigh, 1922).

Organization Pattern

There are at least four general types of organization pattern represented among local interest centers. These pattern types are most clearly revealed among retail trade services, where competition compels the service to accommodate itself to improvements in facilities of communication and transportation.

First there is the *small unit service center* which depends upon primary agencies of communication and transportation for its field of operation. Small retail service centers such as the grocery store, barber shop, and bakery as well as the old fashioned general store belong to this class. In fact, this is the type of organization common to almost all services in the small community. The second type of organization pattern is exemplified by the *department store*. The plan of organization is similar to that of the small unit type except that the range of operation is greatly extended. Instead of relying upon primary means of communication, the department store makes use of secondary forms. It depends upon the streetcar and the daily paper for enlisting patronage. It is centrally located and draws its clientele from all parts of the community. In addition it is specialized in function. It is the local general store departmentalized or specialized.

The third type of pattern is that represented by the *chain store* system. The business is centralized but the service centers are scattered. Instead of the clients going to the service, the service goes to the client. The chain store type of organization is in a way a more advanced organization pattern. It takes advantage of the fact that communication is more speedy than transportation and that business can be more economically centralized than service. It makes use of the same agencies of communication as the department store type, that is, the daily press and telephone, but it operates on the principal that it is less costly to decentralize the service than to centralize the public. The recent trend toward the chain store type of organization is directly associated with the increased use of the automobile, which gives flexibility to the movement of goods but which, on account of traffic congestion, makes it difficult for shoppers to patronize the central shopping establishments.

The fourth type of retail service pattern is the *federation system*. Independent service units unite and establish central offices in which certain business functions of mutual advantage are performed. Small store proprietors are beginning to find themselves at a disadvantage in competing with the chain store system. And in order to obtain the advantage of large scale buying and efficient advertising they are beginning to unite in federated organization. This federated scheme of organization is in principle the opposite to the chain store system. Control is decentralized; it functions from the fringe to the center. Whereas in the chain store system, the control is centralized and the organization functions from the center to the fringe.

Every form of communal organization, whether publicly or privately administered, falls into one or other of these four general pattern schemes. If there is a general trend running through all kinds of communal organization it seems to be in the direction of the chain store pattern. This is the scheme of organization by which our cities are administered. The public administration of protection, police and fire, of health, education, library service, water, telephone, is conducted on this pattern. Private welfare organization is also to a considerable extent organized on the same pattern. This Charity Organization Society has its central offices and scattered branches. Private institutions however such as social clubs, improvement clubs, and churches, are as a rule organized on the federated system. They retain their local autonomy but at the same time have central organizations through which they can act as corporate units when occasion arises. The single unit type of organization is gradually passing; it frequently represents the initial stage of a service which subsequently changes into one or other of the more advanced pattern forms.

6

THE ECOLOGY OF
INSTITUTIONS

1936

"ECOLOGY IS the new name for a very old subject. It simply means scientific natural history," says Elton in his recent book *Animal Ecology*. He then proceeds to show how ecological studies have advanced beyond the old naturalistic story-telling of plant wonders and animal ways, gaining in precision of analysis, terminology, and comprehension of the specific field of investigation. Scientific ecology began with the study of plant life about fifty years ago, attention being focused on the vital linkages that bind living organisms together in mutual dependence and interaction, always in relation to particular environments.

The ecological approach to the study of human settlement is still in its infancy. In a sense human ecology might logically be considered as falling within the scope of animal ecology since *homo sapiens* is a member of the animal kingdom and has vital linkages with the lower organisms, plants, and animals. In fact many students of plant and animal relations have drawn attention to the position of man in the ecological hierarchy. The main reason for considering human ecology as a separate discipline is that man has so gained in dominance over the lower organisms that his relationships with them have, to a large extent, become consciously regulated and controlled. On the other hand, the most significant and least understood aspects of man's symbiotic relations are those which he effects with his fellow men. It is within

Unpublished. Circa 1936. Published by permission of Mrs. Roderick D. McKenzie.

102

this latter sphere of activity that the major problems of human ecology present themselves.

To be sure, various disciplines have already arisen to deal with different forms of interhuman relations—e.g., economics, political science, sociology. But each of these social sciences abstracts a particular system or level of relations for special consideration. Economics centers attention upon the principles involved in the production and exchange of material commodities. Its basic concepts are market, price, and value. Political science restricts its investigation to the theories and problems of government; sociology to the study of social behavior and social process. None of these specialized disciplines views the community as an organic entity in which the human elements are bound together in an intricate and ever changing web of life.

But however we may abstract and classify phenomena to meet our special interests, in reality they are interrelated and interdependent. The component elements which constitute the human community are bound together not merely by common traditions, habits, beliefs, and rules of conduct which have become formally expressed in legislative enactments and enforced by governmental machinery, but also by the vital linkages represented in division of labor and adjustment to physical habitat. It is with respect to the sustenance and geographic bases of its organic unity that the human community most closely resembles the communities of lower organisms. Here we can observe how competition, division of labor, commensalism, parasitism, etc., operate to give form and cohesion to human settlement. The forms in which these fundamental relations express themselves in human society, unlike their natural prototypes in plant and animal communities, are largely determined by the culture and collective controls of the human group concerned. It is for this reason that the diversities and uniformities in the patterns and types of symbiotic relations among different human groups are more pronounced than in communities of lower organisms. A Chinese village differs markedly from an American village although the physical environments of the two may be strikingly alike. On the other hand, the American village in Alaska tends to duplicate in spatial form and economic structure its sister villages in Florida and Southern California. Stated in general terms, plant and animal communal types are related to conditions imposed by the physical environment, whereas human communal types are more closely associated with the characteristics of the cultural setting.

The human ecologist, therefore, unlike his fellow workers in the biological sciences, must always take cognizance of the culture complex in which the symbiotic relations manifest themselves. And since culture is a more dynamic and variable factor than physical environment the task of the human ecologist is much more complicated than that of the plant or animal ecologists.

It is convenient in any type of ecological research to separate the organism-environment relation from the organism-organism relation. This is invariably done by the investigators of plant and animal communities. Likewise in the human field, the ecologist distinguishes between man's relations to the land on the one hand, and his relations to his fellowmen on the other. Down through the ages the major part of human activity has been directed toward the exploitation of the land. With the advance of science and invention, man's relation to the land has increased in complexity in that he has required an ever greater variety of nature's products. Nevertheless, he has become progressively less dependent upon the resources of his local habitat. Moreover, a diminishing proportion of any modern population is required to obtain the raw materials from nature, thus permitting and necessitating a correspondingly increasing proportion of man's activities to be directed to his relations with his fellowmen. These changing ratios of activity are objectively indicated in the census classifications of the gainfully employed. For example, a century ago some four-fifths of the population of the United States was engaged in agriculture. Even as late as 1880 neary half of the working population was thus engaged. In 1920 the proportion had fallen to 27 per cent and in 1930 to 22 per cent. Not only are the interhuman relations increasing in extent, they are also changing in form and complexity. In the simpler societies of the past and in the backward regions of settlement today the family and the local community constitute the basic societal units, and mutual aid, as Kropotkin has so well described it, characterizes the relations among the members of the group. Between communal aggregates hostility and conflict, actual or implicit, define the pattern of relations. In modern society, on the other hand, with its advanced material culture and freedom of movement, the individual and the institution have become the fundamental units of symbiotic activity, and competition and division of labor typify the interrelations of these constituent elements. It is with the growing importance of institutions that I am particularly concerned at present.

Let us digress a moment to define our usage of the term institution as a unit of collective activity performing a specialized social function. While every institution is a cultural form that has become established in the habits and attitudes of the social group, for my present purpose I wish to emphasize the symbiotic rather than the social aspects.

The institution thus conceived represents on the one hand a closely integrated aggregate of individuals performing a specialized social function, and on the other hand an accumulation of cultural artifacts assembled and organized to facilitate the performance of that function. The growth of material culture has at once necessitated and facilitated the rise of social institutions. The machines, mechanical energy, and other technological achievements of civilization have required spatially established centers for their accumulation and use. Thus the institution has acquired a physical structure and a definite locus in space. It likewise has a continuum in time which is not identical with that of its operative personnel. It is less mobile than the individual and less stable than the community, and it has come to constitute the fundamental unit in the ecological organization of modern society.

The advance of civilization has been accompanied by the multiplication and differentiation of social institutions. Indeed, it is through the development of institutions that man has risen above the level of lower animal life. It is by institutions, likewise, that the successive steps in cultural evolution have been attained. The institution is both a symbol of the level of cultural achievement and a ladder up which men may climb to acquire position and status in collective life.

In the more elementary forms of human association the institutions are few in number, relatively undifferentiated in function, and geographically restricted in operation. The primitive village is almost a single institutional unit, so closely integrated are the activities of its members and so narrowly confined is the scope of its activities. The progress of institutional development is closely associated with the growth of the communications and transportation facilities. Routes of movement have been followed by the rise and expansion of social institutions.

To be sure, the process of expansion has not been uniform for all types and classes of institutions. Some have responded more quickly than others to innovations in the transportation system. The historic sequence of the expansion process varies for different peoples and different regions of settlement. In western civilization the development, in broad outline, proceeded from the political religious, and commercial to the industrial, financial, and social forms of institutional expansion, always, to be sure, in a more or less tangled manner.

Needless to say, it is not our purpose to review the history of institutional growth. Everybody is familiar with the early forms of political, commercial, and religious expansion; also with the revolutionary changes brought by the introduction of steam power and other mechanical improvements in the first half of the nineteenth century. The response of these cultural innovations was so rapid and extensive as to warrant the appellation "industrial revolution." The fabrication of goods was taken from the cottage and centered in the newly created factories. Commerce and finance were extended in an unprecedented fashion, bringing different regions of the world into competition and division of labor. Populations concentrated, and cities grew in size and number. However, the development of these new facilities of production and communication did not affect all institutions in the same manner. They encouraged the expansion of industry and commerce but they did not materially affect many of the more local types of institutional services.

The coming of the motor vehicle and electric energy in the early part of the present century, together with the rapid development of communications—the newspaper, telephone, and later the radio—introduced another revolutionary change in the institutional structure of society and one which in its composite effect on the texture of social relations has perhaps been even more significant than that occasioned by the introduction of steam transportation. By enlarging the territorial range of institutional activity, these new agencies of local communication disrupted the established equilibrium, invoked new forms of institutional competition and division of labor, and set the stage for a new spatial pattern of local relations.

Institutional accommodations to the new conditions of technology and communication assume a wide variety of forms, and the process of adjustment is still under way. In the first place there has been a pronounced tendency toward fewer and larger units among all classes of institutions—industrial, commercial, financial, social—followed by increasing territorial concentrations of activity. In the second place there has been a rapid integration of the smaller institutions through the rise of the chain systems of organization and the geographic differentiation of financial and managerial function from that of operative activity. The growth of large-scale organization has had the effect of standardizing the institutional units in different communities and of integrating settlement in a closer functional unity. It has also greatly reduced the proportion of independent workers and made wages and salaries the chief forms of economic income.

Let us now examine the institutional structure of the local community unit. The fact that modern institutions have become discrete entities which may be defined and located makes them amenable to arithmetic and geometric treatment. We now have regular censuses of factories, warehouses, banks, stores, churches, hospitals, and the like, just as we have regular censuses of population. The census classifies institutions by type and by size of the individual units within each type. The type classifications usually exhibit a progressive decrease in numbers as the function or populational appeal becomes more specialized. For example, there are more public schools than high schools, more high schools than colleges, more colleges than universities. Likewise, there are more food stores than clothing stores, more clothing stores than banks, more banks than exchanges, and so on. Accordingly, when we classify the institutions of a community merely on the basis of function—appeal to population—we discover a decreasing numerical frequency of units as activity becomes more specialized. These data when graphed assume a pyramidal form, which has come to be referred to as a pyramid of numbers. This pyramidal structure of institutional aggregates has both populational and spatial implications. On the one hand, the more specialized an institution becomes, the larger the community must be to support it. The situation is somewhat analogous to the life chains in animal communities. We are all familiar with the saying "One hill cannot shelter two tigers," and we are equally cognizant of the fact that one community cannot support two stock exchanges or two grand opera companies.

On the other hand, when we examine the spatial arrangement of institutions within a community we usually find that the larger and more specialized units tend to occupy central positions with respect to the smaller and less differentiated types, presenting a pattern somewhat analogous to an astronomical constellation. Thus every large city has its main business center composed of the more dominant and specialized types of commercial and administrative institutions. This central core is usually girdled by a ring of wholesale, warehouse, and other similar types of institutional structures. Outward from this we find a variety of subcenter formations located at the more strategic points of intersection on the local transportation structure. Each of these business nuclei in turn has its central core and margins of activity as indicated by peaking and decline of land values. Still farther out, if the city happens to belong to the predominantly industrial class, we find a checkered zone of factories, amusement centers, and certain types of public institutions.

While this pattern of distribution is perhaps more ideal than real, it roughly describes the typical form of institutional arrangement in our large American cities. Moreover, it has come about through the operation of natural forces rather than through conscious design. Institutional competition involves, among other things, struggle for the more favorable site locations. Out of this competition institutions become geographically arranged according to function and rent-paying capacity. The process is dynamic and a function of many variables, including the movements and arrangement of population, changes in the routes and agencies of transportation, and the changing function of the institution itself. The study of location factors has received little attention from students of social science. The few who have interested themselves in the subject, notably Alfred Weber, have proceeded on the assumption that the determination of optimal location is merely a problem in mathematics; that is, of discovering the land site which represents a point of equilibrium among cost variables in transportation. By this procedure it is easy to demonstrate that most of our institutions are badly or unscientifically located and that a new system of location is both feasible and desirable. But in spite of these demonstrations, our institutions show no tendency to assume the so-called scientific distribution.

To comprehend fully the forces involved in institutional location we must take cognizance of the vital linkages which exist among the diversified units. In other words, we must take the ecological approach. The spatial patterning of institutions within a community or throughout a nation is not merely a function of the communication system; it is also related to the ties of association which evolve among the institutions themselves. Thus in every large community we find certain classes of institutions clustered together in more or less clearly defined districts, each characterized by the nature of the institutional complex, e.g., financial districts, retail shopping districts, wholesale and amusement districts, and the like. It frequently happens that some of these districts become relatively inaccessible to their clientele. Yet if a single institution were to move to a more accessible location, its chances of survival would doubtless be diminished. The same situation applies to our heavy industries. The tendency of manufacturing to localize in the larger cities has been one of the pronounced features of our settlement process. And it has persisted in spite of all the factors that in themselves would seem to induce scatter. Industrial surveys almost invariably show that the rate of mortality increases with the dispersion of the units. Obviously one of the main reasons for this is the growing interdependence among institutional units. For example, the Detroit region has little if any natural advantages over many another region that might have been taken as locus for the motor industry. But by virtue of its early start in the manufacture of motor vehicles, this section of the country has in cumulative manner attracted a host of subsidiary industries. These in turn have come to furnish the indispensable base for the manufacture of the finished product. The institution, like the plant, tends to build up its own environment.

It is important in the study of any unit of settlement to differentiate those types of activity which furnish the economic base of the institutional hierarchy from those which relate to consumption and the cultural life of the community. The former we may characterize as the basic institutions; the latter as the service institutions. In the first group belong the factories, the large commercial and administrative enterprises, in fact every type of activity which contributes to the total wealth and income of the local population group. Among the institutions of the service category we would group schools, churches, theaters, retail stores, and the like.

Obviously then what is a basic institution to one community may be a service institution to a larger communal area. For example, the University of Michigan is a basic institution to Ann Arbor as it constitutes an important source of income to the local population, yet it is a service institution to the state of Michigan as its economic support is drawn from the basic wealth producing activities. Similar conditions apply to a host of other institutional services. We might generalize and say that every institution which extends its activities beyond the confines of the local community in which it is situated performs a basic function to the community in question.

The basic institutions play a predominant role in the life and character of the local community; in fact, they constitute the very foundation of the community's existence. The size, growth, and geographic distribution of the local population are largely determined by the nature of the basic institutions which cluster together in space. They create demands for labor of specific types and quantity and thus in large measure determine the age, sex, and cultural composition of the community's population. Moreover, it is by virtue of the exchange of products and services of the basic institutions that intercommunity division of labor is achieved and that large-scale economy comes about. This economy is based primarily upon the interchange of physical objects and has become extended to almost worldwide dimensions. The process has been associated with the development of larger and more specialized producing units and more territorial concentration of population.

The community's service institutions, on the other hand, are related to the size and characteristics of the population aggregate drawn to the area by the basic industries. Of course, to the extent that the service institutions are also employment centers they serve as additional population magnets, and in this respect they tend to reduce the abnormalities in population composition resulting from the selective aspects of the basic industries and also to give greater economic stability to the population. Although the basic institutions are paramount in determining the numbers and general geographic distribution of a region's inhabitants, the individual community acquires its characteristic structure or territorial organization from the arrangement and pull of its service institutions.

Whereas communities vary greatly in the character of their basic industries, they show striking uniformities in their complements of service institutions. Communities of a given size-class in our American culture tend to have approximately the same number and types of stores, schools, churches, theaters, and other services. So closely correlated are the service institutions with the size of the population group that given the census of an American town we can predict with a fair degree of accuracy the number and types of service institutions it is likely to contain. Variations in the communal complements of service institutions are more closely related to variations in the size of the local population aggregates than to differences in the character of the basic industries.

Since it is only through having access to service institutions— schools, churches, universities, and other cultural centers—that the individual can participate in the achievements of civilization, every community seeks to develop as adequate a complement of service institutions as the number and economic status of its inhabitants will permit. The small, isolated community is always at a disadvantage in this respect in comparison with the larger city, and various adjustments have been and are still being made to meet this situation. In earlier times these adjustments usually took the form of accommodation to the limitations which small aggregation implies, although even in peasant cultures there has always been more or less supplementation of local institutions by itinerant services as evidenced by the traveling man, entertainers, herb doctors, and the like. Even today we have our circuses, theatrical companies, chatauquas, and dental clinics that make periodic excursions about the country. But in our American culture, under present conditions of mobility and communications and the consequent growing desire for more complete participation in our cultural achievements, our small town and rural inhabitants are no longer content to fashion their lives to the limited cultural opportunities which their communities can sustain. More and more they seek the types of institutional services characteristic of the larger cities. To be sure, the extension of communications has made possible a more adequate institutional organization without entailing actual migration to the larger centers. This is shown by the institutional changes that have occurred in the more sparsely populated areas throughout the nation. There has been a rapid disappearance of the smaller and more scattered institutions and trading centers and a corresponding development of more efficient and selective institutions in the larger towns. However, the chief form of accommodation to institutional inadequacy in the more sparsely populated areas has been migration to territory within convenient access of the institutions of the larger cities.

This desire to participate more fully in the cultural opportunities which large communities afford has constituted one of the main factors in the recent drift to cities. Moreover, the process is cumulative. As population clusters in large aggregates, the communities of concentration become more specialized and more diversified in their institutional structure, catering to more interests and needs of the local population. On the other hand, as population is drawn from outlying territory, the service institutions of the regions concerned become correspondingly weaker and less efficient. Although the decreasing density of rural settlement may, as many of our rural economist suggest, serve to improve the economic status of the rural populations, it tends to weaken their service institutions, for it is important to recognize that optimal economic density may bear little relation to optimal social density.

A modern institution like the ocean vessel requires a rather definite complement of workers to man it at any given time. The larger the institution, the more occupationally differentiated will this complement become. When the employees of an institution are classified according to skill and income, the numbers in each classification show a progressive decline from the least skilled, lowest-paid workers at the base to the most skilled or most responsible control positions at the apex. In other words, the occupational distribution of workers in an institution, like the numerical distribution of institutions in a community, tends to assume the geometrical form of a pyramid of numbers. Obviously no two institutions are exactly identical in these pyramidal classifications of their working personnel, but the hierarchical pattern of symbiotic structure characterizes the institutional form of organization.

To the extent that society is institutionalized, that is, to the extent that individual participation in the collective economy involves employment in some institution, competition takes the form of struggle for the occupational niches which the institutional structure affords, and the general welfare of the employed personnel of any institution is associated with the relative position that institution is able to maintain in competition with other institutions. Since institutions constitute the most dynamic units in our modern social order, ever changing in response to new conditions of competition and cultural change, they continually adjust their staffs in conformity with the changing conditions imposed by competition and social demand. These institutional changes afford stimulus and zest to modern society; they keep the social order from becoming closed and stable, thus stimulating individual ambition and interest in social progress.

But, on the other hand, our institutional adjustments occasion much hardship to the individual and the local community. Compelled by competition to consider its own welfare above that of any of its staff, the institution hires and fires without reference to the effect upon the individual or the community. Unless the displaced persons can find employment in other institutions, they are left stranded, for it is becoming increasingly difficult for the lone individual to secure a livelihood outside the existing institutional system. In this respect our present institutional order differs markedly from that of the simpler economies of the past. In the earlier kinship societies the standard of life of the group might recede to a bare subsistence level, but the individual was always assured of a place in the collective economy; in our modern communities where economic participation in the social order involves employment in some institution, contraction of institutional activity connotes unemployment and complete destitution. To meet the exigencies of this situation, a vast array of charitable institutions have arisen in all of our large cities. In periods of prosperity such institutions multiply and flourish sometimes to the extent of incurring keen competition for clients. To the extent that their relations to one another are competitive and their standards of operation vary from the mores of their clientele, these welfare agencies tend to disrupt the kinship fabric of their local environs and create parasitic attitudes among their clients. It is perhaps for this reason that the slums of western cities, although filled with charitable and character-building institutions, are more disorderly and criminal than are the slums in Oriental cities, where the family and neighborhood forms of conduct still largely maintain.

In periods of extreme contraction of institutional activity, as at present, the local agencies of welfare and relief become unable to cope with their problems; their activities are supplemented by governmental action which proceds as the problem increases from the smaller to the larger politically administrative units and finally is taken over by the national authorities.

I shall abruptly terminate this lengthy paper with a few remarks regarding the problem of social planning in our present institutionalized order. I have attempted to show that the institution has become the fundamental unit in modern society and that the trend is away from individual enterprise in almost every line of endeavor. Competition among institutions has led to larger and larger units and systems of organization. The development has been far from uniform in all lines of activity. It has proceeded more rapidly in those types of industry and business in which the products and services are most amenable to standardized technique. Conversely, it has made least progress in those enterprises which fashion and whim play a predominant role. Our social order still contains a great variety of relatively small institutional units, but to an increasing extent the activities of the small enterprises are being regulated and controlled by the larger and more dominant units and systems of organizations.

The movement in the direction of large institutions and large scale organization has obviously made for greater efficiency in almost every economic and social function. Goods and services have been made available at lower costs and higher qualities than in any former period and have become accessible to a larger proportion of the population.

But this process has reduced the masses of the population to the status of wage-earners and salaried employees and has created a social order in which a relatively small number of powerful individuals direct the economic activities of their fellow citizens. "It is not so much the devices generally associated with modern business control of economic activity—wage system, corporate investment, credit, etc.—that give it its distinctive character, but rather the scope, power and pervasiveness of the system made possible by modern industrialism with its machine technique."[1]

As our institutions have grown in size and range of function, competition has compelled them to consider their own interests above those of their employees and of the communities in which they happen to be located. This pertains especially to our great industrial and commercial enterprises whose products and services extend throughout the nation and in some instances throughout the world. For example, the great motor industries located in the Detroit region adjust their activities to meet competition in

[1]   *Social Science Encyclopedia,* 3:82.

the national and world markets with but a minimum of consideration as to the effects upon their employees or home communities. In general their wage rates are high as compared with other industries, but owing to the irregularity of employment the actual yearly earnings of individual workers attached to the industry are surprisingly low. "The average money wage even in 1923 for full time employment was over $350 below that required to maintain the minimum health and decency budget of the United States Bureau of Labor Statistics' price for the city of Detroit."[2]

Owing to the colossal size of these industries, employing in peak seasons from three to four hundred thousand workers, approximately 90 per cent of whom belong to the unskilled class, it is impossible for the smaller and more stable institutions in the community to absorb the army of unemployed in periods of recession. Hence the community is called upon to supplement the inadequate yearly earnings from the industry itself. This situation, serious even in the most prosperous years, becomes an impossible burden in periods of depression. It is a patent fact that within less than three months' time from the date of peak production in 1929 some 40,000 families were on the relief rolls in the city of Detroit.

It is owing to such conditions in the modern organization of industry that the federal government has been compelled to step in and attempt to regulate a process which, while growing ever more efficient in its institutional enterprises, has at the same time rendered a lot of its employees more precarious and has created the anachronism of poverty and even destitution in the midst of plenty.

"As business has increased in scope and power, governments have supplemented the earlier policy of fostering and protecting it by the adoption of a great variety of measures designed to establish a plane of competition believed to be socially desirable; second, those intended to remove obstructions to competition within the limits set; and finally, measures to regulate the conduct of business enterprises believed not to be adapted to socially satisfactory control by competition."[3] But never beefore in the history of our country has government participation in the direction and control

2 *Ibid.*, 2:327.
3 *Ibid.*, 2:86.

of private enterprise been so extensive as at present, for never before did conditions so urgently demand such extensive governmental participation.

From its earlier position of regulatory action our government has assumed the additional role of general economic and social planner. In adopting this planning function the government has lessened the ability of private enterprises to plan for themselves, for all types of private planning are projected upon past trends and prediction of future conditions. Consequently, the more public planning we have with its consequent disturbance of the natural tendencies, the less private institutional planning is possible. One of the most common indictments against public planning at present is the affirmation that it prevents individual enterprises from projecting its activities. This is the dilemma which confronts us and for which at present we see no solution. One thing seems obvious and inevitable, namely that unless our private institutions can more adequately stabilize and synchronize their various activities to effect greater economic and social security for their employees and local communities, the government must of necessity increase rather than lessen its participation and control.

III. Interregional Expansion
and Interracial Contacts

7

INDUSTRIAL EXPANSION AND THE INTERRELATIONS OF PEOPLES

1933

THE RISE, spread, and subsequent "fall" of peoples is a commonly recognized sequence in historical phenomena. "Rhythms, pulsations, or cycles," says Huntington, "seeem to be the law of organic life."[1] Modern students of demography have come to recognize this cyclical tendency in population growth. Pearl summarizes the results of his experimental and statistical research in the statement: "Growth occurs in cycles";[2] Gini has developed an elaborate theory to account for this phenomenon.[3] Whatever position one may take with regard to the factors involved in the pulsatory tendencies of growth and spread of population, it is apparent that history is largely the record of a succession of empires. Civilizations have evolved through a long series of conquests and invasions in which different peoples have risen and fallen, each contributing elements of race and culture to the larger moving complex. That such periodic advances and recessions occurred even among preliterate peoples is evidenced by the complex mixture of races and the wide diffusion of cultures which prevail throughout the primitive world.

Reprinted from *Race and Culture Contacts*, ed. E. B. Reuter, pp. 19–33. Copyright, 1934. Copyright renewed 1962, by McGraw-Hill, Inc. Used by permission of McGraw-Hill Book Company.

1   Ellsworth Huntington, *The Pulse of Progress*, p. 6.
2   Raymond Pearl, *The Biology of Population Growth*, p. 22.
3   Corrado Gini, "The Cyclical Rise and Fall of Population," *Population, Lectures on the Harris Foundation*, 1929.

The Expansion of Settlements

The early wanderings of tribal peoples, however, is hardly parallel with the expansion of established settlements. They represent rather the processes of dispersion typical of the lower forms of life. The concept expansion, on the other hand, connotes movement outward from a spatially determined center of settlement without loss of contact with that center. It presupposes a sufficient development of the center or core of settlement to insure reciprocal relations within an ever-widening range of territory. The center may be a single city, as in the case of the ancient city state, or it may be a more complex economic and cultural unit, such as the modern nation. In either case the extension of the margin involves closer integration of the core and a higher development of settlement structure. Thus great cities and closely knit national states are the natural concomitants of expanding peoples. Considered from the point of view of movement in space, expansion implies both centrifugal and centripetal processes. To the extent that the expanding group effects a division of labor with outside peoples, movement becomes cyclical rather than purely linear. In other words, it takes the form of circulation rather than mere migration; and the strategic points of outside contact, in turn, tend to develop into new centers of dominance.

The expansion of one group almost invariably involves contacts with other groups and occasions movements and rearrangements of the peoples affected. As a pebble thrown into a pond starts a series of waves which move outward to the shore line, so the expansion of a people into a territory already occupied induces a succession of migrations frequently of far-reaching proportions. The human migrations thus occasioned, however, do not possess the symmetry of the ripples on the pond; on the contrary, they may assume opposing tendencies and divergent directions.

Expansion has assumed many different forms in the course of history; but the general trend has been from military and political to economic and cultural dominance. The ancient empires were based primarily upon military conquests and subjugation of surrounding settlements.[4] Tribute rather than trade characterized the relation of the center to the fringe. For this reason Pericles could boast of ancient Athens: "Because of the greatness of our city the fruits of the whole earth flow in upon us, so that we may enjoy the goods of other countries as freely as our own." It is significant that he stressed the inward flow of goods and failed to mention the outward flow. The modern city depends quite as much upon its ability to export as to import goods; it is the product of a division of labor between center and hinterland.

The transition from military and political to economic and cultural expansion has followed a slow and devious course. Even in the present day there is a close relation between the movements of trade and the flag. On the whole, however, the flag has assumed a position subordinate to trade; and military conflict has become less important than "peaceful penetration" in the expansion of peoples and cultures.

The history of modern civilization is largely the story of European expansion, which, slowly at first, then with increasing momentum, brought different regions and peoples within a common economic order and a common cultural milieu. While this development, extending over four centuries, is a single process, it is by no means a simple one. The rate of change has not been uniform; there have been periods of rapid expansion followed by periods of relative stagnation. Different European peoples have taken the lead at different times. Frequent changes have occurred in the political and economic alignments of centers and frontiers. The general trend, however, has been toward a constant thickening of the web of relationships, the development of a more clearly outlined settlement structure, a contraction of space as measured in time and cost, an extension of territorial limits, the inclusion of an ever-increasing number and variety of peoples, and a general leveling of cultural differences. Mantoux has likened the expansion of industrial society to a river, "which does not always flow at the same pace, but sometimes slackens its course, sometimes rushes

[4]   "There was never a period in the whole life-time of the City State when war could be regarded as exceptional" (Alfred Zimmern, *The Greek Commonwalth*, p. 346).

on, now running through narrow gorges and now spreading back over the plain, now breaking up into many divergent branches, and now winding about, so that it seems to curve back on itself."[5]

Marginal Settlements

Historians and economists, in tracing the evolution of Western civilization, invariably divide it into periods or stages of development, the number of divisions depending upon the special interest of the investigator. For the purpose of this report, which is to indicate in broad outline the development of the present ecological organization of world society, the history of Western expansion may be divided into three successive stages.

The first, beginning with the age of discoveries in the fifteenth century and extending into the nineteenth century, represents an era of transoceanic rim-settlement development. During this period various European peoples—Spanish, Portuguese, English, French, and Dutch—established outposts at different points along the seacoasts of the New World, Africa, and Southern Asia. These marginal settlements were of three general types: (a) farm-family colonies of European migrants in the temperate belts; (b) sugar and spice plantations in the tropics, owned and operated by European capitalists but worked by colored slaves; and (c) the trading stations along the coasts of India and Southern China.

Trade consisted primarily of articles of luxury—precious metals, spices, sugar, tea, and manufactured commodities of handicraft production. The attitude and practice of the different European powers throughout this period were predatory and exploitative. Knowles states:

Overseas possessions were regarded at this time by all the colonizing powers as estates to be worked for the benefit of the mother country, and the "colonial system" was designed so to shape the development of colonies that they should become producers of raw materials or

5   Paul Mantoux, *The Industrial Revolution in the Eighteenth Century*, p. 488.

tropical products, such as sugar and spices, and should provide good markets for the manufacturers of the mother country.[6]

Almost to the close of this era the plantations and Eastern trading posts were considered by the home countries to be of greater importance than the agricultural colonies in the temperate belts. The great distances, as measured in sailing time, that separated the European centers from the overseas frontiers prevented the development of an effective geographic division of labor and created conditions favorable to piracy and exploitation. On the other hand, the lucrative trade in plantation and Eastern products furnished certain of the European powers, notably England, with the capital reserves necessary for the subsequent development of manufacturing.

Industrial and Commercial Development

A second phase of European expansion began early in the nineteenth century and continued with increasing momentum almost to the outbreak of the World War. This era was initiated by the succession of mechanical inventions which brought about a transformation in methods of production and means of transportation. It is characterized by the rise of industrial cities, by increasing movements of European peoples to overseas settlements, by an inland expansion of those settlements,[7] and by a more extensive and varied interchange of products between centers and frontiers.

England assumed the lead in the industrialization process. As the power-driven factory displaced handicraft production and the steamboat and railway became the leading agencies of transporta-

---

[6]   M. I. Knowles, *Economic Development of the British Overseas Empire*, 1:10.

[7]   During the whole of the past century it has been a question of the development of interiors—the moving inland from a port or coast line to control the land behind, and then the continuous pushing of the frontier, a process enormously quickened by railways in the last half century" (M. I. Knowles, *op. cit.*, p. 79).

tion, a new basis for a geographic division of labor was introduced. The process was cumulative, advancing with accelerated speed throughout the nineteenth century. Industrial cities sprang into existence, first in England, later in surrounding European countries and in the United States. Population moved inward to the growing centers of industry and commerce, and outward to the expanding frontiers. The complementary exchange of products which ensued, consisting mainly of the exchange of manufactured goods for food and other raw materials, furnished the most effective territorial division of labor the world has ever known. It made possible the doubling of the white race in the course of half a century, coupled with a substantial increase in the material standard of living.

Meanwhile the rising dominance of West European centers and the increasing concentration of industry and wealth stimulated a demand for larger quantities and greater varieties of plant and mineral products, also for the luxuries of the Orient. This caused an extension of European capital and business enterprise into a wide range of territory occupied by peoples of different race and culture. It likewise led to an extensive transportation of colored peoples, first African slaves, later East Indian and Chinese contract coolies, to meet labor requirements in the new plantation and mining areas. Thus the number of interracial settlements increased, each organized on the pattern of white direction and control of colored labor.

The mid-century gold discoveries on the Pacific coast of North America and in Australia and New Zealand gave rise to a somewhat different type of interracial settlement. These new mining ventures became magnets inducing spontaneous migration of both white and colored—mostly Chinese—people and provided the initial stimulus for settlement in previously undeveloped regions. They expedited railroad construction and hastened the extension of the frontiers of Western civilization. Their chief significance, however, inheres in the fact that they introduced an era of interracial conflict, which quickened national racial consciousness among peoples bordering on the Pacific and eventuated in the rise of legislative barriers against all Asiatic immigration to those countries.

Concurrent with the rise of these interracial plantation and mining settlements, another type of European outpost suddenly acquired new economic and cultural significance, namely, the commercial center in Oriental countries. For several centuries different European powers had traded with the peoples of India and Southern China but after the middle of the nineteenth century—with the advent of the steamboat, cable, telegraph, and railway—power-driven factories began to appear at shipping points along the coast of Asia; Japan was opened to Western commerce. The completion of the Suez Canal in 1869 and of a trans-American railway line in the same year opened a new transportation route around the world. By cutting in half the time required to encircle the globe, the completion of this thoroughfare reduced correspondingly the distance between the East and the West.

The effect of these various developments was revolutionary in character. Whereas the earlier contact of Western traders and missionaries with the peoples of the Orient made but slight impress on these older civilizations, the coming of power-driven factories, railways, banks, and other elements of the furniture of modern capitalism initiated a succession of economic and cultural changes in Asiatic countries the repercussions of which have been worldwide. Japan, owing perhaps to her more efficient internal organization, responded more quickly than her Oriental neighbors to the impact of Western culture. Within a single generation this country has risen from a feudal state to the rank of a world power.

By the beginning of the twentieth century the basic structure of modern civilization had been laid. The steamboat had brought the land masses of the earth into easy economic access and the railways had penetrated the inland regions. Consolidated national states had been formed by the coalescing and federation of formerly isolated settlement units. Great cities had arisen along the coast lines and at strategic inland points of the New World and Asia integrating extensive hinterlands and coming into competition with European centers. Tariff barriers—symbols of the growing consciousness of nationality and interregional competition—had been introduced in the United States and the British Dominions. England alone of the European powers still maintained a policy of free trade.

Cultural Maturation and Economic Nationalization

The third and present phase of industrial expansion developed early in the twentieth century and was accelerated by the dislocation occasioned by the World War. This may be styled an era of cultural maturation of frontier settlements and general emergence of economic nationalism. It is characterized, on the one hand, by the decline of European dominance in Western civilization and a decrease in the transmaritime movements of European peoples, capital, and goods and, on the other hand, by the rise of the United States and Japan as centers of world expansion, by the growth of manufactures in hitherto backward countries, and by the extension of tariff barriers and immigration restrictions.

While some of these tendencies were in evidence during the latter part of the nineteenth century, they have all increased in tempo since the turn of the century and particularly since the close of the war. They are, of course, related to the utilization of petroleum and electric energy in industry and communication. The advent of these new forms of energy furnished the basis for the extensive succession of economic and social changes that have come to characterize the "second industrial revolution."

Economic Expansion of the United States

Inasmuch as the United States led the world in the mechanization of industry, she rapidly acquired a dominant position in the territorial organization of modern civilization. By the early twenties this country had shifted her role from a debtor to a creditor nation and, during the decade preceding the depression, became the world center in the export of capital. With the surplus of wealth accruing from mass production and the optimism engendered by a rapidly rising material standard of living, capital flowed out of the United States in unprecedented amounts.[8]

The extensive foreign loans, especially the capital investments in the younger and more backward countries, stimulated settlement development in those areas. In response to the increasing demand for raw materials, new plantation and mining settlements suddenly burst forth and older ones expanded. Each such development invoked fresh movements and mixtures of peoples entailing economic and cultural adjustments to large-scale capitalistic organization. To the extent that these expanding settlements have come to depend upon the United States as a source of capital and as a market for their export products, they have come under the economic dominance and, in some cases, the political hegemony of this country.

A significant aspect of the rapid and in many respects artificial expansion of American industry during the twenties is the fact that it hastened the economic maturation of many of the younger countries and extended the economic frontiers of Western civilization too rapidly for their effective incorporation within the world economy. Particularly does this pertain to regions specialized in the production of a single export product such as sugar, cotton, coffee, rubber, wheat, and various types of minerals.[9] The adjustment of these specialized producing areas to normal market conditions constitutes one of the most serious problems facing West-

[8] "At the beginning of 1931 the foreign investments of the United States were distributed as follows: $5,600,000,000 was in Europe, Germany alone being indebted to the extent of nearly $1,500,000,000; $4,000,000,000 in Canada; $3,000,000,000 in Central America; and an equal amount in South America. Over half of the capital placed in various American countries was represented by direct investments, while at least three-fourths of the capital exported to Europe was represented by American investments in bonds" (M. Palyi, "Foreign Investment," *Encyclopaedia of the Social Sciences*).

[9] In thirty of the fifty-one non-European countries listed in the United States *Commerce Yearbook*, 1932, vol. 2, one product comprises over 50 per cent of the total exports.

ern civilization today.[10] Whereas most of the large cities of the modern world can accommodate their economies to changing markets without involving substantial shifts of population, the regions specialized in the production of raw materials, particularly those located outside the national boundaries of their leading markets, find it difficult to do so. This difficulty is aggravated by the fact that the older countries are tending to exploit more intensively their own resources and are erecting tariff walls against foreign products and, in some instances, even against those from their own colonies.

It should be noted also that many of the monoexport regions are interracial settlements into which immigrants have been drawn in response to outside enterprise. Population numbers have increased beyond the possibility of support by a self-contained economy. It is not surprising, therefore, that interracial conflict and political revolt have in recent years become endemic throughout the so-called backward regions of the world. Nor is it possible any longer to impute blame or responsibility to parent countries for the adverse conditions prevailing in their colonies. The interrelations of modern peoples have become depersonalized; they are now determined more by the vicissitudes of world markets than by the policies of imperial powers.

The Rise of Japan

While the economic expansion of the United States has accelerated the development of settlements throughout the New World and induced various realignments of peoples, the rising dominance of Japan has produced effects in modern world relations of almost equal importance. Whereas the expansion of the United States has been largely confined to the export of capital and machine-made products, that of Japan has involved the emigration of people as well.

[10]   "In 1905 one ton of rubber was exported from British Malaya, in 1907 the figure had risen to 885 tons, in 1917 to 79,831 tons. By 1921 over half the rubber of the world came from Malaya and there was an overproduction which prevented remunerative prices" (M. I. Knowles, *op. cit.*, p. 127).

The expansion of Japan, unlike that of any other Oriental nation, has assumed a typically European aspect. Her citizens have emigrated as family colonists to the New World, first to the Pacific coast of North America and later to certain South American countries, notably Brazil. Her merchants, capitalists, and administrators have established trading posts, factories, and plantations along the coast of Asia. Meanwhile she has extended her political jurisdiction, directly or indirectly, over an ever-widening range of near-by territory.

As Japan has developed industrially, she has reached out into the larger world to secure raw materials for her factories and markets for her finished products. In this connection she has effected a division of labor with certain countries—notably the United States, where raw silk is exchanged for cotton and lumber —but she has come into keen competition with other countries, especially England, in the extension of her markets into Asiatic territory. Japan's location at the outer margin of European contact with the Asiatic peoples affords her a strategic position from which to wage commercial warfare against Europe's eastern front. Already she has captured much of England's trade with India and the South Pacific regions. She is pushing westward into Africa and South America. This, coupled with the fact that other Asiatic peoples are "coming of age" in the new industrial regime, is causing a general recession of European trade and peoples from all Eastern territory.

Summary

Surveying the world today, we see its land surface divided into about a hundred major political areas or countries.[11] These countries range in area from a few thousand to over four million square miles and in poulation from a few thousand to over four hundred million inhabitants. If we consider each country as the

---

[11]   The United States *Commerce Yearbook*, 1932, vol. 2, lists 103 "principal countries." Of course, a number of these countries are political dependencies, but each is sufficiently distinct to be treated as a separate economic unit.

home of a people possessing sufficient cohesiveness and consciousness of common destiny to be thought of as a unit, the human population of the globe may be conceived as an aggregation of peoples,
geographically and politically set apart but economically and culturally bound together.

These different human groups vary greatly in the influence
they exert in the modern world. Some are aggressive forces pushing out beyond their own political domains; others are playing
a defensive role, seeking either to free themselves from foreign
political entanglements or to guard the territory they occupy
against the intrusion of foreign commerce. Some are entering
upon a new cycle of expansion; others seem to have reached their
crest and are beginning to recede; still others are in a condition
of relative stagnation. All, however, are being drawn closer together with the advance of communication and each is becoming
more conscious of the presence of the others.

A more realistic way, perhaps, to view the present world order
is to disregard the political map and direct attention toward cities
and their hinterland alignments. For whether we think in terms
of peoples or nations, cities constitute the engines which drive
the expansion process. The expansion of industrial civilization is
both creature and creator of cities. At the beginning of the nineteenth century the world contained not more than 20 cities that
had reached the 100,000 mark and not one that could boast of
1,000,000 inhabitants. Today there are at least 530 cities with
populations ranging from 1,000,000 to 10,000,000. Each of these
great cities, and many of the smaller ones also, may be considered
as an active center of expansion. For as populations become concentrated in cities, they tend to become more alert to the conditions
of the larger environment. There is obviously a close relation between the growth of cities in the younger and more backward
countries and the rise of nationalism in those regions.

In the present alignments of centers and frontiers of settlement two outstanding tendencies are observable: (a) the tendency
for the city or city region to become more diversified and more
closely integrated in its industrial and commercial structure, (b)
the tendency for the region of raw-material production to become

more specialized in its economic base and more dependent upon distant markets. These two opposite yet complementary processes have important bearing upon the interrelations of peoples and the diffusion of modern culture. As the economic base of the city region becomes more diversified, there is greater opportunity for an interracial division of labor, occupational mobility, and cultural assimilation. But as the scattered areas of primary production become more specialized and more enslaved by the dominance of world markets, their inhabitants tend to become more dependent upon outside forces, and the opportunities for cultural advance become correspondingly lessened.

The pioneer belts of our present industrial civilization, with few exceptions, occupy very different positions from those of the earlier economic frontiers of the nineteenth century. Instead of being located along the seaboards of undeveloped hinterlands, our modern frontiers occupy the margins of inland expansion and many of them are prevented by geographic and marketing factors from developing that economic diversification that forms the basis of a rounded cultural achievement.

8

MOVEMENT AND THE
ABILITY TO LIVE

1926

LIFE DIFFERS from death in the matter of movement. And the scope of life is defined by the facilities used for overcoming distance. The cycle of growth from infancy to old age may be measured in terms of spatial movement. Starting life with a minimum of activity, the child gradually extends his sphere of movement and of environmental control until he reaches his maximum attainment somewhere in adulthood. Then his range of movement gradually declines as old age creeps on until it arrives again at the point from which it started.

The quality of life is also related to the ability to move. The fundamental difference between the plant and animal lies in the realm of movement. The stationary plant must adapt itself to the conditions of the environment circumscribed by the reach of its roots and leaves, or die. The mobile animal lives in a larger world. His power of locomotion enables him to exploit a larger food area, and in this respect the animal represents a higher form of life than the plant.

Man as an animal possesses, in addition to his native power of locomotion, the ability to extend his environment by calling to his aid secondary agencies for overcoming distance. And his progress in world dominance has gone hand in hand with the increasing efficiency of the agencies of fluidity that he has been able to call to his assistance. The unequal development of different racial and cultural groups throughout the world is fundamentally associated

Reprinted from *Proceedings of Institute of International Relations*, 1926.

with the comparative efficiency of the agencies used in transportation and communication.

The great difference between the East and the West at the present time is in the matter of movement. In comparison with the West, the East is sluggish, stagnant, immobile. Although Asia possesses over half the world's population, nevertheless, she has less than nine per cent of the world's motor cars, less than three per cent of the world's telephone instruments, and sends about one per cent per year of the world's telegraph messages.

But the degree of stagnation of China and India cannot be measured by statistics showing facilities of communication and transportation. These two great countries are even more immobile than such statistics would imply. The great majority of their people die in the villages in which they were born. The last census of India, taken in 1921, showed that of the 43,000,000 people enumerated in the Madras presidency, ninety-nine per cent had been born in the local census district in which they were then living.

The secret of environmental control lies in the ability to conquer distance, that is, in the ability to go to the sources of food supply or to transport food to the source of consumption. The former is the way of the animal, of primitive man, and of the lower cultural groups. Historic migrations have been largely of the movements of people to the source of food, as in the case of the Lombards, Goths, Danes, and Normans, who swept into different parts of Europe, displacing their predecessors and occupying the food producing regions.

Civilization, however, presents a different pattern. It is based on fixity of place and mobility of products. In a word, civilization implies fixed centers, primary and secondary, associated with integrated regions and tied together by lines of communication and transportation. The city has ever been the symbol of civilization and it has grown in importance and dominance *pari passu* with the evolution of facilities for conquering distance. The early civilizations of the Euphrates, the Nile, and the Mediterranean seaboard emerged around dominant centers coordinated with tributary productive regions by means of water and land transportation. The great empires of ancient Greece and Rome were of a similar pattern, but tribute rather than trade defined the relation of the subordinate provinces to the urban centers. These civilizations crumbled when the lines of communication between their integrated parts were broken by outside invaders. From the later Middle Ages down to the present time, a new European Civilization has been expanding over the earth, gaining in power and momentum as each new agency of communication has evolved to give further control of distance. Temporarily retarded in its eastward expansion by the power of the Ottoman Turk in the fifteenth century, European expansion turned to the West and found a greater outlet in the Atlantic, over which it poured its surplus capital and population until the American frontiers became more dominant and aggressive than the parental source from which they sprang.

A new era of Euro-American world dominance commenced about the middle of the nineteenth century when the application of mechanical energy to transportation revolutionized distance in the movements of people and commodities, and when electrical mechanisms of communication annihilated space in the transmission of intelligence. The power of world control which this revolution of spatial distance has introduced is almost beyond comprehension. Not only has it made possible a wider and more intelligent utilization of the resources of the world, but it has brought the races and peoples of the world into a united relationship of competitive cooperation.

The recent emergence of a world market for the more important agricultural and industrial products is, of course, a direct effect of our efficient mechanism of communication. The expansion of the market has had very great significance with reference to human migration and regional integration. In the first place it has occasioned regional specialization of production, which not only brings different parts of the world into competition with one another but which also produces regional interdependence. The world is becoming territorially divided into wheat belts, corn belts, sugar, coffee, rubber, and tobacco areas. Canada competes with Argentina and Australia in the production of wheat; Egypt, with Georgia and our other Southern States in the production of cotton;

Brazil with Ceylon in coffee; Cuba with Hawaii in sugar; British Malaya with Java in rubber.

Likewise the extended market has brought the industrial areas of the world into a condition of interregional competition. Manchester competes with Bombay and Osaka in the manufacture of textiles; Pittsburgh and Gary with Birmingham and Essen in the manufacture of steel and iron products; Glasgow with Amsterdam and Osaka in the construction of ships. The point I wish to emphasize is that modern communication, by transcending all our old local and political boundaries, is bringing the world into a single economic unity in which competition is between *natural geographic regions* rather than between political, cultural, or racial groups as such.

Under the dominance of the greater market, it is the movement of capital that determines the movement of people rather than the reverse. Human migrations are no longer to the sources of food supply, but rather to the regions where capital is invested. And since the capital of the world comes from the West and is seeking investment in enterprises which cater to western consumption, the present direction of flow is not into the food producing regions (Canada, Argentina, and Australia have scarcely begun to develop), because the West has all the food it needs and the East cannot make its need effective, but rather, capital flows into the regions where luxuries may be produced, wherever those regions may be located.

This sweep of western capital into the remote corners of the world is of profound importance with reference to human migration. Not only are people washed hither and thither over the world in obedience to the dictates of capital—from the villages to the cities, from the sleepy valley of the Pearl river and the palmy plains of Southern India to the rubber plantations of Malaya and the sugar cane fields of Hawaii—but they are forced into a new economy in which the machine replaces the artisan and the product of toil is consumed far from the source of production. The little kinship and communal groups of the old regime are being reduced to individual atoms, and the herd is replacing the family as the pattern of social organization All the great cities of China and India are predominantly male. Women and children cling to the delapidated villages in the vain hope that the old order will one day be restored.

The great problem of the modern world is the problem of equilibrium. The agencies of fluidity have developed faster than those of control. In a static world, equilibrium is maintained by the operation of natural forces. The death rate fluctuates in accordance with the conditions governing local food supply. Population balance is maintained by the operation of positive checks— premature death, famine, war, pestilence.

But in the dynamic western world, local birth and death rates have but slight relation to equilibrium. Economic balance is maintained by movement. Surplus population moves to the regions of better economic advantage as is evidenced by the seasonal movements of labor along our Pacific Coast, as well as by the less conspicuous migrations from rural to urban districts in general.

Such movements of population take place for the most part within national boundaries. International migrations are impeded by legal restriction, as well as by cultural and linguistic barriers. This is illustrated in the case of England's surplus population at the present time. Her population is quite fluid within the national boundaries, but it does not readily flow into neighboring European countries, nor into the sparsely inhabited colonies.

The problem of equilibrium is still considered as a national problem, despite the fact that the forces which disturb the equilibrium are international in character. Regional prosperity or depression is determined largely by forces which operate in parts of the world and over which the region itself has little or no control.

If the region affected happens to be part of a large national unit, equilibrium may be attained by movement; but if it happens to be a part of a small political unit, such as Belgium or Japan, then the problem of adjustment is much more difficult.

The problem of equilibrium is in reality fast becoming a world problem. As the world increases in economic interdependence, it becomes one dynamic whole that cannot be controlled by the national autonomy method. The problem is similar to that of municipal government. Prior to the introduction of efficient intramural transportation, the ward system of government prevailed; but as soon as the city became tied together by rapid communication and reorganized into a single economic complexity, central control displaced the ward system.

By tariff walls and immigration restrictions the modern state attempts to maintain economic equilibrium. However, by closing the arteries of movement, the equilibrium thus attained tends to throttle further development and forces the world into the old self-sustaining regional pattern, in which the smaller territorial units suffer most.

Controls of international functions are gradually shifting from the periphery to the center in conformity with the actual facts of life and the more efficient utilization of world resources. Already in the sphere of private business, international cartels are superseding the national units. Centralization of economic control will undoubtedly be the trend in the future.

Although competition has become interregional, nevertheless cooperation has also, and to the great gain of mankind. Climatic and resource variations have made different parts of the world interdependent. One region supplements another. Moreover, the very fact of racial difference, instead of being a world calamity, is a fortunate evolution. Racial difference makes possible a much more efficient utilization of world resources. It is no longer necessary for the races to come into physical contact in order to compete or to cooperate. The most direct competition or cooperation may take place between racial groups located at opposite poles of the earth. The Tamils of Malaya cooperate with the workers of Akron in the production of rubber tires, and the jute growers of Bengal cooperate with the capitalists of Dundee in the production of jute bags. England has learned that Malaya is a more lucrative possession than Australia, although less than one per cent of its population is white. And Japan has learned that Formosa is a much more valuable possession than Korea, although the latter provides a source for emigration.

At present, however, the cooperative relation between the East and West works largely to the advantage of the latter. It is the kind of cooperation that exists between labor and capital when labor is plentiful and capital is scarce. But present conditions will not last. Change is rapid in these days. Before long the countries of the East will assume the western pattern and will demand their rights in a world economy. Japan, in the short span of a single lifetime, has wrought a change in her national economy as great as that which it took Europe 200 years to accomplish. China and India, by the very fact of massive size, yield more slowly to western penetration. But even these two great countries are gradually laying aside their medieval garments and donning the western uniform.

The West still treats the East as though it were a subordinate outpost. Economic dominance has carried with it the attitude of social and political dominance. Both must change. Asia cannot indefinitely remain as the reservoir of labor for the luxury consuming West. Her illiterate masses will arise, as the proletariate of the West have arisen, and demand a share in the achievements of science. And gradually, as the millions of Asia are able to make their wants effective, the food producing areas of the world will become the richest fields for investment, and the now sparsely settled plains of Canada, Argentina, and Australia will bustle with life and activity.

The world is still primitive, exceedingly so. Primitive barriers impede movement at every turn, throttling the efficient utilization of world resources. China is the example *par excellence* of this condition. Almost every district has its different system of weights and measurements and of money as well as its own dialect and customs. It is a strange paradox that on one side of the Pacific lies the most mobile country in the world, while on the other side lies the most stagnant country in the world. These two great nations—America and China—are much alike in size, climate, and physical resources. But while the former is a united whole, every part integrated and related to every other part in one great national economy, the latter is a disjointed and disintegrated mass, helpless in its poverty, while much of its resources lies undeveloped. The difference lies in movement. America, without its railways, its automobiles, its electrical communication, would be another China. And so the whole world might be much like America if the primitive barriers which now exist were removed and a system of world communication installed with as little impediment to movement as now exists in this country.

9

MIGRATION IN THE PACIFIC AREA

1930

THE *Survey*, 1929, contained an examination of United States immigration policy, beginning with the minor conditions or limitations imposed by the states of the young republic, continuing with the assumption of control by the federal government, and concluding with the erection of barriers against the rising waves of immigration, as the demand for unskilled labor decreased and Congress reached the conclusion that the "new" and growing immigration from east and southeast Europe was less assimilable than that which preceded 1890.

That study took into account the conditions and impulses which have determined the volume and character of immigration from Europe, and discussed the biological theories which have been advanced in favor of a free or a restrictive immigration policy, and the various proposed bases of restriction. Oriental immigration was considered only in so far as it contributed to the development of an American exclusion policy and sequent legislation. The following account is intended to round out the subject by giving the movements of population which directly interest the United States in the vast stretches bordering on the Pacific.

The subject gains an additional interest from the effect of population growth and movement on political attitudes. In the time of the Grand Monarque, Vauban said that "the number of their subjects measures the grandeur of kings." Napoleon expressed the

Reprinted from *American Foreign Relations, 1930*, ed. C. P. Howland (New Haven: Yale University Press, 1930).

same idea more brutally in answering Madame de Staël's question as to who was the greatest woman of all time, "She, Madame, who furnished the most cannon-food at her country's need."[1] A twentieth-century Mussolini sees power in the same terms: "In disciplined, enriched, cultivated Italy there is room for 10,000,000 more men. Sixty million Italians would make their weight felt in the world."[2] Vaguely but generally associated with the numbers of citizens is state power. European nationalism includes the idea that the surest measure of a country's greatness is a rapidly and continuously waxing population; as between strong nations, well organized, equal in national genius and possessing equal resources, superiority in war may well lie with the nation which has preponderant numbers. Ignoring the conditions under which this thesis is valid, the popular mind has applied it to the comparison of strong nations with those loosely organized and has persuaded itself that numbers measure strength and that the nation which multiplies the fastest outfoots all other in the contest for existence. The contrast between the nine hundred and fifty millions of Asia and the one hundred and twenty millions of the United States inspires a genuine apprehension no less than the more rabid fears associated with the "yellow menace."

Apprehension is felt in certain quarters regarding an alleged decline of the old American stock. In the early period of English settlement in America the population grew rapidly by natural increase. The early American families justified, with remarkable frequency, the estimate of Matthews Duncan that "a normal woman among civilized races living in wedlock throughout the mature period under favorable circumstances should bear from ten to twelve children."[3] But in the course of fifty years the increase and wider distribution of prosperity, the growth of inherited wealth, and the various factors associated with a higher standard of living, though stimulating certain cooperative and collectivistic practices, yet have induced a spirit of individualism and loosening of tradi-

---

[1]   Both quotations are from Edward M. East, *Mankind at the Crossroads*, p. 51.

[2]   *Gerarchia*, September, 1928.

[3]   A. M. Carr-Saunders, *The Population Problem*, p. 100.

tions. In consequence there have appeared in this country the population tendencies that have long characterized France and now characterize most of Europe, i.e., a decline in the number of births averaged to each woman of breeding age. As yet the declining death rate still permits an actual increase of population but the composition of the population is changing; there are relatively fewer women of child-bearing age, and the present maintenance of gross numbers may mask the potentiality of a future decline.[4]

Dwelling fondly in the past, political imagination can be easily excited by a contemplation of former cataclysms, and the suggestion of a historic parallelism. The population pressure of yellow multitudes is supposed to threaten the same dangers to American civilization as came to Rome from

> those fair warriors, the tall Goths, from the day when they led their blue-eyed families off Vistula's cold pasture-lands . . . and in the incontaminate vigor of manliness, . . . tore at the ravel'd fringes of the purple power. . . .

and Malthus' classic picture of the "clouds of Barbarians"[5] still affects men's minds. Such events afford no parallel to present conditions. The hammer-strokes recorded by Malthus are barbarian conquest-migrations in which whole races or segments of races were on the move. The conditions of such events is the uprooting of a whole tribe or the breaking off of an integral segment, driven by restlessness and supported by hardy enterprise, powerful motives operating upon races of tremendous will. There is little danger that to the assistance of individuals migration organized conquest will be brought by "yellow" people against "white" people who have encompassed and organized a territory politically and socially.

Certainly there is no reason for governments to come into conflict over such an issue. Experience has left no doubt that emigration affords no more than the briefest relief to an increasing population pressure. The fecundity of China or Italy does not de-

[4]   R. R. Kuczynski, *The Balance of Births and Deaths* (New York, 1928), vol. 1.
[5]   Malthus, *Essay on Population*, chap. 3.

cline because Chinese or Italians emigrate, whether to Malaysia, Brazil, California, or Italian colonies; population may even increase until it reaches the former pressure point. This was reported and understood in the eighteenth century:

> The population of the thirteen American states before the war was reckoned at about three millions. Nobody imagines that Great Britain is less populous at present for the emigration of the small parent stock that produced these numbers. On the contrary, a certain degree of emigration is known to be favorable to the population of the mother country.[6]
>
> Who can now find the vacancy made in Sweden, France, or other warlike nations by the Plague of heroism forty years ago; in France by her expulsion of the Protestants; in England by the settlement of her colonies; or in Guinea, by one hundred years' exportation of slaves that has blackened half America?[7]

The solution of population congestion lies more in the direction of freedom of trade than of freedom of migration. Density of population becomes of less consequence under free specialized production and ease of communication and transportation. The term "over-population" implies the acceptance of some such criterion as Carr-Saunders calls an optimum number of people. Presumably this optimum is taken to be the number of people in a given area who with existing resources and arts of production can obtain the highest standard of living. The optimum population probably means increasing density as the arts of production become more efficient. It is also highly characteristic of the most prosperous modern nations that the densities of populations within their borders vary widely from place to place.

Atlantic Versus Pacific

Migration in the Pacific area is still in its infancy. As against the fifty-five million Europeans who traversed the Atlantic during

6   *Ibid.*, chap. 6.
7   Benjamin Franklin, *Observations Concerning the Increase of Mankind, People of Countries, etc.* (Boston, 1755).

the years 1820–1924, not more than one million Asiatics have crossed the Pacific to take up residence in the New World since the beginning of recorded migrations.[8] For the ten-year period preceding the World War the average yearly immigration from Europe, with its five hundred million people, was greater than the recorded immigration of all time from those Asiatic countries which lie in the western Pacific area and have an equal population.

Conditions of relatively recent origin account for these contrasts in the flow of people. A hundred years ago the masses of Europe were almost as immobile as are those of Asia today. But a movement of liberation was born of the industrial and political revolutions. People's minds were awakened to the possibilities of individual enterprise, and with ease of movement of goods came the movement of human beings. Steam navigation afforded a ready means of transportation to the New World, which needed strong arms and promised a more stable existence.

Asiatic migration also was restricted by traditional and political barriers. Chinese overseas migration began in the seventh century with the settlement of Formosa and the Pescadores Islands. The resulting trade routes to British Malacca, the Dutch East Indies, and the Philippines led to the second migration beginning with the fifteenth century. The Malay Archipelago, Java, Sumatra, Borneo, the Sulu Archipelago, and the Philippines were colonized. In 1712 Chinese residing abroad were prohibited from returning home under penalty of death sentence.[9] As Chinese ports were

[8]   "Prior to the establishment of current systems of migration statistics in the nineteenth century (Great Britain, 1815; United States, 1820) records and lists of emigrants were frequently kept" (*International Migrations* [National Bureau of Economic Research, 1929], 1:78).

In China, records were started at Amoy in 1845; for Japanese, records of passports were begun in 1868, and emigration statistics are available since 1898.

"Genuine migration statistics, distinguishing overseas from continental migrants and taking account of the more important movement of native labor, were introduced after the War" (*Ibid.*, footnote, p. 223).

[9]   Ta Chen, *Chinese Migrations, with Special Reference to Labor Conditions* (Washington, 1923), p. 20.

opened by treaty, the third period of emigration began; the numbers leaving the treaty ports were small at first, but when, about the middle of the nineteenth century, Spain, Portugal, Holland, and Great Britain began looking for labor for the industrial and commercial development of their colonies and contract-coolie emigration was legalized, they increased and by 1873 amounted to 13,016.[10]

"From 1636 to 1866 emigration from Japan was a capital offense, and the stream did not begin to flow freely until the eighties of the last century."[11] Indian oversees emigration began soon after the abolition of slavery in the British Empire in 1838. By a series of acts since 1837 the Government of India has provided for the welfare of the emigrant and controlled the number to meet opportunities abroad.[12]

Unlike the early European migrants—yeomen colonists who crossed the Atlantic to till their own holdings in the New World—the early Asiatic migrants were mainly indentured laborers who were imported to work on plantations in the West Indies or southern Pacific, or free laborers who came to assist the white pioneers in the development of their settlements in the coastal regions of North America, Australia, and New Zealand. Discoveries of gold stimulated immigration into California, Australia, New Zealand, and Canada, but even in these cases the number of arrivals was soon adjusted to the white pioneer's conception of his labor requirements. Remote from the centers of population and political control, the western white settlements had developed an unusual degree of local consciousness and corporate behavior, and they acted with great vigor in regard to Oriental immigration. Additional population was wanted for purposes of labor only. The Asiatics who came to the western seaboard of America or to the white settlements of the southern Pacific, found themselves associated with peoples of strikingly different racial and cultural traits which had developed during a long period of semi-isolation.

10   *International Migrations, op. cit.*, 1:151.
11   *Ibid.*, p. 160.
12   *Ibid.*, pp. 140 ff.

Settlement Areas

Considered from the standpoint of population changes, the various Pacific regions vary greatly. Of the western Pacific countries only Japan and Java show rates of natural growth comparable with those of European peoples. Since Japan was open to western commerce its population has risen from 32,000,000 to 60,000,-000,[13] and in fifteen years (1905–20) the population of the Netherland East Indies increased from 38,070,389 to 49,350,834.[14] Neither of these populations has as yet shown any pronounced tendency toward emigration. In many respects the Japanese are more European than Asiatic. Their migrations bear a much closer resemblance to European migrations than to those of other Asiatics; a western standard of living bars them from the plantation regions of the South Seas except in the capacity of Europeans, that is, as commercial and industrial promoters. Only within recent years have the people of Japan begun to seek homes in foreign lands, and up to the present few Javanese have gone further than the plantation regions in neighboring islands. Two regions are notable for immigration—British Malaya and Manchuria. The increase in the population of the former from slightly over a million in 1901 to 3,332,603 (census data) in 1921, and of the latter from about 14,000,000 in 1900 to 30,000,000 in 1928, is almost wholly attributable to net migration.

In the Caucasian areas of the Pacific nearly all the settled regions attract immigration. About 30 per cent of the net annual gain in the population of Australia is due to migration.[15] In the three Pacific Coast states of the United States the population has a still larger proportion of newcomers. In 1920 only 30 per cent of the native white population of Washington was born within the

13   *Problems of the Pacific* (1927), Proceedings of the Second Conference of the Institute of Pacific Relations, Honolulu, 1927, p. 340.
14   *Commerce Yearbook*, 1928, 2 (Foreign Countries): 439.
15   Phillips and Wood, *The Peopling of Australia* (Melbourne, 1928), p. 52.

state; the ratios for Oregon and California were 37.8 and 37.3 respectively.

Although climate influences not only the economic structure of an area but also the white man's appraisal of its fitness for settlement, both change with the growth of science and the improvement of communications. At one time the Pacific Coast was thought to be too remote for white settlement. A commission, appointed to inquire into making "an establishment" at the mouth of the Columbia River in order to reap the benefits of the fur trade, recommended the importation of Chinese, with their wives and children, as settlers. Experience had shown, the commission said, that family life keeps men's minds "from pursuits which often in frontier countries lead to strife."

And though the people of that country (China) evince no disposition to emigrate to the territory of adjoining princes, it is believed they would willingly, nay, gladly, embrace the opportunity of a home in America where they have no prejudices, no fears, no restraint in opinion, labor, or religion.[16]

But once steamships and railways had made these salubrious areas accessible to western settlement a sudden change of attitude took place, and "white" immigration policies were developed.

White People in the Non-Caucasian Pacific

Although Europeans have been in contact with the peoples of eastern Asia for several centuries and in continuous intercourse since the middle of the nineteenth century, at present only a few western white people are resident there, and despite trade expansion between eastern and western countries their number shows little tendency to grow. Moreover, except for a part of the missionary population, they are almost exclusively confined to the large modern coastal cities which contain European quarters of an official or unofficial character. The European and American populations of Japan are almost stationary, the latter declining slightly from

[16]   *Annals of Congress*, Sixteenth Congress, Second Session, January, 1821, pp. 956–57.

1926 to 1927—2,134 as against 2,012;[17] the British population increased slightly in this interval but almost all the other European nationalities remained the same or decreased slightly. In China the total white population, excluding Russians, was only about 32,000 in 1927, of whom 11,714 were British, 6,970 Americans, 2,588 French, 2,719 Germans, and 2,061 Portuguese.[18] Although Americans have had contact with China since clipper-ship days, not until after the Civil War did they begin to take up residence in China, and even then largely in the capacity of missionaries. According to Dr. Otte's figures there were 1,153 United States citizens in China in 1890 but only thirty-two American firms. During the next decade the number of firms increased to ninety-nine but the number of persons scarcely doubled. From 1900 to the present the ratio of American firms to persons has steadily increased, amounting to one firm to every thirty-six persons in 1890. In 1923, the peak year of American population in China, about half of the total of 12,530 were missionaries. By the beginning of 1928 the number had dropped to 8,569 of whom nearly half were in Shanghai.[19]

The West entered the East at the top of the occupation pyramid; the East entered the West at the bottom. This contrast in levels of invasion has imporant bearing not only upon interracial attitudes, the individual being taken as representative of his race, but also upon the duration of stay and the territorial distribution of foreign residents. The Oriental immigrants who came to America as unskilled laborers are gradually working up the economic ladder, and as they rise they become more widely distributed throughout the country. But the Westerner who enters Asia at the top of the occupational pyramid cannot descend in the economic scale; when he fails to maintain his original status his homeland is his only refuge. On the other hand, his position at the top is

17   Foreign office figures.
18   See Dr. Friedrich Otte, "Foreigners in China, A Statistical Survey," *Chinese Economic Journal*, 3, no. 6: 993–1002.
19   See the succinct analysis of the present distribution and activities of the American population in China, by Mr. Julean Arnold, United States Commercial *Attaché* in Peking: *China, a Commercial and Industrial Handbook* (1926).

usually temporary; in course of time the local people learn his technique and gradually displace him.

According to the Committee on Industry and Trade,[20] the foreign trade of Japan until about thirty years ago was almost entirely in the hands of non-Japanese merchants, mostly British. As the Japanese realized that a large share of the resulting prosperity was going into foreign pockets, they organized firms, in some cases with indirect governmental aid, which gradually established branches in all parts of the world. A similar situation has evolved in China, although because of political instability the Chinese have not yet been able to organize business to the same extent. The white populations of Hawaii and Malaya have been able to maintain their position at the peak of the occupation pyramid but are gradually being displaced by other races in mercantile and professional services.[21]

Japanese Migration[22]

Japanese immigration may be divided into three periods: (1) prior to 1907, the year when the Gentlemen's Agreement went into effect; (2) from 1907 to the introduction of the exclusion measure in 1924; (3) from 1924 to the present. Japanese migration has been much more definite and measurable than Chinese. From 1868, the year when the Secretary of State for Foreign Affairs began to issue passports to Japanese passengers going abroad, until 1924, when exclusion from the United States became effective, the Japanese Government has issued a total of 1,187,566 passports to passenger citizens. Of this number 197,902 were issued to persons going to continental United States, and 238,291 to persons going to Hawaii—together constituting 36.7 per cent of the total passports issued. During the same period 30,491 passenger citizens left for Canada, 12,261 for Mexico, and 49,668 for various

20   *Survey of Overseas Markets* (1927), p. 412.
21   Andrew W. Lind, *Journal of Social Forces*, December, 1928, p. 293.
22   For a more extensive discussion of Japanese immigration, see *Survey*, 1929, pp. 501 ff.

South American countries, mainly Brazil and Peru.[23] Inasmuch as emigrants constitute a large percentage of the total outflow, the statistics are significant in showing the leading streams of emigration.

Although Japanese overseas emigration began about 1866, it did not amount to more than 1,554 until 1885, when 3,461 left the country, of whom 1,959 went to Hawaii. Arrangements were made by the Kingdom of the Hawaiian Islands with the Empire of Japan for the bringing in of contract laborers to work on sugar plantations. This marked the beginning of Japanese migration to those islands, and Hawaii remained the leading destination until 1908, receiving until 1891 almost half of the total number of Japanese going abroad. In 1893 the total number of passports issued by the Japanese Government to citizens going abroad was 13,669, in 1895 it increased to 22,411, and in 1896 to 27,565. Ten years later, during the Russo-Japanese war, 19,466 passenger citizens left Japan. The following year, 1906, was the peak year of Japanese immigration to Hawaii, and 58,851 passports were issued, of which 30,393 were to persons going to Hawaii and 8,466 to persons going to continental United States.[24] Inasmuch as Hawaii was by this time an integral part of the United States, many of these crossed to the continent without any official record being made of their entry. Their arrival occasioned alarm in the Pacific Coast states and resulted in an Executive Order of March 14, 1907, which ordered that

Japanese or Korean laborers, skilled or unskilled, who have received passports to go to Mexico, Canada, or Hawaii, and come therefrom, be refused permission to enter the continental territory of the United States.

A short time later the so-called Gentlemen's Agreement was consummated according to which the Japanese Government agreed to refuse passports to laborers, skilled or unskilled, seeking to enter continental United States. Similar restrictions were made applicable to the Hawaiian Islands and Mexico. By 1906 streams of

23   Facts compiled from *International Migrations, op. cit.*, 1:934.
24   *Ibid.*

migration had developed to Canada, Mexico, and Peru. The movement to Mexico lasted only two years, but by 1912 Brazil was receiving over a thousand passenger citizens. Meanwhile the migration to the south Pacific and other regions fluctuated in volume and varied in direction in response to legal limitations and economic conditions. The following table, furnished by the Japanese Embassy, shows the general distribution of Japanese in foreign countries according to the latest statistics compiled by the Government:

JAPANESE RESIDING ABROAD

	Male	*Female*	*Total*
Asia	163,225	136,469	299,694
Europe	2,741	202	2,943
North America	89,984	45,671	135,655
South America	30,256	17,266	47,522
Africa	49	23	72
Oceania	69,108	48,374	117,482
	355,363	248,005	603,368

The census returns by decades give a brief but significant account of the growth of the Japanese population in continental United States and Hawaii.[25]

Year	*Continental United States*		*Hawaii*
1870	55		------
1880	148	(1884)	116
1890	2,039		12,860
1900	24,326		61,111
1910	72,157		79,675
1920	111,010		109,274
1922	115,186		112,221

[25]   Prior to 1900, the first census in which Hawaii was included in United States data, the figures for Japanese in Hawaii are taken from Romanzo Adams, *The Peoples of Hawaii* (Institute of Pacific Relations, Honolulu, 1925), p. 7.

Net Immigration

The characteristic desire of Orientals to return home seems to warrant special consideration, as net rather than gross immigration is significant.[26] From 1909 to June 30, 1929, 19,356 more Chinese left the United States than entered it, at least so far as official records are concerned, while the net increase in the Japanese population due to immigration was only 1,640. Undoubtedly the outward movement during this period was relatively much greater than in earlier years. By 1908 laborers of both groups had been excluded, the Chinese by the Act of 1882, and the Japanese by the Gentlemen's Agreement of 1907. These restrictive measures had reducd th inflow of Japanese immigrants from a total of 133,557 (1900–1908) to 60,308 (1909–17), and perhaps accentuated the return movement to the Orient as they implied agitation and prejudice on the part of Americans toward Orientals already here.

Age and Sex

The age and sex composition of Oriental immigration merits some consideration, not only because it concerns the Oriental population of the country but also because it affects the

[26] A word of caution should be given with regard to the interpretation of migration statistics. The common practice has been to gauge net immigration by subtracting the number of emigrant aliens from the number of immigrant aliens and to assume that the difference represents net immigration. While this practice is fairly sound with reference to European migration, it is misleading when applied to Orientals. A more nearly reliable criterion of net Chinese and Japanese immigration is found by subtracting the total departures from the total arrivals irrespective of status classification. Data for this are available only since 1908. "Taking the figures for a recent period as a guide, aliens of the returning resident class comprise over three-fifths of the Japanese nonimmigrants, about one-fourth of the Chinese nonimmigrants, and a little over one-half of the European nonimmigrants" (From a letter written by Harry E. Hull, Commissioner General).

administration of the immigration law. Chinese immigration tends to be predominantly male, as indicated by the sex ratios in the different regions of settlement. In Australia the ratio of Chinese males to females is 16 to 1; in New Zealand about 14 to 1; in Canada, 35 to 1; in British Malaya, 12 to 1. This sex disparity is striking also in continental United States, although there is a tendency toward equalization. In 1900 the ratio of Chinese males to females was 21 to 1; in 1910, 16 to 1; in 1920, 8 to 1. The ratio for Hawaii is more nearly normal; in 1920 there were only about 2 males to 1 female. In all places from which further immigration is barred, the effect of this sex disparity tends to leave the Chinese a declining population until the proportion of the sexes is approximately equalized in the second or third generation. The Chinese population of the United States has shown a substantial decrease in each of the last three census returns, and the 1930 census will doubtless show a still further decline.

Maintenance of their families in China by Chinese men in America adds to the burdens of immigration officials. Under present legal restrictions, the two main classes of Chinese admitted are the children, mostly males, of "treaty merchants" (Treaty of 1880), and Chinese United States citizens who have acquired citizenship by virtue of the fact that either they themselves or their fathers were born here. The latter constitute about a third of the total number of Chinese admitted. Between 1925 and 1929, 15,405 Chinese American citizens entered the United States. The problem of proving legal right to entry is the source of much irritation and misunderstanding.[27]

In the case of Japanese immigration the early preponderance of males was temporary. As soon as the young men became settled in the country they straightway sought to establish family life. Although the percentage of married males, fifteen years and over, to all males, was about the same for the Chinese and Japanese in 1920, 49.7 and 54.5 respectively, the proportion of married Japanese having their wives in the United States was almost six times that of the Chinese.

[27]   See R. D. McKenzie, *Oriental Exclusion* (Chicago, 1928), chap. 5; and *Survey* (1929), p. 500.

This tendency on the part of Japanese immigrants to establish family life has an important bearing on their selection of occupation as well as upon the growth of the local Japanese population. It has contributed to the withdrawal of Japanese from Hawaiian sugar plantations, Alaskan canneries, and western camp life, and to their adoption of more settled occupations. In 1907, 2,685 Japanese were employed in logging camps in Washington, but by 1924 the number had declined to 1,458, although the total number of employees in the industry had increased 30 per cent during this period. Moreover, the Japanese who remain in the logging industry have to an unusual extent settled in the more stable camps where they could live with their families. Thus while the Chinese population in the United States is steadily declining, the number of Japanese is gradually increasing owing to excess of births over deaths.

East Indian Migration

As far as the United States is concerned, Chinese and Japanese are the only Asiatic groups in the Pacific area which in the past have caused immigration problems. East India migrations in the Pacific have been largely confined to British possessions; only an insignificant number have found their way into the United States. The census does not record East Indians separately, but the Commissioner General of Immigration reports only 8,474 East Indian immigrant aliens between 1899 and 1929; between 1908 and 1929, 2,691 emigrant aliens departed. Prior to 1907 East Indian migrations to the United States and Canada was negligible, never more than one or two hundred a year and usually less. The increase in 1907 to 1,072 cause no alarm in the United States, but in Canada an increase to 2,124[28] resulted in the Continuous Passage Ordinance (Order in Council, P. C. 23), an order which caused 372 Indians to be denied admission upon arrival at Vancouver on board a Japanese ship, the *Kamagata Maru*, chartered by a Sikh labor contractor.

[28]   As the system of recording migration statistics was changed in this year, this figure is for nine months only.

Although Indian migration to the United States showed no tendency to increase, the Canadian incident and the fear of probable East Indian immigration at the conclusion of the World War sufficed to bring about the Barred Zone Provision in the Immigration Act of 1917. By this Provision no immigrants were allowed to enter from India or other parts of the western Pacific not already covered by restrictive measures.

The Philippine Islands

Coming to the Philippines in the tenth century, the Chinese competed with the Arabs there and by the twelfth century had driven them out. During the two and a quarter centuries of Spanish occupation the policy toward the Chinese "alternated between contemptuous toleration, attained apparently by wholesale bribery, and brutal attempts to exterminate them by massacre."[29] In 1898 there was a resident Chinese population of about 40,000 (41,035 in 1903). As soon as the islands came under the jurisdiction of the United States, measures were taken to exclude the Chinese. On September 26, 1898, General Otis "issued a military order applying the American exclusion laws to the islands."[30] Despite the protest of the Chinese Minister, the United States Government in 1902 ratified the order by officially extending its Chinese exclusion laws to the Philippines.

During the first two decades of American occupation, the resident Chinese population showed little tendency to increase, the official census of 1918 recording 43,802, only 2,767 more than the census of 1903. In recent years Chinese residents in the Philippine Islands seem to be increasing more rapidly, as in 1926 their numbers were estimated at 60,000.[31] The estimates of smuggled entries vary widely, but in any case the recorded net increase of Chinese aliens between 1925 and 1929 was 14,430; in 1929, 18,385 Chinese aliens arrived and 15,062 departed.[32]

[29]   H. F. McNair, *The Chinese Abroad*, p. 88.
[30]   *Ibid.*, p. 89.
[31]   W. Cameron Forbes, *The Philippine Islands*, 1:17.
[32]   *Annual Reports of the Commissioner General of Immigration.*

As in many other parts of the south Pacific, the Chinese in the Philippines serve as middlemen between the Malay peoples and their western rulers. Their experience, industry, and clannishness have put most businesses into their hands. They are engaged extensively in the retail and interprovincial services, distributing imported merchandise and collecting from the natives most of the export products.[33]

Japanese immigration is of relatively less significance, mostly confined to Davao province on Mindanao. The census of 1903 recorded only 921 Japanese, that of 1918, 7,806, and the latest official information, October, 1928, furnished by the Japanese Foreign Office, puts the number at 14,000. Between 1925 and 1929 a total of 13,002 Japanese entered the Philippines and 5,781 departed, a net increase of 7,321.[34]

Filipino Migration

. . . . Filipinos—and Mexicans also, in the case of the Alaska fisheries—are replacing the Chinese and Japanese as laborers in the industries cited. The process is a replacing rather than a displacing one. The earlier immigrants have graduated to independent agriculture or are concentrated in urban centers. Although going on for years, this "ascensive process" does not become apparent until legislation stops the stream of new recruits. The labor vacuum thus developed at the base of the occupation pyramid is filled by the importation of a different ethnic stock. Wave after wave of different cultural and racial groups has been brought into Hawaii as plantation workers. Portuguese, Chinese, and Japanese have served their apprenticeships in the sugar-cane fields and then moved to the urban centers or withdrawn from the islands entirely; now Filipinos are filling in the ranks. When the Act of 1883 imposed restrictions on Chinese immigration, Japanese laborers were imported to Hawaii. Again, when the Agreement of 1907–8 cut off the supply of Japanese

[33]   See *Philippine Islands, A Commercial Survey* (U. S. Bureau of Commerce, 1927).

[34]   *Annual Reports of the Commissioner General of Immigration.*

workers, the planters of Hawaii turned their attention toward the Philippines, which by this time had become a territorial possession of the United States. In 1910 and 1911, 4,930 Filipinos were introduced into Hawaii by the Hawaiian Sugar Planters' Association. Between 1912 and 1924, 52,626 Filipinos went to Hawaii.[35] In 1929, 8,369 Filipino emigrants left for Hawaii, and 3,991 returned. Most of this migration is the result of a highly organized system of recruiting carried on by the Hawaiian Sugar Planters' Association, and, in accordance with an Act of 1915, under the supervision of the Philippine Government. The planters are required to give free transportation, to pay a minimum wage "of 40 pesos per month of 26 days . . . to give free rent, water, fuel and medical attendance" during the period of employment.[36]

A considerable part of the Filipino migration to Hawaii passes on to the mainland, where wages are higher and opportunities for advancement more promising. As late as 1910 the census recorded only 160 Filipinos in continental United States; by 1920 the number had increased to 5,603. Since 1920 and especially since the passing of the Exclusion Act in 1924 the stream of incoming Filipinos has increased rapidly with a proportionately diminishing number of returns. In recent years it has taken two courses, one flowing from Hawaii and the other direct from the Philippines. From July 1, 1924, to June 30, 1929, inclusive, 26,006 Filipinos,[37] mostly young male laborers, arrived in continental United States; during the same period 9,790 came from Hawaii. In 1929, 11,360 Filipinos arrived in Pacific Coast ports of continental United States, of whom 8,689 came from the Philippines, 2,654 from Hawaii, and 17 from other places.[38]

In December, 1929, there were approximately 50,000 Filipinos in continental United States, the great majority of whom were concentrated in California and Washington. Unlike the Chi-

---

[35]   *International Migrations*, 1:1022.
[36]   *Monthly Record of Migration*, April, 1927, pp. 146–47.
[37]   War Department, Bureau of Insular Affairs, Communication, June 2, 1930.
[38]   *Annual Report of the Commissioner General of Immigration*, 1929, p. 230.

nese and Japanese groups who maintain their own local institutions and services, the Filipino immigrants rely upon the institutions of the larger community, coming into contact with the organized charities, the public health service and other welfare organizations. These of the new arrivals who succeed in finding employment enter the unskilled occupations vacated by the rising group of Orientals who preceded them. Although definite occupational data are lacking, general observation and report indicate that the Filipino immigrants are concentrating in the unorganized domestic services, as waiters, house-boys, elevator operators, and hospital attendants; they are also serving as transient laborers in the truck-gardening areas, in the canneries, and railway gangs. They come into competition with Mexicans, Negroes, and to a certain extent with female workers. Representative leaders of the Negro colony in Seattle assert that as a result of Filipino competition the colored population of that city has decreased by about two thousand during the last four years. Ever since the Philippines became a possession of the United States a small but increasing number of Filipino students have come to continental United States to enter the higher institutions of learning; the return movement has usually balanced this immigration.

The problem of dealing with Filipino immigration is fraught with legal difficulties. The Filipinos are not aliens as defined by the 1924 Act and are therefore not subject to exclusion, but they are as different in culture and race from the people of continental United States as are any of the Asiatics already excluded. And now that they have begun to evince a tendency toward spontaneous migration—the movement to the mainnland is entirely spontaneous, and since 1927 considerable number have come to Hawaii of their own accord—it is not surprising that the anti-Oriental organizations in the Pacific Coast states should direct their attention toward Filipino exclusion. In May, 1928, a bill to exclude Filipino immigrants was introduced by Congressman Welch of California,[39] and organized labor has gone on record as favoring "the immediate grant of indepenednce to the Filipino people" chiefly for the reason that if the Philippines were an independent

[39]   See Paul Sharrenberg, *Pacific Affairs*, February, 1929, pp. 49–54.

country Filipinos would be automatically excluded from the United States as aliens to citizenship.[40]

The British Dominions

During the development of policy and methods of dealing with Oriental immigration to the United States similar attitudes and legal devices, designed to stem Asiatic invasion, were forming in a number of other regions throughout the eastern and southern Pacific. The similarity of devices employed by the British Dominions suggests the contagion of fear and the reciprocal borrowing of procedure. The damming of the immigration stream at one point tended to divert it to others; this caused alarm, and the erection of barriers spread. Canadian experience with Oriental immigration has been almost identical with that of the United States. Attracted by the discovery of gold on the Fraser River sand bars, Chinese began entering British Columbia shortly after their first arrival in California. It is estmated that as early as 1860 over 2,000 Chinese had entered.[41] In 1882 organized importation of Chinese coolies to work in the construction of the Canadian Pacific Railway began, and during the next two years 15,701 were brought into the Province.

By 1900 Japanese immigrants had begun to arrive in British Columbia. The white settlers became apprehensive and protested to the Dominion Government. The matter was brought to the attention of the Japanese Minister with the result that instructions were issued to Japanese local authorities to prohibit temporarily the migration of Japanese laborers into Canada and the United

[40] The problem thus arising has a legal aspect as long as the Philippine Islands are under the political jurisdiction of the United States. Judge D. R. Williams, formerly a judge in the Philippines, has expressed the opinion that Congress is without constitutional authority to exclude Filipinos; Attorney General Webb of California finds nothing to prevent Congress from taking whatever action it chooses with regard to Filipino exclusion. "Filipino Immigration," *The Commonwealth, Commonwealth Club of California*, November 5, 1928.

[41] R. E. Gosnell and E. O. S. Scholefield, *A History of British Columbia*, p. 185.

States. This order virtually stopped migration from Japan to Canada for the next five years although it had little effect on Japanese migration to the United States,[42] but following President Roosevelt's proclamation which stopped the movement of Japanese laborers from Hawaii to continental United States, a new crisis arose in Canada, and riots occurred in Victoria and Vancouver. A "Gentlemen's Agreement" between Canada and Japan was then concluded which was similar in substance to the agreement between the United States and Japan, except that the number of passports to be issued by the Japanese Government to the admissible classes was not to exceed 400 a year. In March, 1924, as a result of further negotiations between the House of Commons and the Japanese Government, the number of passports to be issued annually was reduced from 400 to 150.

Meanwhile Chinese immigration into Canada, which had been checked in 1885 by the imposition of a head tax of $50 which was doubled in 1901 and raised to $500 in 1903, rose again in 1907–8, 1,482 paying the head tax in 1908; increasing numbers continued to arrive, 7,445 entering in 1913. Agitation arose, and an Order in Council, December 8, 1913, reduced Chinese immigration. During the World War only a few hundred arrived annually, but in 1918, 4,233 entered. The numbers decreased during the next years and the Chinese Immigration Act of 1923, which prohibits Chinese immigration to Canada other than the usual exempt classes of government representatives, students, and merchants ("defined by what regulations the Minister of Immigration and Colonization may prescribe") shut off immigration; only a few hundred Chinese, all belonging to the exempt classes, have entered since the law became effective.

Australia and New Zealand

The history of Oriental migration to Australia and New Zealand is strikingly like that of Oriental migration to the United States and Canada. Starting about the same time, it was also lured by gold, and passed through a similar cycle of local conflicts, re-

[42]   See *Survey*, 1929, p. 502.

strictive measures, and national exclusion founded on a policy of racial selection. In the beginning Victoria, South Australia, and New South Wales attempted to control Chinese competition by poll taxes and legislative measures limiting the number of Chinese immigrants that could arrive on a ship. This checked the movement at certain points only to increase it at others. Gradually the different colonies learned that concerted action was necessary.

Up to the last decade of the nineteenth century the action of the various colonies toward Chinese immigration was directed toward avoiding the evils which were supposed to be connected with a large Chinese element in the community. Between 1891 and 1901 the feeling evinced gradually developed the "White Australia" policy which excludes all colored people. On the consummation of federation this policy was expressed in the Commonwealth Immigration Act of 1901.[43]

The act, as amended, provides that no person shall be admitted who fails to write out "in the presence of the officer," and from his dictation "not less than fifty words in any prescribed language."[44] This indirect method of excluding Asiatics was first suggested to Australian colonial legislatures by the Imperial Government in 1897 in order to spare the susceptibilities of British Indian subjects of the Crown as well as of foreign Asiatics.[45]

At the time of its inception the Act of 1901 met with vigorous protest from the Japanese Government. Although few Japanese had gone to Australia, Japan did not wish to see the continent locked against it. In response to its protests the Australian Government in 1904 concluded an informal arrangement, a sort of Gentlemen's Agreement, "whereby *bona fide* students, merchants (engaged in oversea trade), and visitors from Japan were permitted to enter the Commonwealth for a stay of 12 months without liability to the dictation test on passports issued by the Japanese authorities and viséed by the British Consul at the port of embarkation."[46] Subsequently similar arrangements were made with the governments of India and China.

[43]   *Official Year Book of the Commonwealth of Australia*, 1925, p. 955.
[44]   Immigration Act 1901–1925, Sec. 3a.
[45]   *Problems of the Pacific* (1927), p. 483.
[46]   Phillips and Wood, *The Peopling of Australia*, p. 84.

During the early years of Oriental immigration to New Zealand the procedure used to check the stream was similar to that of the colonies in Australia. At first head taxes and ship limitation measures were imposed. Later, alarmed by the influx of Chinese following the passage of the Australian Commonwealth Immigration Act of 1901, the Government of New Zealand in 1908 likewise introduced a dictation test. An Act passed in 1920 repealed this measure and left it to the discretion of the Governor-General to determine what "nation or peoples" might be admitted.[47]

Latin America

Although many of the smaller Latin-American republics have followed the fashion set by the Anglo-Saxons of erecting legal barriers against Asiatic immigration, some of the countries, notably Brazil and Argentina, encourage Asiatic colonization, especially Japanese.

Mexico has no discriminatory legislation against Orientals as such, but the general requirement of the Migration Act of June 1, 1926, that all immigrant workers must produce a contract of employment in conformity with Mexican law and at the same time possess "sufficient funds to maintain themselves . . . during three months," serves to restrict Asiatic immigration.[48] Organized labor in the United States and Mexico has unsuccessfully attempted to persuade the Mexican Government to enact exclusion legislation against "peoples of Oriental birth or extraction."[49] Naturally the interest of American labor in such legislation is to close what it considers a back-door entrance for Orientals, although there is no evidence that Mexico has been used to any great extent by Orientals as a mode of surreptitious entry to the United States. Between 1911 and 1924 the net immigration of Chinese to Mexico was 10,036 and the net immigration of Japanese, 2,125.[50] According to the 1921 census there were 14,813 foreign-born

[47] Immigration Restriction Act, 1908, Amended, November 9, 1920.
[48] *Monthly Record of Migration*, December, 1926, p. 501.
[49] *Ibid.*, November, 1927, pp. 435–36.
[50] *International Migrations, op. cit.*, 1:503, 504.

Chinese in Mexico.[51] The Japanese population in 1927 was only 4,530.[52]

Panama, owing perhaps to United States influence, prohibits by an Act of 1927 the immigration of Chinese, Japanese, East Indians, and certain other non-white peoples.[53] Guatemala forbids the entry of Asiatics in general; Salvador prohibits the immigration of Chinese citizens; Nicaragua forbids the entrance of citizens of Asiatic races; Costa Rica likewise does not allow Chinese to settle in the country; Honduras is the only Central American republic which as yet has no discriminatory legislation against Orientals.[54] Colombia and Ecuador definitely exclude Chinese. For a time the Peruvian Government forbade the entrance of Chinese immigrants, but in 1909 the restriction was canceled "on condition that the Chinese authorities restrict the immigration themselves."[55] Chile will not receive Asiatics who come *via* Panama. The other countries of South America have no legislation against Orientals that does not pertain equally to other immigration. Asiatic immigration to South American republics, save that to Peru, Brazil, and Argentina, has been negligible.

Post-Exclusion Migration

Restrictive legislation has proved effective. During the four-year period prior to the passing of the Immigration Act of 1924 a total of 17,226 Chinese immigrant aliens entered the United States, whereas during the four years following its enforcement only 5,078 Chinese immigrant aliens entered. The figures for the Japanese for the corresponding periods are 28,025 and 2,462. Moreover, since the passing of the 1924 Act 4,464 more Chinese have departed from the United States than have entered it, and Japanese total departures have exceeded total entries by 18,402.[56]

---

51   *Statesman's Year-Book*, 1928, p. 1100.
52   *Japan Year Book*, 1929, p. 48.
53   *Monthly Record of Migration*, December, 1927, p. 470.
54   See Ching-ch'ao Wu, *The Chinese Social and Political Science Review* 13, no. 2: pp. 161–62.
55   *Ibid.*
56   *Annual Reports of the Commissioner General of Immigration.*

An analysis of the Chinese arrivals shows how few Chinese are actually added to the United States population annually. Of 8,402 Chinese who applied for admission, 8,018 were admitted of whom 4,507 were in transit, 519 temporary visitors, 1,795 domiciled residents who were returning from visits abroad and 699 merchants permitted to carry on trade. And of the remaining 498 Chinese who would be added to the population, only 14 were admitted for permanent residence, that is, "only those who were ministers of a recognized religious denomination or professors of colleges or seminars, together with their wives and minor children."[57]

Similarly in Canada[58] there has been a decided reduction in Oriental immigration since restrictive legislation has gone into effect. During the years 1922–24 a total of 3,133 Chinese entered the Dominion, whereas after the 1923 Chinese Immigration Act became effective only two Chinese entered in the years 1925–27. For the three years prior to the Gentlemen's Agreement, 1906–8, 11,565 Japanese immigrants entered Canada, whereas during the next three years, 1909–11, only 1,203 immigrants entered. During 1926–28 Japanese entries to Canada have been about the same as immediately after the Agreement, a total of 1,374 having entered. East Indian immigration to Canada has been practically nil since the *Kamagata Maru* was refused permission to land in 1914; between 1915 and 1928 only 309 Indians have come to Canada, most of whom have been students or tourists.

The dictation test, as used in Australia, seems to have proved a barrier to Asiatic immigration. Only a few Asiatics have attempted to take it and up to 1929 none had passed. The fear of the test and its mode of administration is said to operate as a "stand-off signal"[59] to prospective immigrants. "During the last five years the number of persons who desired but were not permitted to land was 18 in 1922, 49 in 1923, 50 in 1924, 35 in 1925, and 58 in 1926."[60] Those admitted without the dictation test were as follows:

[57]   *Annual Report of the Commissioner General of Immigration*, fiscal year ending June 30, 1929, p. 17.
[58]   *Canada Year Book*, 1929.
[59]   *Problems of the Pacific* (1927), p. 485.
[60]   *Official Year-Book of the Commonwealth of Australia*, 1928, p. 899.

	1923	1924	1925	1926	1927
Chinese	1,974	1,917	1,235	1,780	1,767
Filipinos	25	15	22	15	7
From India and Ceylon	141	174	186	188	190
Japanese	222	240	440	328	251

The majority of the persons of Asiatic or other non-European nationality shown in the table are former residents of Australia who have returned from visits abroad or are persons who have been admitted temporarily under exemption certificates for business, education, or other purposes.[61]

The numbers of Asiatics arriving in New Zealand since the system of permits required by the Immigration Act of 1920 went into effect, do not indicate much change from the preceding years, as shown by the following table.[62]

	CHINESE		INDIANS	
	Arrived	*Departed*	*Arrived*	*Departed*
1917	272	313	92	12
1918	256	214	138	19
1919	418	238	193	18
1920	1,477	380	225	54
1921	255	368	137	100
1922	345	362	32	125
1923	365	378	115	66
1924	548	451	128	128
1925	517	524	216	165
1926	613	541	239	164

Between 1921 and 1926 only 119 Indians and 19 Chinese were added to the population.

Besides reducing the volume of Oriental immigration, restrictive legislation has had a selective influence. During the early stages of Asiatic immigration, not only to the United States but to other countries bordering on the Pacific, it was primarily the coolie who migrated, for the frontiers required his labor. His character-

61   *Ibid.*, 1929, p. 928.
62   *New Zealand Official Year-Book*, 1928, p. 88.

istics were taken as typical of Oriental civilization and all Orientals were commonly thought to belong to the same class.

Exclusion legislation, wherever it has been applied, has practically eliminated this type of immigrant. As noted above, the Asiatics now arriving in the United States under the exemptions provided in the 1924 Act belong almost exclusively to the upper social and economic classes, such as students, government officials, tourists, and merchants. The only Oriental coolies arriving at present are former residents who have been granted return permits. In this respect there is a fundamental difference between the Chinese and Japanese who enter the United States. Owing to the fact that two classes of Chinese—United States citizens and children of "merchants"—enter in larger numbers than do similar classes of Japanese (the definition of a Chinese merchant is that of the Chinese Exclusion Laws which were in effect prior to the Act of 1924), a much larger percentage of Chinese than of Japanese entries since 1924 has been of the coolie class. By the older laws Chinese engaged in local forms of business are allowed to enter as merchants; whereas the only Japanese merchants allowed to enter are those engaged in international trade as defined in the 1924 Act. Moreover, the fact that the Chinese maintain their families in China while the Japanese have established homes in the United States makes for a larger immigration of Chinese who assert they are United States citizens.

By changing the character of Asiatic immigration, the Act of 1924 is also changing its distribution within the country. The coolie immigrants of pre-exclusion days almost invariably found employment close to the Pacific ports of entry and only as they advanced economically and entered trade did they tend to spread into other districts. The exempt classes who now enter go wherever their business or professional interests call. An increasing proportion of post-exclusion migration goes direct to eastern United States. During the two years before the 1924 law went into effect 54.8 per cent of the Chinese who arrived gave one of the three Pacific Coast states as the place of future permanent residence, but for the four-year period (1925–28) since the 1924 Immigration Act only 43.8 per cent of the Chinese entries indicated Pacific

Coast states as the place of future residence. The corresponding percentages for the Japanese are 52.9 and 40.4. New York is becoming an increasingly frequent destination for Chinese and Japanese of the non-immigrant classes. For the two-year period, 1923–24, 11.1 per cent of the Chinese and 5.2 per cent of the Japanese who entered the country went direct to New York state while for the four-year period since the Immigration Act, 1925–28, 13.6 per cent of the Chinese and 25.8 per cent of the Japanese arrivals gave New York as their destination. In 1929, of the 1,071 immigrant alien Chinese admitted, 412 gave California as the state intended future permanent residence, 56 Washington, and 14 Oregon; and 106 gave New York state. Of 716 Japanese, 224 gave California, 79 Washington, 9 Oregon, and 195 New York state.[63]

This new type of Oriental immigration, more widely distributed, is developing tolerance for itself. The merchant, professional, and student classes of the new immigration come into contact with a class of the American people which the earlier immigrant scarcely touched except in the role of servants or laborers. This, in conjunction with better trade contacts in the Pacific area, is tending to break down prejudice and to build up more cordial attitudes. The recent emergence of good-will groups, such as China Clubs and Japan Societies, as well as numerous trade and business agencies, indicates that organization is no longer a one-sided affair as it was during the period of agitation for restriction and exclusion. This does not imply a probable change of policy with respect to the admission of Oriental laborers, but it means that more consideration is now given to the sensibilities of Asiatics and the nations they represent.

Occupational Succession

Partial restrictive legislation, however, protects a prospering region only temporarily. Inasmuch as migration is largely a response to economic conditions, the damming of one stream usually releases another. Exclusion of the Chinese in 1882 created a

63   Compiled from Table 28, p. 78, *Annual Report of the Commissioner General of Immigration*, 1928, and similar reports for other years.

vacuum which was filled by immigration from Japan. Similarly restriction of the Japanese by the Gentlemen's Agreement of 1907 and the Act of 1924 has been followed by a tide of Filipino and Mexican immigration, which is now causing as much alarm as did the Chinese and Japanese immigration of previous years. Organizations formed to combat this earlier immigration are now actively opposing the influx from the Philippines and Mexico.

Occupational requirements play a large role in the selection of immigrants. Throughout the Pacific Coast states, as well as in Hawaii, a considerable part of the prevailing economy requires a high proportion of relatively unskilled mobile labor. The general high standard of living and the competition for individual progress effect a continuous graduation process. Few individuals are content to remain at the base of the occupation pyramid. As soon as they acquire sufficient competence and skill they seek more desirable occupations. This frequently means a move to other districts. The Chinese who began as laborers in the mines and fields of California are now concentrating in the great cities throughout the country, engaged for the most part in business and domestic service. The Japanese, who followed them, spent even less time as migratory unskilled laborers. They entered agriculture as independent cultivators, and when thwarted by alien land legislation, concentrated in cities and engaged in wide range of business and professional enterprises. The occupations thus vacated by the earlier immigrants are being filled by Mexicans and Filipinos.

10

CULTURAL AND RACIAL DIFFERENCES AS BASES OF HUMAN SYMBIOSIS

1931

I. *Human Symbiosis and Segregation by Race and Occupation*

PLANTS LIVE in symbiotic relations by virtue of differences in species. Human beings effect similar sustenance relations within their own species by means of division of labor. Human division of labor, however, has but little relation to inherent biological differences. It is based, for the most part, on cultural and geographical dissimilarities and is, therefore, ever in process of change. Whether the basis of the division of labor be cultural or geographical it is never a permanent condition. The dynamic cultural process is ever changing the trade relationships between regions and the pattern of division of labor among individuals.

Modern science and invention have effected a revolution in the symbiotic relations of human beings, both interregionally and in the division of labor within the region. Man is learning to utilize an ever-increasing variety of the materials of the earth. He is also learning how to organize the racial and cultural differences that have emerged within his species, to promote his own well-being. Instead of slaying or enslaving the stranger, civilized man seeks to exploit him in a division of labor relationship. Human symbiosis, like that of lower organisms, represents a wide range of sustenance relations; competition, mutualism, parasitism. The

Reprinted from *Social Attitudes*, ed. Kimball Young (New York: Henry Holt, 1931).

form of the relationship between different ethnic groups varies with changing conditions and circumstances. In the early stages of contact between high and low cultural groups or between the metropolis and the frontier, the tendency toward parasitism is pronounced; the dominant group exploiting the backward group or region.

In the evolution of the great economy the pattern of territorial expansion has been from the center to the rim, from the metropolis to the frontier. In the initial stage of contact the trade relationship is usually characterized by the exchange of manufactured articles for raw materials. But sooner or later the frontier "comes of age" and begins to produce commodities it previously imported, sometimes becoming a competitor of the metropolis for outside markets. In other words, as the technical development of the frontier approaches that of the metropolis, the primary forms of trade tend to disappear. New forms may arise of a specialized nature in accordance with the principle of comparative advantage. The trend in interregional symbiosis is from a relationship based on different levels of culture to one based on specialization of production in a uniform level of culture. In fact, as a result of cultural obsolescence, the pendulum may, for a time, swing the other way and the frontier have an advantage over the metropolis owing to its more modern technical equipment.

Occupational division of labor as relating to different ethnic groups within a region seems to have a natural history similar to that of the metropolis and the frontier. In the beginning the more sufficient cultural group dominates the symbiotic relationship. Through superior technical knowledge and managerial skill it effects a division of labor with the backward group that approximates a parasitic relationship. In other words, the superior group occupies the apex of the occupational pyramid and directs the energies of the lower cultural group at the base. This initial pattern of ethnic division of labor, however, is never lasting. Gradually members of the lower cultural group acquire the technique of their directors and begin to push up the occupational ladder, displacing some of those above them, and effecting a new pattern of division of labor.

Every economic region develops an occupational pyramid of greater or less complexity, according to the nature of its resources and the stage of settlement development. The pyramid is always changing; certain occupations decline or disappear altogether and new ones come into existence. But despite the fact of change there is always a tendency toward equilibrium. The complexity of the division of labor and the number that may enter any occupation is determined not by design but by interregional competition and the nature of settlement structure.

Under present conditions of mobile equilibrium there is constant regional exchange of population. Each region selects or ejects population in accordance with the requirements of its occupation pyramid. The enterprising frontier, proud of its educational system, graduates its native sons and passes them on to the metropolis or out to initiate new frontiers and imports people of a different cultural level to fill the gaps in the occupational succession. Wave after wave of European peasants, each time from a remoter source, has come to America to enter the unskilled labor tasks left vacant by the upward climb of their predecessors or created by new industrial expansion.

In the expansion of the "great economy" different racial stocks as well as different cultural groups come together in symbiotic relations. The racial factor tends to complicate the division of labor pattern. In the beginning, occupational succession takes place in about the same way as among different cultural groups of the same racial stock. But as the invading race pushes upward from the base of the occupation pyramid, it tends to segregate occupationally. To be sure, more or less segregation is common even when the immigrants are of the same racial stock as the local group. This is obviously the case with regard to different immigrant groups from Europe. It is common knowledge that Greeks, Italians, Irish, and Poles, as well as many other nationals, tend to segregate in certain occupations far beyond their numerical proportions. In mobile societies, such as ours, however, this form of occupational segregation tends in time to disappear unless there is some racial trait sufficient to differentiate the immigrant group from the general population. In this event occupational segregation seems to be lasting. It may change in form but it is persistent. This is exemplified by the occupational distribution of the Jews, Chinese, Japanese, Negroes, and Mexicans in the United States. In more static societies, such as India, it becomes the basis of a caste system of social organization.

The form of occupational segregation that an ethnic group assumes in settlement structure tends to determine its spatial distribution pattern. Wherever different ethnic stocks come together in symbiotic relations they tend to segregate spatially as well as occupationally. American and some Asiatic cities have their "little Europes" and in some cases almost little worlds, each ethnic group tending to segregate residentially in that part of the communal structure where it is allowed or able to live. The ethnic spatial pattern, however, is as changeable as the occupational distribution pattern. As individuals graduate from occupations so also do they graduate from districts, and unless the colony like the occupation is maintained by fresh recruits of the same ethnic origin it becomes the habitat of a different group.

II. *Ethnic and Occupational Symbiosis in the Pacific Basin*

With this theoretical statement let us examine some phases of ethnic symbiosis now in process of formation in the Pacific basin. The new constellation of Pacific settlements is superimposed upon an indigenous racial and cultural garland which developed under a rudimentary system of communications and which represents a wide diversity of cultural and racial structure. The new frontiers, which owe their origin to Western enterprise and capital, have, in almost every case, developed with a rapidity far beyond the rate of natural biological increase. Population has been drawn from many different racial and cultural areas and has evolved a division of labor pattern of great complexity and usually of high productive efficiency. The division of labor pattern varies from region to region according to the racial and cultural composition of the population and the stage of settlement development.

In order to illustrate some of the characteristics of ethnic symbiosis in such frontier regions I shall briefly survey the conditions in three widely separated settlement areas, namely, British Malaya, Hawaii, and Alaska. These regions have many features in common but they are sufficiently different in regard to location, resources, population, and stage of settlement development to make comparison profitable.

As to location, British Malaya is a gateway to commerce. Singapore, the island tip of the peninsula, is the apex of the great triangular route of traffic connecting Europe, the South Seas, and the Far East. The Malay peninsula is an interstitial, racial, and cultural zone lying between the great civilizations of India and China. Hawaii, located near the center of the Pacific, is remote from the great centers of population but lies at the crossroads of movement, at the intersection of the diagonal trade routes that cross the Pacific. Alaska occupies a peripheral location, away from natural routes of movement and beyond the margin of established settlement.

Climatically these three regions would be classified by the geographer as "areas of debilitation," that is, so far as white settlement is concerned. They are regarded by their metropolitan directors as regions of exploitation to be developed and used for their contributions to settlements elsewhere.[1] All three regions have been developed within recent years by outside capital and enterprise. Each has evolved a highly specialized economic base organized on a commercial pattern; each produces commodities to be consumed elsewhere and, judged by trade statistics, each represents a highly efficient symbiotic unity. British Malaya leads the world in per capita foreign trade, both exports and imports. In 1927 these ratios were $179 and $172 respectively. Hawaii ranks higher than Malaya when domestic trade is included with per capita exports listed at $334 and imports at $266. But Alaska is the most efficient of the three when judged by trade statistics in relation to resident population. In 1927 her per capita exports were $941 and imports $661, largely, of course, domestic trade.

---

[1]   Hawaii is gradually passing out of this stage.

The three regions in question represent different patterns of settlement structure and different stages in communal development. Malaya is a highly integrated settlement unit. Its commercial activities are oriented around three important urban centers; Singapore, Malacca, and Penang. The former is a city of over 400,000 inhabitants and is the dominant commercial center not only for the Peninsula but for the entire archipelago round about. The other two are subordinate shipping points; Malacca an exit for rubber and tin, and Penang, the doorway to India.

Hawaii has a simpler settlement structure. The commercial activities of the nine islands which comprise the archipelago are integrated in Honolulu, the only city of any size on the territory.[2] Movement is impeded by the insular nature of the land area. Accordingly Hawaii is not so highly integrated a settlement unit as is the peninsula of Malaya with its unbroken system of motor roads and railways. Alaska represents a much more rudimentary pattern of settlement structure than either of the other regions. It contains no dominant urban center to integrate the scattered settlement units. Juneau, the largest town, is barely of urban size, having only 3,034 inhabitants in 1920. The scattered towns and villages of the vast territory, are, for the most part, individually integrated with the port cities of Puget Sound rather than with one another.

Each of the regions has evolved an occupation pyramid which indicates the nature of its economy and the stage of its settlement development.

It will be observed from the foregoing broad classification of occupations that the three frontiers in question are definitely regions of basic production rather than of manufacture or residence. Each region has its own structural peculiarities. Malaya and Hawaii, being plantation areas, have more than half of their occupied males engaged in agriculture. Next to agriculture, Malaya emphasizes commerce, while Hawaii stresses manufacturing. Alaska ranks high in mining and manufacturing, the latter on account of the salmon canneries located there. All three regions fall

2   Honolulu 83,327; Hilo, 10,431 (1920) ; the former reports 137,582 for 1930.

TABLE I

PERCENTAGE OF MALES ENGAGED IN EACH SPECIFIED OCCUPATION
(CENSUS DATA)

Occupation	British Malaya [3] 1921	Hawaii 1920	Alaska 1920	United States 1920
All occupations	100.0	100.0	100.0	100.0
Agriculture	52.9	51.0	21.1	26.3
Manufacturing	8.6	17.6	15.5	30.8
Trade	12.6	6.8	4.9	10.2
Transportation	9.5	7.8	9.6	7.4
Mining	6.2	0.2	21.3	2.6
Public service	3.5	6.4	5.3	1.9
Clerical service	...	2.8	2.0	7.5
Professional service ...	1.4	2.3	2.8	5.2
Domestic service	5.2	5.2	17.5	8.2

below the norm afforded by the United States classification in the ratios of their populations engaged in clerical and professional services. The large percentage in the "Domestic Service" class in Alaska is due to the fact that guides and trappers are classified under this heading.

The ethnic composition of the population of the three regions may be roughly ascertained from official census data.

Table II does not, of course, give an adequate picture of the racial and cultural complexity of the regions. For instance, in British Malaya the "Europeans" represent 19 different nationalities; the Malays are divided into 11 sub-classes; the Chinese into 11; the Indians into 12; and the class "All others" includes Siamese, Japanese, Arabs, Sinhalese, Jews, and five different divisions of Aborigines. Then there are the local-born offspring of each immigrant group, usually known as the "second generation," who represent cultural diversities of symbiotic importance.

[3]   Straits Settlements, Federated Malay States, and Johore.

TABLE II

RACIAL COMPOSITION

British Malaya (1921)		Hawaii (1920)		Alaska (1920)	
Population, 3,358,054		Population, 255,912		Population, 55,036	
Class	*Per Cent*	*Class*	*Per Cent*	*Class*	*Per Cent*
All classes	*100.0*	*All classes*	*100.0*	*All classes*	*100.0*
European	0.4	Caucasian:		White:	
Eurasian	0.4	Portuguese	10.6	Native	29.6
Malay	48.6	Porto Rican	2.2	Foreign-born..	21.2
Chinese	35.3	Spanish	1.0		
Indian (Br.)	14.2	Other Caucasian .	7.7	Chinese	0.1
All others	1.1			Indian (Am.) ..	48.3
		Caucasian-Hawaiian	4.3	Japanese	0.6
		Asiatic-Hawaiian ..	2.7	Negro	0.2
		Hawaiian	9.3	All others	0.2
		Chinese	9.2		
		Japanese	42.7		
		Korean	1.9		
		Filipino	8.2		
		Negro	0.1		
		All others	0.1		

The facts for Hawaii are in more detail, but here, too, numerous subgroups are omitted. The Alaska table is the most incomplete of all chiefly because the employees of the fishing industry are not included. This is largely a seasonal population that goes to Alaska in the spring and returns to the coast cities of the states in the autumn, hence it is not enumerated in the census reports. In 1920 there were 28,534 persons engaged in all branches of the fishing industry in Alaska. Of this number 57.3 per cent were whites; 13.5 per cent were natives; 9.8 per cent Chinese; 6.6 per cent Mexicans; 5.5 per cent Filipinos, and 5.3 per cent Japanese.

We shall now attempt to indicate some of the main features of the ethnic division of labor in these three frontiers. Let us begin with British Malaya where racial intermixture is most complicated and where symbiotic relations have developed with least restriction on movement. The following table (III) shows the racial

TABLE III

RACIAL DIVISION OF LABOR IN THE STRAITS SETTLEMENTS AND THE
FEDERATED MALAY STATES, 1921

Total Occupied Males and Percentage Distribution by Groups

Occupations	Europeans	Eurasians	Malays	Chinese	Indians
Total employed	7,681	2,935	239,138	569,718	248,782
All occupations	*100.0*	*100.0*	*100.0*	*100.0*	*100.0*
Fishing	... }	6.3	7.9	1.8	.3
Agriculture	27.9 }		63.3	26.6	48.4
Mining	4.0	...	...	10.7	1.1
Engineering and metal and wood	7.1	10.9	2.0	7.6	1.4
Commerce	20.2	41.5	3.8	18.5	9.7
Transportation	...	...	9.7	10.4	6.9
Shipping	2.3	...	...	...	...
Government	12.2	20.9	4.4	1.5	9.2
Professions	12.6	10.0	1.3	.9	.9
Personal service ...	...	...	1.4	6.6	6.3
Army and Navy ...	9.9	...	...	...	...
Other occupations ..	3.7	10.2	6.1	15.2	15.7

division of labor by industries according to the census data of 1921.

While this table indicates considerable ethnic segregation in the broad occupational classifications it does not, of course, reveal the details of the symbiotic pattern. In agriculture, for example, the Malays and Indians bunch conspicuously; the Europeans and Chinese show less than normal quotas and the Eurasians are not listed at all. The "agriculture" in which the Malays are engaged, however, is the cultivation of primitive rice paddies, whereas the Indians are almost exclusively confined to work on the rubber plantations. In 1921 Indians constituted 79 per cent of the total estate population of British Malaya. The Europeans and Chinese in agriculture are also occupationally segregated; the former are estate managers, the latter are, for the most part, coolies engaged in clearing the land and planting the rubber trees. A few are independent owners of small holdings.

In mining the Chinese predominate. A few Europeans are engaged as managers in certain phases of the industry, but the work is almost exclusively done by Chinese. Of 82,195 laborers engaged in tin mining in 1922, 76,449 were Chinese.

Under the heading "commerce" it will be observed that the Eurasians lead in degree of segregation, Europeans come second, and Chinese third. Here, too, however, there is pronounced ethnic division of labor. The Eurasians are predominantly clerks. "In the Colony and the Federated States the bulk are engaged in clerical work either in Government or commercial offices, while those employed in agriculture are for the most part clerks in rubber estates."[4] The Europeans concentrate in shipping, finance, and governmental functions. The Chinese in "commerce" are largely confined to retail services. In Singapore alone, almost 20,000 Chinese are listed in the 1921 census as "proprietors and managers of business," and there are about 6,000 similarly listed for Penang and 1,500 for Malacca. Moreover, the Chinese have a practical monopoly of the retail trade in the smaller inland towns and villages. "The Chinese general shopkeeper is ubiquitous in the Federated States; 32,673 persons were returned under this heading."[5] The Indians also participate in retail service but to a much less extent. Pro rata to respective populations the Indians have only one-fourth as many shopkeepers as the Chinese in the Federated Malay States.

In transportation a similar ethnic segregation is observable. The Chinese furnish practically all the rickshaw coolies—23,000 in Singapore alone in 1921; no other race is listed under this occupational heading. The Indians, on the other hand, especially those from the Punjab and other parts of northern India, are the bullock cart drivers; and the native Malays are the chauffeurs and horsemen of the Peninsula.

The analysis of ethnic division of labor in Malaya might be extended almost indefinitely. Not only do the major racial groups interlace in a division of labor complex but each tribal or cultural unit within the race tends to segregate in particular occupational lines. For instance, "The majority of the Malay-born Chinese are

4   Census of British Malaya, 1921, p. 119.
5   *Ibid.*, p. 117.

traders or shopkeepers, and not laborers or agriculturists, and they are proportionately more numerous in the towns."[6] The Hokkiens (Chinese) "form the bulk of the trading and shopkeeping classes."[7] The Cantonese "form a high proportion of the mining population."[8] The "Hailams in the towns are mainly engaged in domestic service, nine out of ten servants in European houses belonging to this tribe."[9] Similar tribal segregation is conspicuous among the Indians, "More than four-fifths of the Indian population on estates is Tamil."[10] The "Sikhs and other Punjabis have been attracted to this country (Malaya) by either military or semi-military employment."[11] They are employed as watchmen, guardians, and to some extent as police. The Bengali, on the other hand, "are employed as clerks, artisans and shopkeepers"[12] and are found almost exclusively in the larger cities.

The ethnic division of labor in Hawaii has been studied rather intensively by Adams and Lind, so I shall merely summarize some of the facts assembled by them. In a recent article[13] Lind has presented occupational indices which show the general pattern of ethnic symbiosis in the Islands. His indices for three broad occupational divisions compiled from 1920 census data are given below.[14]

It will be observed that the base of the occupation pyramid is occupied largely by Japanese and Filipinos, the more recent arrivals in the Islands. The data, however, are for 1920. Since then Filipinos have come to the territory in large numbers as plantation workers. According to Adams they outnumbered the Japanese two

6   *Ibid.*, p. 96.
7   *Ibid.*, p. 79.
8   *Ibid.*, p. 80.
9   *Ibid.*, p. 83.
10   *Ibid.*, p. 138.
11   *Ibid.*, p. 89.
12   *Ibid.*, p. 89.
13   Andrew W. Lind, "Occupational Trends Among Immigrant Groups in Hawaii," *Social Forces* 8 (1928) : 290–97.
14   "An Index of 1,000 indicates that a given race has exactly its proportion of members within the particular occupation."

TABLE IV

TOTAL POPULATION 10 YEARS OF AGE AND OVER ENGAGED IN SE-
LECTED OCCUPATIONS, TOGETHER WITH "INDEX OF OCCUPANCY"

	Laborers		Retail Dealers		Professionals	
	Number	Index	Number	Index	Number	Index
Native Hawaiians ..	3,604	0.8405	27	0.1311	315	1.037
Part-Hawaiians ...	743	0.3645	37	0.3789	474	3.304
Other Caucasian[15] .	840	0.1318	263	0.8598	1,888	4.210
Portuguese	2,808	0.7402	73	0.4007	199	0.7452
Porto Rican	1,614	1.641	1	0.0212	6	0.0867
Chinese	4,824	0.7953	1,051	3.609	249	0.5832
Japanese	28,286	1.108	1,322	1.079	892	0.4966
Filipino	13,641	1.103	5	0.0132	42	0.0758
Korean	2,039	1.330	26	0.3820	41	0.3387
Other	88	3.148	....	.....	12	0.9705
Total	58,487	....	2,805	.....	4,118	.....

to one in 1926 and constituted more than half of the entire labor force on sugar plantations that year.[16]

As in Malaya, the Chinese lead as retail dealers, having more than three times their due proportion in this service. The Japanese come second, being slightly over par; while all other races fall well below their normal ratios. It is noteworthy that native Hawaiians should have such slight participation in retail business. In this respect they are like the native Malays of British Malaya, who rank below all other races in commercial activities.

The professional services of the Islands are largely in the hands of whites and part-Hawaiians. The situation is quite similar to that of Europeans and Eurasians in Malaya. So far, the white man has been able to maintain his position at the peak of the occupation pyramid in such frontier zones. He cannot withstand the open competition in the simpler service lines, but as the representative of outside political and capitalistic enterprise he is hard to dis-

[15]   Includes American, British, French, German, and Norwegian.
[16]   Romanzo Adams, *Education and Economic Outlook for the Boys of Hawaii* (Honolulu, 1926), p. 11.

lodge. The hybrid seems to play an intermediate role in the occupational hierarchy. Like the members of the indigenous population who participate in the new economy, he tends to segregate in the sheltered services, bridging the gap between the ruling and the competing classes.

Of course, the pattern of ethnic symbiosis in Hawaii is only slightly indicated by the foregoing facts. Racial division of labor expresses itself in scores of different ways. Within each industry, trade, or other service the races segregate in a competitive-cooperative division of labor complex. A few examples will suffice to illustrate the general picture. The Japanese predominate in the minor basic industries; they comprise over 90 per cent of the coffee farmers and are rapidly displacing the Chinese as rice planters and fishermen. They tend to segregate also in certain skilled occupations and trades such as carpentry, barbering, garage work, and dress making. "The Koreans have specialized in the furniture business" . . . and "They now virtually monopolize the tailoring for the military population."[17] The Chinese are found in all forms of retail business but especially in grocery shops and bakeries. They also predominate in the tailoring trade. The Hawaiians and part-Hawaiians, as already indicated, are segregated in government service occupations as clerks, policemen, postmen, etc. They are gradually withdrawing from the tasks of teamsters and fishermen in favor of the Portuguese and Japanese.

While ethnic division of labor in Alaska is less complicated than in either of the other regions still it is a pronounced characteristic of the occupation pyramid.

Having a "white man's climate" and being more accessible to white settlements elsewhere, Alaska shows less occupational segregation of whites than either Malaya or Hawaii. The white population, both native and foreign-born, is found in all the occupational divisions, even constituting over half of the labor engaged in the fishing and mining industries. The few Oriental residents of the Territory are segregated in domestic service tasks, especially in the restaurant and hotel business. The Indians, too, are concentrated in domestic service but simply because guides and trappers

[17]   Lind, "Occupational Trends," p. 299.

are so classed in the census. Like the indigenous populations of Malaya and Hawaii the Indians of Alaska play a very minor part in the new economy. Those listed under "Agriculture" are really engaged in their traditional occupation of fishing; a few work in the canneries and mines, but only at marginal tasks.

TABLE V

OCCUPATIONAL DISTRIBUTION OF RACES IN ALASKA, 1920

Total Occupied Males and Percentage Distribution by Groups

	Native Whites	Foreign-born Whites	Negro	Chinese	Japa-nese	Indian and All Other
Total occupied males	8,470	9,608	56	53	237	6,288
All occupations	*100.0*	*100.0*	*100.0*	*100.0*	*100.0*	*100.0*
Agriculture	12.1	19.8	5.4	....	9.3	36.1
Mining	21.2	34.4	10.7	....	2.9	2.3
Manufacturing	18.9	15.5	17.8	22.6	16.0	10.9
Trade	8.1	4.5	1.8	7.5	3.4	1.4
Transportation	11.5	13.2	8.9	....	2.9	1.7
Public service	11.4	3.2	7.1	....	.4	.3
Professional	5.6	1.7	1.8	....	.4	.7
Domestic and per-sonal service	6.9	6.4	44.6	69.8	64.1	46.1
Clerical	4.2	1.2	1.8	....	....	.3

Of course, the main form of racial symbiosis in Alaska is found in the fishing industry. The labor for the canneries is recruited seasonally in the Pacific coast cities of the United States and transported to and from the canneries. About half of the laborers employed in this industry are engaged under what is known as the Oriental contract system, that is, Oriental residents of Pacific coast cities contract to pack the fish. They engage their own labor, transport it to the canneries and furnish it with food and lodging. The composition of the labor force depends upon the supply available for such seasonal work. Of the 28,872 employed in all branches of the fishing industry in 1927, 58.8 per cent were whites; 16.8 per cent were local Indians; 3.8 per cent were Chinese; 4.6 per cent, Japanese; 9.9 per cent, Filipinos; 4.7 per cent, Mexicans.

The racial division of labor within the industry is complicated. It varies from district to district and to some extent from plant to plant. The ratio of white labor employed seems to vary inversely with the distance from the coast cities of the states. For instance, many of the canneries bordering on Puget Sound use nothing but white labor. Those in southeastern Alaska, the first judicial division of the Territory, get from 35 to 50 per cent of their labor force locally, "about 10 per cent of those so employed being native Indians."[18] The canneries located farther north in the third division employ very few whites. Native Indians constitute from 50 to 80 per cent of the labor secured locally, which, however, is only about 15 per cent of the total labor force. The remainder of the labor is made up of Orientals, largely Chinese and Japanese, imported from Seattle or San Francisco. Mexicans and Filipinos prefer to work in the more accessible canneries of southeastern Alaska.

The racial division of labor within the plant likewise is variable. In general, however, white laborers are employed as machinists, pile-drivers, sub-bosses, dock men and at other such tasks. The colored labor segregates occupationally according to skill and experience. The older participants in the industry, the Chinese and Japanese, are assigned most of the tasks requiring responsibility and skill, while the more recent arrivals—the Mexicans and Filipinos—do the routine within the factory. An incidental factor making for occupational segregation is the difference in food habits of the various racial groups. For instance, Chinese and Japanese contractors prefer Filipinos to Mexicans because the former live on rice and fish, while the Mexicans insist on meat, vegetables, etc., thus complicating the diet problem.

III. *Socio-Economic Change*

The foregoing facts indicate the symbiotic patterns of our three regions only for specific dates. They do not include the process of change. Succession is rapid in such pioneer belts. Not only is the region constantly changing in economic structure, but indi-

[18]   Annual Report of the Governor of Alaska, 1928, p. 85.

viduals and ethnic groups keep changing position in the occupation pyramid. The regions under review have responded in different ways to forces from the outside world. Malaya and Hawaii are passing rapidly from frontier outposts to areas of established settlement. Their basic industries are becoming more diversified and their population pyramids less abnormal. Alaska, however, is still a frontier in the rudimentary stage of development. Its resources are exploited for the most part by a non-resident population that comes and goes with seasonal requirements. The settled population of the Territory is practically stationary if not declining. Most of the business and office people who direct the economic activities of Alaska reside in Seattle or other Pacific port cities of the United States.

But more important than change in settlement structure, at least from the standpoint of this paper, is the occupational succession of the different ethnic groups. The external occupational shell of a region is a relatively stable thing, but the human units that give it content are highly variable elements. This pertains especially to frontier regions, where the human material is excessively mobile and where much of the division of labor is based on transitory cultural differences. The form of occupational succession is much the same for all three regions. The white man enters at the peak of the pyramid and maintains his position by using his homeland as a reservoir for new recruits and a refuge for those displaced in the competitive struggle. The lower cultural groups enter, or are brought in, as unskilled laborers at the base of the pyramid. But they seldom remain long in their initial capacity. They either return to their native habitats or press upward in the occupational ladder. Employers in such regions are always confronted with the problem of recruiting fresh workers. They never succeed in building up a "permanent labor force" within the region itself. Sometimes, as in Malaya, the source of labor remains relatively constant within the same racial stocks; other times, as in Hawaii and Alaska, the new recruits are brought from different ethnic and cultural groups.

In each of the regions under consideration there is a tendency for one ethnic group to succeed another at the base of the occupation pyramid. Racial displacement, however, furnishes but meager evidence of the process of occupational succession as a large part of the succession takes place within the same racial group.

TABLE VI

ESTATE POPULATION IN THE FEDERATED MALAY STATES [19]

| | *1911* | | *1921* | |
	Number Employed	Percentage of Total Estate Population	Number Employed	Percentage of Total Estate Population
Malays	23,158	14.5	13,933	5.8
Chinese	40,026	25.0	33,135	14.0
Indians	94,950	59.4	186,550	78.8

While there is noticeable racial displacement in favor of the Indians, this table does not show the extent of labor turnover within this race itself. The fact that "the average stay of an estate laborer is from two to three years"[20] indicates that the mobility is high.

Clearer pictures of racial succession are presented by the facts for Hawaii and Alaska.

The process of occupational succession is much the same for Hawaii and Alaska. In these regions where legal restrictions have interrupted the continuous flow of certain ethnic groups, we find one race gradually superseding another in the basic industries—first the Chinese, then the Japanese, and now the Filipinos, and in Alaska, the Mexicans also. What becomes of those who leave the occupation is difficult to state. Some undoubtedly return to their native land, a few continue within the industry itself, usually in the capacity of skilled workmen, but many press upward in the occupation pyramid into more congenial and individualistic forms of work. The rate at which the upward trend takes place varies for each region and race. It seems to take place more slowly in Malaya than in either Hawaii or Alaska, and more slowly for the Indians

[19] Cf. *Census of British Malaya*, 1921, p. 137.
[20] *Labor in British Malaya* (London, 1924), p. 13.

TABLE VII

HAWAII—SUGAR PLANTATION LABORERS [21]

	1886		1908		1926	
	Number	Per Cent	Number	Per Cent	Number	Per Cent
Total workers	*14,539*	*100.0*	*46,918*	*100.0*	*46,056*	*100.0*
Native Hawaiian and part Hawaiian	2,255	15.5	1,309	2.8	445	.9
Portuguese	3,081	21.2	3,807	8.1	1,341	2.9
Porto Rican	....	...	1,989	4.2	1,073	2.3
Spanish	....	...	750	1.6	70	.01
Other Caucasian	379	2.6	970	2.1	62	.01
Chinese	5,626	38.1	2,916	6.2	1,242	2.7
Japanese	1,949	13.4	32,771	69.8	13,603	29.5
Korean	....	...	2,125	4.5	741	1.6
Filipino	....	...	141	.3	25,848	56.1
All others	1,249	8.6	140	.3	1,631	3.5

TABLE VIII

ALASKA—FISHING INDUSTRY LABORERS [22]

	1914		1918		1927	
	Number	Per Cent	Number	Per Cent	Number	Per Cent
Total workers	*21,200*	*100.0*	*31,213*	*100.0*	*28,872*	*100.0*
Whites	11,178	52.7	17,693	56.7	16,972	58.8
Natives	4,184	19.7	5,251	16.8	4,857	16.8
Chinese	2,138	10.1	2,734	8.7	1,102	3.8
Japanese	1,318	6.2	1,509	4.8	1,353	4.7
Filipinos	} 2,382	11.2	1,338	4.3	2,882	9.9
Mexicans			1,709	5.4	1,373	4.7
Miscellaneous			979	3.1	333	1.1

21 Adams, *Education and the Economic Outlook*, p. 11.
22 *Annual Reports of the Governor of Alaska*. The miscellaneous group includes Negroes, Koreans, Puerto Ricans.

than for the Chinese in Malaya. If we take the rate of urbanization as a rough index of the vertical occupational trend it is apparent that the Chinese "graduate" from the primary forms of employment more rapidly than any other colored race in the Peninsula. In 1921, 52.8 per cent of the Chinese population of British Malaya were classified as urban dwellers as against 27.4 per cent of the Indians and 9 per cent of the Malays. Although the Chinese constitute less than one-third of the total population of British Malaya, they constitute more than four-fifths of the population of Singapore. Their tendency toward urbanization has been more rapid than that of any other ethnic group. In the larger towns of the Federated Malay States they increased from 50 to 123 per cent during the decade 1911 to 1921. Of course, many of their town population are coolies but they do not seem to remain long in this capacity. As D. M. Fraser observes: "The coolie of yesterday is the hawker and small shopkeeper of today, his son is a tamkay, substantial merchant and capitalist, using the telephone, occasionally wearing the white man's clothes. His children are in school, speaking English."[23]

The Indians do not seem to rise so rapidly, probably because they are brought direct from India to the plantation and do not have occasion to come in contact with other groups in urban life. Moreover, they do not have within their own ethnic group so large a representation as do the Chinese in the different rungs of the occupational ladder. They, therefore, lack the traditions of occupational advancement that fall to the lot of their Mongolian competitors.

The educational system of Malaya is not such as to hasten the disappearance of original cultural differences. There is no free and compulsory educational system in the Peninsula for all classes of people such as prevails in Hawaii or Alaska. The British pursue the policy of educating only for the needs of the region. They provide a few English schools to train an adequate supply of clerks, and some vernacular schools for the indigenous people, but they are frankly opposed to "any ideal of education, not adjusted to lo-

[23]   *The Nation* 128 (March 7, 1928): 180.

cal wants" as it must inevitably "lead to economic dislocation and social unrest."[24]

In Hawaii the opposite ideal of education prevails. A free and compulsory school system is maintained, and all races are compelled to learn the English language and stimulated to strive for individual improvement. Consequently, in Hawaii, the desire for more congenial occupations is dominant and occupational succession is rapid. In referring to the school system of the Islands, Adams says:

It presupposes the American political and social order and American opportunity. The children respond to the teachings much as do children on the Mainland, only there is more enthusiasm for our old American ideals—liberty, democracy, political and civil equality, even-handed justice and economic opportunity for all. They like to make speeches and to write rhetorically on such themes. In general their education is preparing them not for the common labor of Hawaii and not for the kind of work most will find if they go to the Mainland. It is not mainly a matter of knowledge or of skill but of attitude and expectation. Nearly all are looking forward to the upper third of the places.[25]

The occupational succession of the different ethnic groups participating in the fishing industry in Alaska is of the same general pattern, and for the same reasons, as that in Hawaii. The fact that the labor is recruited from Mainland cities to which it is returned at the close of each season stimulates the trend to other forms of employment. The United States affords so many occupational outlets that the enterprising individual does not need to depend upon the canning industry for long. In fact, in the off-season he is compelled to supplement his Alaska earnings by other forms of employment. It is interesting to note how quickly members from each racial group graduate from the role of laborers in the canneries and become contractors or subcontractors and employers of labor. As we have already noted, about half the labor supplied to the fishing industry in Alaska is furnished by Oriental contractors,

[24] *Educational in Malaya*, London, 1924, p. 15.
[25] Adams, *Education and Economic Outlook*, p. 13.

Chinese, Japanese; and now the Filipinos are beginning to enter the contracting game. At present there are six Filipino cannery contractors in Seattle.

It is when the upward process begins that invasion and displacement take place. It can hardly be said that the substitution of one race for another as unskilled laborers in the plantations or in the canneries implies invasion or displacement. The initial participation is seldom spontaneous; it almost always involves recruitment. "During the decade 1911 to 1921 the total number of immigrants from southern India was 908,100, of whom 714,175 were assisted immigrants brought in by the Fund."[26] Labor for the plantations in Hawaii has likewise been recruited throughout the years by the plantation operators. At present the Hawaiian Sugar Planters' Association has its paid agents in the Philippine Islands recruiting labor for work on the plantations in accordance with regulations imposed by the Government of those islands. While the labor for Alaska is not obtained in quite the same way, still the function performed by the labor contractor is fundamentlly of the same character.

As soon as the upward process begins, competition and reaccommodation take place, producing ethnic occupational concentration and spatial redistribution. We have already noted the tendency toward racial occupational segregation in various service lines throughout our regions and the trend toward urbanization of the older racial groups. Adams observes, "In general, the peoples who have been longer in the Islands are more often found in the cities while the newly arrived are mainly on the plantations. . . . According to the way workers see it, going from rural employment to city employment is progress."[27] A similar tendency is apparent for the Chinese on the Mainland. In 1920 four-fifths of the Chinese population of the United States were urban dwellers, mostly concentrated in the great cities throughout the nation. In retiring from the unskilled labor tasks the Japanese have shown a tendency to concentrate in agriculture as individual owners or tenants. Since legal restrictions have limited their activities in this

[26]   *Labor in British Malaya* (London, 1924), p.13.
[27]   *The Peoples of Hawaii* (Honolulu, 1925), p. 10.

vocational outlet, they have begun to drift into the cities, concentrating in specific service occupations such as grocery store proprietors, fruit and vegetable dealers, hotel and restaurant keepers, etc.

The upward pressure from the base of the occupation pyramid sooner or later affects the white population at the top. Displacement takes place in the minor services first, notably in clerical and retail functions. Whites are practically excluded from such occupations in Malaya. The high remuneration which the white man must receive to continue residence in such a region disqualifies him for participation in any of the service tasks. He maintains his position at the peak of the pyramid simply because he performs an essential function in the symbiotic process for which the lower cultural groups have not yet acquired an adequate technique. The Japanese, however, are beginning to play the "white man's" role in British Malaya. They are decreasing as laborers in the Peninsula but increasing as estate owners and managers. "Japanese estates are numerous in Johore, but only the superintending staffs are Japanese, and no successful attempt has yet been made to introduce Japanese labour." In this state the Japanese population increased from 173 in 1911 to 1,287 in 1921.[28] Although the European population of British Malaya increased about 35 per cent (including military), during the decade, 1911–1921, the ratio of Europeans to the total population of the peninsula remained constant, namely .4 per cent, notwithstanding the fact that the trade of the Peninsula increased 230 per cent during the decade.

According to Lind's indices the white population of Hawaii is playing a role quite similar to that of the Europeans in Malaya. It is maintaining its position at the peak of the pyramid but is gradually losing ground to other races in a number of the mercantile and professional services it previously performed. "The 'whites' who came as 'conquerors' have maintained their superior position in the professions to a remarkable extent. Nevertheless their stronghold is being gradually invaded by the other immigrant groups; and the 'Other Caucasian' index of occupancy is slowly declin-

[28]   *The Census of British Malaya*, 1921, p. 91.

ing."[29] There is no indication, however, of white displacement in Alaska. Even in the fishing industry whites are maintaining their quotas with other races, and in the residence population of the Territory they greatly outnumber all of the other immigrant peoples. Orientals are barred largely because the settlement structure of Alaska provides but few occupational outlets for the small mercantile classes. Most of the white inhabitants of the Territory occupy government positions or are representatives of firms located in the United States proper.

Occupational succession in such frontier zones seems to be largely confined to immigrant peoples and their descendants rather than to the indigenous population. While some of the indigenous peoples of our three frontiers have risen in the occupational ladder, the ratio of advancement is much lower than that of immigrants. We have already seen that the indigenous populations play but a minor role as laborers in the basic industries. The Comptroller of Labour in Malaya writes in his report of 1924:

> Local Malay Labour in the Colony is not of importance. The Malays are not as a rule anxious to earn more than is sufficient to support them . . . They are mainly useful in supplementing the regular labour forces and doing temporary work. They prefer to live in their kampongs as much as possible, and do a little estate work when in special need of food or clothing.[30]

In Hawaii the situation is somewhat different. The indigenous economy is almost completely supplanted by the new economic structure, and the native Hawaiians are being absorbed in the general populations. They have never played a very important role as estate laborers and at present they are scarcely represented at all. Neither have they participated extensively in the professional occupations. Like the Malays they are less urbanized than any of the other ethnic elements of the population, and their occupations are largely of the sheltered type such as government and public service positions. Adams summarizes their occupational status thus: "They hold most public positions—official and clerical—and are

---

29   *Social Forces* 7 (1928) : 293.
30   *Annual Report of Labor Department*, Singapore, 1925, p. 13.

employed largely in public or quasi-public enterprises such as road building and in the service of the public utility corporations."[31] In Alaska as in Malaya the indigenous inhabitants not only comprise the largest numerical division of the population but retain their own traditional economy, participating only in the fringes of the new system. As we have already seen, the native Indians play but a minor part in the fishing industry.

Occupational participation, of course, is a question of attitudes and conditions. The indigenous peoples of many of the frontier zones of modern industrialism are surrounded by their own web of culture and their own economic structure. Consequently they are slow to take part in the new economy especially as unskilled laborers. It is the individual widely removed from his native habitat that is most adaptable to the conditions imposed by capitalism in frontier regions. Imported labor cannot so easily escape to its home village when conditions are distasteful as can the local population. Moreover, frontiers, such as the three in question, require a high degree of mobility of labor—workers who will go to the location required and remain there during the season of activity. Imported labor fits into this condition better than any type of local labor. For instance, Filipinos are often preferred as workers in the hop and berry district in the state of Washington because once they are brought to the field of activity they are less likely to leave when their services are required than are the American workers, most of whom have automobiles and their own homes to return to. On the other hand, imported labor is expensive to the employer as it has to be recruited and transported. The employer is always interested in building up a permanent labor supply. But as no form of labor remains "permanent," he is confronted with the alternative of the cost of recruiting and importing foreign labor or putting up with the undependability of the local supply.

IV. *Mobility and the Pacific Area*

The striking characteristic of the three frontiers in question is the high mobility of their immigrant inhabitants. Popula-

[31]   *Education and Economic Outlook*, p. 8.

tion shuttles in and out in ceaseless process. From 1911 to 1926 inclusive, 1,343,840 Indians arrived in British Malaya and 796,-680 departed, leaving a new gain of 574,160. The back and forth flow of Chinese has been even greater. During the eleven-year period 1916–1926, 1,821,639 entered Malaya and 804,423 departed, making a net immigration of 1,017,216.[32] A considerable part of the Chinese movement in and out of Singapore is in passage to and from surrounding islands, Singapore serving as an *entrepôt* station in human movement, as in the movement of commodities, for the adjacent islands.

Movement in and out of Hawaii is equally high but somewhat more difficult to trace as the Islands serve as a half-way station to a considerable migration to and from the Mainland. From 1911 to 1926 inclusive 51,911 immigrant aliens were admitted to Hawaii and 11,398 emigrant aliens departed[33] from the Islands. The figures, of course, do not include the movements of citizens, or Filipinos. "From 1909 to the end of 1925, 72,242 Filipino laborers emigrated to Hawaii and 15,601 returned from Hawaii."[34] This outflow, however, does not account for the number that migrated to the Mainland, definite figures of which are difficult to obtain.

Movement to and from Alaska, while on a smaller scale, is even more extensive in comparison with the total population of the Territory. According to the reports of the Governor of Alaska, 277,860 persons entered and 293,182 left the Territory during the eleven-year period 1917 to 1927. These figures include tourists as well as other migrants, the former varying from three to five thousand per year for the last few years.

Much of the human ebb and flow associated with these three regions is directly related to the fluctuations in their basic industries. This applies particularly to Malaya and Alaska, Hawaii being relatively stable. In the case of Malaya the yearly fluctuations in the gross value of exports varies from 10 to 25 per cent, due chiefly

[32]   *Census of British Malaya*, 1921, p. 93; and *Monthly Records of Migration.*
[33]   *Annual Report of the Commissioner General of Immigration*, 1926, p. 196.
[34]   *Monthly Record of Migration*, April, 1927, p. 146.

to changes in the price of rubber. For instance, in 1927 the average price of rubber was 36 cents gold per pound; in 1926 it was 46 cents; in 1925, 65 cents, and in 1921, only 15 cents. Even more drastic fluctuations take place in the fishing industry of Alaska, but due to variations in output rather than in exchange value of products. In 1924 the pack of canned salmon was, in round figures, 4 million cases; in 1926 it was 6 million cases; and in 1927 it dropped to 3 million cases, a decline of approximately 50 per cent below the previous year.

But in addition to the periodic variations in the regional demand for labor as a cause of the high mobility, consideration must be given to the factors of retirement and graduation. A large part of the immigrant inhabitants of such frontiers—from the unskilled laborers at the base of the pyramid to the professional and administrative classes at the apex—look upon the region as a place of temporary domicile, as area of exploitation rather than one of permanent residence. This applies especially to the non-native peoples of Malaya and Alaska and to a less extent to those of Hawaii also. No European looks upon Malaya as his permanent home. Sooner or later he expects to return to his native land to live on his savings or pension. Meanwhile he returns there every three or four years for temporary furlough. The Indian population likewise consider Malaya a place of temporary domicile rather than a permanent home for themselves and children. "Probably not one Indian laborer in 1,000," writes the Superintendent of the Census, "comes to British Malaya with the idea of making this country his home; in two or three years he must answer the call of his village in India, though poverty may keep him here longer."[35] The Chinese of Malaya seem to take a somewhat different attitude. A larger proportion of them make the Peninsula a place of permanent residence. This is shown by the fact that the Chinese have a higher proportion of Malay-born than the Indians (220 per mille as opposed to 124 per mille), although their ratio of females is considerably less (384 per 1,000 males as against 405 per 1,000 for British Indians).[36]

[35] *Census of British Malaya*, 1921, p. 98.
[36] *Ibid.*, p. 98.

Hawaii, owing to its more equitable climate, invites more permanent domicile. A considerable proportion of the white population maintain established residence in the Territory, and Asiatics seem quite ready to become permanent residents also as far as conditions will permit. But despite the more favorable settlement features of Hawaii a large part of the population look upon residence there as of temporary duration. Most of the Filipino plantation workers come in on a three-year contract with the provision that they shall be given free return transportation to their homes in the Philippines provided they have worked 720 days during three consecutive years.[37] And under the Immigration Act of 1924 the only other Orientals that are permitted to enter the Islands are those of temporary domicile. While there is a stable core of white residents, the majority go to the Islands for the "experience," with the expectation of returning to the Mainland later on.

Alaska even more than Malaya is exploited by a non-resident or temporarily resident population. Owing to the seasonal nature of its industries and its accessibility to Puget Sound ports, the Territory has succeeded in maintaining and even increasing its production with a declining resident population. Alaska is a good example of a modern frontier that may be exploited under modern communications by a non-resident population. Of 133 firms engaged in the fishing industry in Alaska only 47 have offices in towns within the Territory. All the rest are located in coast cities of the states, mostly in Seattle.

But more important than the attitude of temporary domicile as a basis of mobility is the phenomenon of occupational "graduation" and its coercive significance. The frontier is continuously "graduating" certain elements of its population. We have already noted the process of racial succession in the basic industries As wave after wave of immigrants serve their apprenticeship in the unskilled occupations and acquire familiarity with the language and cultural technique of the region, they press upward in the occupation pyramid only to find, in many instances, that the opportunities decrease with each successive rung in the ladder. And as it seems impossible for the individual to return to the lower occu-

37   *Monthly Labor Review*, October, 1926.

pational status, either on account of age or attitude, he is forced
to leave the regions and seek opportunities elsewhere. Regional
change seldom takes place as fast as cultural change in the individual. To be sure, the rate of individual development in the
cultural complex varies with the settlement conditions and the
nature of the educational system. The early arrivals in the frontier
have better opportunities to rise in the occupation pyramid than
those who come later. Winstedt describes the situation in Malaya:

> Until recently the demand for pupils from the English schools as
> clerks was greater than the supply, and a Cambridge Certificate or the
> Standard VII Certificate was a commercial asset, ensuring a com-
> petency in adult life. Today the supply is growing greater than the
> demand and parents are beginning to realize that the son of a shop-
> keeper, for example, may have to seek his living in his father's shop,
> even though he has done well at an English school. With the spread
> of English education, knowledge of that language will cease to be an
> open sesame to fortune or even to a livelihood, and one of the gravest
> problems today is to devise for the coming generation types of instruc-
> tion fitting the young of Malaya for such careers as the country offers.[38]

The frontier everywhere, and especially the frontier in which
the educational status is high, is carrying on a trade in population
of a character just the opposite to that of its trade in commodities.
Whereas in goods it exchanges raw materials for finished products;
in population it exchanges the skilled or tutored individuals for
unskilled, illiterate people whose cultural status compels them to
accept the jobs vacated at the base of the pyramid. Over- or underpopulation in the frontier is fundamentally related to occupational
adjustment rather than to resources. There may be over-population
in the upper rungs of the occupation pyramid and at the same time
a dearth of labor at the base. Social mobility among immigrant
peoples is largely a one direction movement. Even the failures
seldom revert to the base of the pyramid; instead they tend to return to the native habitats.[39] The white man has succeeded in
maintaining his status at the apex of the pyramid in the plantation

[38]   *Education in Malaya* (London, 1924), p. 15.
[39]   Decrepit estate laborers of British Malaya are returned to their
native land.

frontiers largely for this reason. In regions where such return is not feasible as in South Africa a "poor white" class emerges.[40]

The assumption that, if a different racial group of lower cultural level moves in volume into a region already occupied, it will soon displace the resident population and completely possess the territory, is not borne out by the facts. Sooner or later the outflow becomes greater than the inflow. This has been the cast with respect to both Chinese and Japanese migration to continental United States and Hawaii. Even now when residence in the country should be at a premium, considering the difficulties in obtaining entry, the yearly number of Oriental emigrants always exceeds that of immigrants. As resident Orientals become culturally disqualified for participation in the unskilled occupations, they find competition keener and the problem of making a living more difficult. A few find niches in the upper rungs of the pyramid, but not of sufficient importance to enable many to live according to cultural attainment. The occupational problem of second-generation Orientals is fundamentally of this character. Time alone will reveal what form of racial symbiosis they will succeed in developing with other groups in the country.

Graduation from the frontier is not equally facile for all classes of the population. The cultural change which unfits an individual for participation in the occupation pyramid frequently unfits him for migration elsewhere. Outward movement is easiest for the short-term immigrant. He may return to his native village with comparatively little difficulty. But the long-time residents, and more especially those born within the region, find outward movement hazardous. The local-born Orientals of Malaya and Hawaii find it difficult to move elsewhere. The racial hybrid is even more immobile. Eighty-nine per cent of the Eurasians of Malaya, in 1921, were natives of the Peninsula. The migration of this class into or out of the Peninsula is exceedingly small. Facts are not available to indicate the mobility of the hybrids of Hawaii, but general opinion is that but few have left the Islands.

Of course, the indigenous population of the frontier is the

[40]   See R. L. Buell, *The Native Problem in Africa* (1928), 1:15.

least mobile of all. The native Malays, Hawaiians, and Alaskan Indians scarcely ever leave their native habitats.

The number of Malays who were enumerated outside the Settlement or State in which they were born forms 6.9 per cent of the total Malay population . . . and in the majority of cases migration merely means a removal of a few miles over the State boundary. . . . The Malay peasant is conservative in the extreme, and the construction of roads and railways and greater ease and rapidity of communication have not made him eager to try his fortune outside his native State. In any of the Unfederated Malay States one may meet hundreds of Malays who have never travelled more than 20 miles from their own home . . . the great majority of the Malays still live and die not merely in the State but in the village in which they were born.[41]

Likewise the emigration of native Hawaiians or Alaskan Indians, even to continental United States, is practically zero. They do not offer a sufficient inducement to the labor recruiter to be transported as workers and they are too bound to locality to emigrate of their own accord.

As the settlement core, or population delta, of the frontier increases, either through natural increase or net immigration, the local attitude toward the region changes. The native sons and immigrants of established residence develop a sense of territorial possession or local patriotism which sooner or later expresses itself in political action. Efforts are made to save the region for its own inhabitants, usually by the imposition of restrictions on the inflow of foreign peoples and goods. The local Chinese are developing this sense of possession of Malaya. They are demanding participation in administrative activity and limitations on the freedom of movement. Likewise the established residents of Hawaii are developing pride and local patriotism in the Islands. Institutions are being erected on a basis of permanent settlement. Alaska is still largely a non-resident frontier. But here too the attitude is growing that the resources and development of the region must be considered from the standpoint of its established residents rather than from that of non-residents who seek only to exploit it.

[41] *Census of British Malaya*, 1921, p. 100.

Selected Bibliography

Adams, Romanzo, *The Education of the Boys of Hawaii and Their Economic Outlook*, Honolulu, 1926.

Adams, Romanzo, *The People of Hawaii*, Institute of Pacific Relations, Honolulu, 1927.

Arnold, Julien, *China, A Commercial and Industrial Handbook*, 1926.

Bogardus, E. S., "The Mexican Immigrant," *Journal of Applied Sociology* 9 (1927) : 470–88.

Bogardus, E. S., "Mexican Immigrants and the Quota," *Sociology and Social Research* 12 (1928) : 371–78.

Buell, Raymond L., "Japanese Immigration," *World Peace Foundation Pamphlets*, vol. 7, nos. 5–6, 1924.

Condliffe, J. B., ed., *Problems of the Pacific*, Chicago, 1928.

Coman, Katherine, *The History of Contract Labor in the Hawaiian Islands*, Publications of the American Economic Association, August, 1903.

Coolidge, Mary Roberts, *Chinese Immigration*, New York, 1909.

Coolidge, Mary Roberts, "Chinese Labor Competition on the Pacific Coast," *Annals of American Academy of Political and Social Science* 24 (1909).

Emigrant (pseudoynm), *Indian Emigration*, London, 1924.

Gamio, Manuel, *Mexican Immigration to the United States*, Chicago, 1930.

Hinton, W. J., *Government of Pacific Dependencies, British Malaya*, Institute of Pacific Relations, Honolulu, 1929.

Hourwich, I. A., *Immigration and Labor* (2d ed.), New York, 1922.

Inui, Kiyo Sue, *The Unsolved Problem of the Pacific*, Kamakura, Japan, 1925.

Lind, Andrew W., "Occupational Trends Among Immigrant Groups in Hawaii," *Social Forces* 7 (1928) : 290–97.

Mears, E. G., *Resident Orientals on the American Pacific Coast*, Chicago, 1928.

Otte, Friedrich, "Foreigners in China, A Statistical Survey," *Chinese Economic Journal*, vol. 3, no. 6 (December, 1928).

Phillips, P. D., and Wood, G. L., ed., *The Peopling of Australia*, Melbourne, 1928.

Scholefield, G. H., *Asiatic Immigration in New Zealand*, Institute of Pacific Relations, Honolulu, 1927.

Taylor, Paul S., "Mexican Labor in the United States: Imperial Valley," *University of California Publications in Economics*, vol. 6, no. 1, 1928.

Taylor, Paul S., "Mexican Labor in the United States: Valley of the South Platte, Colorado," *University of California Publications in Economics*, vol. 6, no. 2, 1929.

Taylor, Paul S., "Mexican Labor in the United States: Migration Statistics," *University of California Publications in Economics*, vol. 6, no. 3, 1929.

Thompson, Warren S., *Danger Spots in World Population*, New York, 1929.

Toynbee, A. J., *Survey of International Affairs*, London, 1925.

Winstedt, R. O., ed., *Malaya, The Straits Settlements, and the Federated and Unfederated Malay States*, London, 1923.

Wu, C. C., "Chinese Immigration in the Pacific Area," *Chinese Social and Political Science Review* 12 (October, 1928).

Young, K., *Social Psychology of Oriental-Occidental Prejudices*, New York, Institute of Pacific Relations, 1929.

Annual Reports of the Commissioner General of Immigration, Washington, D.C.

Annual Reports of the Governor of Alaska.

Census of British Malaya, 1921.

Filipino Immigration, The Commonwealth Club of California, San Francisco.

Philippine Islands: A Commercial Survey, U. S. Bureau of Commerce, 1927.

"East by West" (Papers on Orient), *The Survey Graphic*, vol. 66, no. 3 (May 1, 1926).

IV. Dominance and the Region

11

THE CONCEPT OF DOMINANCE
AND WORLD-ORGANIZATION[1]

1927

CHILD IN his interesting book, the *Physiological Founda-tions of Behavior*,[2] develops the thesis that the primary physiolog-ical factor connected with organismic reaction is the relation of dominance and subordination between integrated parts, cells, tis-sues, organs. As the organism develops from the simple to the multicellular form, the integration of parts increases in complexity and the relation of domination and subordination becomes more pronounced and localized. The type of interrelation of parts at any particular stage of development is designated as the "organismic pattern." This varies in complexity from the integration in the amoeba to that in man.

Toward the end of his book Child points out that social groups, whether animal or human, seem to develop spatial pattern forms similar to those of organismic pattern. This is, the living units become integrated in a dynamic relation of dominance and sub-ordination, leaders and followers. This is the pattern of the pack, the herd, the flock of migrating birds, as well as that of all human groups. Even social organization in its broader significance seems

Reprinted from the *American Journal of Sociology* 33 (1927) : 28–42.

[1]   No attempt is made here to stress the biological analogy, but simi-larities of structure seemed worth while pointing out. It goes without say-ing that the thesis of this paper is presented as a speculative line of de-parture rather than as a finding from inductive research.
[2]   New York: Henry Holt & Co., 1924.

to present the same fundamental pattern forms of dominance and subordination as are found in biological organisms.

Child does not attempt to trace the identity of principle operating on the more fixed aspects of economic and cultural organization. He restricts his remarks to pointing out the identities of pattern among social groups. But since the same relation of dominance and subordination of parts is even more striking in communal pattern than in social behavior pattern, I shall attempt in this paper to point out how spatial integration of human institutions takes place under different conditions of communication and transportation. It is common knowledge that all the spatially fixed aspects of our communal structure, such as roads, homes, shops, factories, institutions, become integrated into rather definite pattern forms with the relation of dominance and subordination as the dynamic organizing principle.

Communal Spatial Pattern or Ecological Organizations

Child differentiates several general types of organismic pattern. The simplest of these he calls the surface-interior pattern. In certain lower organisms the region of dominance or area of greatest activity is connected with the external surface. This is where the organism is most alive and also where it is most directly concerned with its environment. As we ascend the scale of animal life, however, we find an increasing differentiation of parts and concentration of the area of dominance, until we reach the human animal, in which the brain or cerebral cortex has become a highly specialized center of dominance coordinating and controlling the complexly integrated parts of the body.

In social evolution somewhat similar steps stand out in the spatial pattern characteristics of human aggregations. Primitive human communities, like organismic forms, are livest at the periphery or part that is most exposed to the hazards of the environment. The primitive village is usually a mere aggregation of dwellings without any specialized center of activity save that which is associated in some cases with a temple or shrine. The chief region of attention is the outer edge, where, at night, watchmen are usually stationed to guard against marauders. This pattern of village structure exists today in all parts of the world where central government is weak and where brigands infest the region, as, for example, in many parts of Asia.

A similar type of spatial pattern is represented in the walled city, which has existed everywhere in the past and which still exists in China and Asia Minor. In such cities the outer edge is the live or active part; the gates are usually the spots of greatest activity. The streets, as a rule, decline in importance as one proceeds from the gate inward. Even the more modern nation is organized somewhat on this form of spatial pattern. The political boundary, especially in the old highly fortified European states, constitutes a sort of wall or periphery of heightened activity inclosing a region of more advanced ecological pattern.

The trend of social evolution, like that of organismic evolution, is toward the axiate form of spatial pattern with dominant center and subordinate integrated parts. Wherever modern means of transportation and communication are introduced, the symmetrical undifferentiated pattern of spatial grouping is replaced by the axiated and differentiated pattern. All our cities have developed on the principle of dominant centers and subordinate, interdependent parts, which represent different forms of land utilization and different levels of land value. This familiar axiate pattern of our communal life is accepted by us as the normal and inevitable thing. However, this is not the spatial pattern of the old cities of Asia. In fact, the symmetrical pattern characterized by absence of dominant centers constitutes the structure of most of the oriental cities at the present time. For instance, cities like Soochow, Hangchow, and Foochow, to mention only a few have, generally speaking, no centers of dominance. The narrow winding streets are of almost uniform importance throughout. The gates which give ingress and egress to the important outlying regions are the spots of leading activity. Of course, such cities have inner sections of concentrated activity, such as the open space surrounding temples and shrines, where bazaars are usually held; but such areas do not dominate the structure of the city to the extent of creating coordination and integration of parts.

The introduction of the railway and modern mechanisms of communication tends everywhere to produce similar results with reference to spatial redistribution. As a rule the railroad penetrates the old city wall and locates its terminus at or near the geographical center of the community. Immediately spatial reorganization begins. The new center of the community gains in relative importance over all other parts. Axiate intramural transportation systems are introduced. Central land values rapidly increase. Hotels, office buildings, banks, and department stores arise in or near the center. Population and utilities become redistributed with reference to the new center of dominance and land-value levels.

This process of transition from the symmetrical to the axiate pattern is well illustrated in the growth of Tokio. The pre-railroad city was a loose federation of villages clustered around the shogun's castle, now the imperial palace. The villages were connected by narrow, winding roads, which in course of time became lined with small shops of every description. On the advent of the railroad in 1872 and the construction of the big central depot,[3] a new center of specialized activity commenced to develop. An undeveloped tract of land which lay between the railroad station and the imperial grounds immediately became the site of many important banks and office buildings, constructed on Western lines and built high above the rest of the city. Wide streets have been opened in all directions from this new region of dominance. Street cars and motor busses have been introduced, effecting a profound reorganization of the spatial pattern of the city. In a word, Tokio is rapidly assuming the structure of any Western city of its size. All the "districts" normal to a city of two millions are emerging in Tokio. Population is rapidly being segregated according to income, and the domestic economy is yielding to the factory. The shuttling process of workers and shoppers in and out from periphery to center is increasing apace. However, large districts of the

3   Completed in 1914.

city still belong to the old type of spatial pattern and the handicraft stage of economy.

The axiate pattern of spatial distribution with the relation of dominance and subordination among the interdependent parts is becoming a world distribution pattern. As the agencies of communication improve and as the impediments to movement are overcome, the world becomes organized on the pattern of a spider's web. The entire physical shell through which civilization functions is becoming a complexly interrelated entity in which the fundamental relation of parts is that of dominance and subordination. All the old boundaries, both local and national, are gradually losing their significance; routes, rather than rims, are becoming the subject of stressed attention. Modern competition is between regions and centers rather than between cultural and political areas. While political boundaries continue to receive much attention, nevertheless their modern significance is with reference to the movements of commodities and peoples rather than the movements of armies. Since the areas of consumption may now be far remote from those of production, the imposition of artificial impediments to movement seems to be an effective way of preventing regional exploitation.[4]

Dominance a Function of Communication

The expansion of Western civilization is a result of the development of transportation and communication. The region of dominance expands as the agencies of communication improve. The city has ever been the symbol of civilization, which, even in its crudest form, represents a spatial pattern of a fixed center of dominance with tributary subordinate districts. As Jeudwine rightly says, "All effective expansion begins from a town and begins in a town. It is the great towns such as London which provide our great trading companies which created our Empire; it is with the establishment of forts and trading places, whether on the

---

4   The recent rush on the part of many nations of the world to impose artificial barriers to movement, such as tariff walls and immigration restrictions, is an attempt to solve problems arising from modern fluidity.

Hooghly or the St. Lawrence and Potomac or on the Hudson Bay, that our Empire began."[5] The ancient empires of China, Greece, and Rome represent military and political forms of dominance centered in fortified cities and operated through ability to utilize successfully the crude forms of communication available at the time. Tribute rather than trade, however, defined the relation of the subordinate regions of the dominant centers.

The shift of emphasis from political to economic or ecological dominance came with the rise of the trade centers on the Mediterranean and Baltic seaboards. It is not necessary here to trace the successive stages of rise and decline of the different trade centers of Europe. History shows that the various rendezvous of trade and commerce varied in relative importance in proportion as they were successful in maintaining efficient lines of communication with outlying parts of the world. Spanish, Portuguese, Dutch, English, and French vied with one another in extending their commercial relations with Asia, Africa, and America. The final supremacy of England was due to the fact that she succeeded in developing and maintaining the most efficient system of communication between her home ports and the outlying parts of the world. The advantage gained over her competitors in the early part of the nineteenth century was greatly accentuated when new forms of communication and transportation were introduced. England led the way in the extension of the new agencies of communication. She not only developed the greatest merchant marine and navy to protect it, but she laid most of the cables of the world and built or financed most of the ports and railroads outside of Europe and the United States. Through her efficient system of communication, therefore, she learned more quickly than any other nation how to utilize the undeveloped parts of the world for the benefit of her own people. This concentration of the main arteries of world communication in the little island in the North Sea has given to it a dominance in international commerce that is very similar to the dominance of the business center of the modern city with respect to the local integrated districts. During the last fifty years England

[5]   *Studies in Empire and Trade* (Longmans, Green & Co., 1923), p. 59.

has become the business center of Europe and America with reference to much of the trade and commerce with Asia, Africa, and the islands of the sea.

Communication Versus Transportation

Prior to the middle of the nineteenth century, communication and transportation were practically synonymous terms. Intelligence was transmitted by the same agencies as commodities and people; but the introduction of the telegraph, telephone, and wireless forms of communication has completely changed the situation and produced revolutionary results in spatial reorganization. The first effect of this divergence in the rate of speed as physical objects. Industries and other business enterprises may now be located at great distances from the source of their management and control. This is illustrated by the tendency of European and American firms to establish plants in India, China, and other parts of the world where conditions warrant it.[6]

In the second place, the tendency toward concentration of intelligence has given to the centers of our cities an importance or dominance quite unknown in the past. It is the exchange, the office building, the transportation and communication establishments, rather than the retail business institutions, that differentiate the centers of our cities from all other parts. In other words, the city's center or area of dominance is where the intelligence is received and transmitted, where brains and ability concentrate, where the community is most alive.

This centralization of intelligence and control resulting from the annihilation of space by modern means of communication has given to individual cities or chains of cities specialized roles as collectors and distributors of different kinds of information. The great produce and financial exchanges centralize in strategic cities or groups of cities and thereby create primary and secondary centers of dominance with respect to the differentiated functions. For instance, Chicago, Winnipeg, and Liverpool far outdistance all

---

[6]   Over half of the cotton mills in China are foreign owned. See *Chinese Economic Monthly*, February, 1926.

other cities of the world in dealing in futures in wheat; while New York, New Orleans, and Liverpool are the dominant trio that deal with futures in cotton. Similarly, London and New York are the world's financial centers.

The extension of the market made possible by modern communication is producing regional specialization of production, and therefore territorial integration, to a degree unknown in the past. The modern world is integrated through information collected and distributed from fixed centers of dominance. However, as intelligence becomes centralized and coordinated, commodities are exchanged on more direct or geometrical lines. The old forms of entrepôt trade are gradually giving way to direct trade, the route of which is determined by cost-time factors.[7]

Many impediments of a primitive nature still serve as limiting factors to the most direct or geometrical exchange of commodities. Regional boundaries, differences in language, customs, monetary systems, weights and measures, business ethnics, etc., serve as barriers to the most efficient utilization of world-resources. Standardization is essential for free and unimpeded regional coordination. A vast amount of standardization has been achieved within the limits of national boundaries, but the primitive character of the world is still amply demonstrated with reference to international

---

[7] The following figures (*Report of Committee on Industry and Trade-Survey of Overseas Markets*, H. M. Stationery Office, London, 1926, p. 452) relating to two commodities of some importance to United States import trade indicate the extent to which direct trade is superseding entrepôt trade:

IMPORTS IN THOUSANDS OF POUNDS WEIGHT

	1910–14 (Average)	1923
Crude tin:		
From United Kingdom	57,700	25,014
Straits Settlements	38,226	105,137
Rubber:		
From United Kingdom	28,737	66,612
From British East Indies	8,315	462,112
From Dutch East Indies	133	112,305

movement.[8] Nor need we go to the backward parts of Asia to find examples of primitive barriers that stand in the way of economic progress. Europe, with its twenty-six political boundaries, with its score of different languages or dialects, its regional jealousies and cultural differences, furnishes ample evidence of how sentiment overrides interest as a factor in spatial pattern.

Dominance and the Frontier

The concept "dominance" suggests a center and a margin of activity, an inner locus and an outer periphery. In a world that is not yet closed there are areas that are just coming under the influence of the great society pattern and areas that still lie outside the sphere of dominance. The marginal regions that are in process of development or reorganization are commonly known as frontiers.

There are many types of frontiers. They may be grouped, however, into three general classes according to the nature of their economic relation to the centers of dominance.[9] First there is the trade frontier, characterized for the most part by the exchange of primary products for manufactured goods. This has been the relation of the far-flung parts of the British Empire to the mother-country. It is the relation of regions of agriculture everywhere to those of manufacturing. Second, there is the plantation type of frontier, a species of the first class, but sufficiently different to merit separate consideration. The plantation frontier is usually located in or near the tropical zone. It implies large-scale finance and organization and an abundance of cheap labor supplied by subject

---

[8]   China is the example *par excellence* of how the lack of standardization impedes the economic and political reorganization of the country. Local likin charges (in Shansi province there are twenty-two stations where likin dues are collected) impede the free movement of goods. Lack of standardization with reference to money, weights and measures, and quantity of goods makes exchange almost impossible.

[9]   Omitting the consideration of the settlement and the more recent amusement-center types of frontiers. These do not have as pronounced a relation to specific centers of dominance as the three classes discussed.

peoples. Typical examples of the plantation frontier are found in Cuba, Jamaica, Hawaii, Malaya, the Dutch East Indies, Assam, and Ceylon. The third type of frontier may be designated as the industrial frontier. This is the most recent development in the expansion of Western dominance. It implies the introduction of machine industry under outside finance and management into the less industrialized parts of the world, as for instance, the recent invasion of European and American factories into China, India, Latin America, and Canada.

Whatever the nature of the modern frontier, it is usually more intimately connected with its distant centers of dominance than with its local *hinterland*. The Western world has established its outposts along the water rims of the backward continents and islands of the sea. Lines of transportation and communication connect the frontier with the foreign centers of control. Docks, godowns, banks, office buildings are constructed as the essential mechanisms of control. The coast cities of China, Malaya, and India wear these European masks which give the visitors the impression that he is traveling along the shores of Europe or America. A short distance from the waterfront, however, he discovers the "native" city with its pristine organization and form, apparently unaffected, although not actually so, by the foreign invasion.

Modern dominance penetrates new parts of the world in catastrophic fashion; that is, large-scale industry or business breaks into undeveloped or differently developed parts of the world in a sudden and mature form. It is only the large organization that can afford to invade new parts of the world. Consequently the invasion comes, not as a slow growth, but as a sudden burst of power producing revolutionary effects upon the space and sustenance relations of the indigenous inhabitants.

Dominance and the Ecological Reorganization of the Frontier

As soon as an area comes under the dominance of Western centers it undergoes profound changes in the spatial and occupational distribution of its population. Western forms of communication—railroads, highways, motor cars, cables, telegraphs, and telephones—are gradually introduced and effect a new scale of spatial distance, which, in turn, makes for a redistribution of the population. All Oriented cities which have been subjected to Western influence have commenced a redistribution of population and an inauguration of a new spatial pattern of communal structure similar to that of Western cities. The household and domestic industries gradually yield to the competition of the factory and the cheaper imported merchandise. The family structure disintegrates as division of labor and separation of work from residence redistributes the familial group. The population of the city tends to become redistributed on the basis of economic status and occupational interest. Surrounding villages deteriorate as their young men and women are drawn into the city workshops.[10]

In plantation frontiers the reorganization is different but quite as pronounced. In the first place, the region changes from its simple self-sustaining agricultural form to a condition of high specialization in the production of a product which is consumed in other parts of the world. The indigenous population usually participates but slightly in the new economy. They are universally branded by the invading foreigner as unambitious, shiftless, and lazy. Consequently outside labor is imported from the most practical source of supply, which in most cases is India or China. In the first half of the nineteenth century such labor was imported as slaves; later, as indenture; but now for the most part under government supervision. The imported racial groups, under the pressure of competition, gradually assume racial division of labor, as for example in the rubber plantations of Malaya and the sugar plantations of Cuba and Hawaii. The agricultural specialization of the region, whether in tea, rubber, sugar, or tobacco, places the entire area in a relation of interdependence with other parts of the world. Its prosperity rises and falls in accordance with the rise and fall of

10   The industrial cities of Japan recruit girls from the villages to work in the textile factories; while those of China and India for the most part select men.

the world-price for the product which is produces.[11] Regional competition tends to produce cycles of agricultural specialization. For instance, the island of Ceylon first specialized in spices, then in coffee, then in tea, and now rubber is tending to become the leading product for export.

Perhaps the most significant thing about the plantation frontier is the mobile character of the population. Both the labor and the management consider the plantation as a place of temporary domicile where money is to be made as rapidly as possible to enable early retirement to the homeland. The effect of this is that most of the wealth produced in the district is consumed elsewhere, with the result that improvements in the way of roads, homes, schools, and other institutions are developed only to meet temporary needs.

Dominance and Settlement

In the course of time most frontiers grow up. They pass from a pioneer to a settled condition, and in turn become new centers of dominance creating other frontiers. During the first half of the nineteenth century most of the world was a frontier region to the centers of dominance in Western Europe. It was an open world which could be exploited by Europe as rapidly as the agencies of communication could be extended. England, especially, took advantage of this situation. Her superior technique of communication enabled her to import raw materials from the ends of the earth and ship back manufactured products to the frontier settlements. In this way she learned how to sustain a population far in excess of the limits of her local food supply.[12]

But this pioneering stage is rapidly passing. Many of the old frontier regions, including this country, have become manufacturing centers, supplying most of their own needs and at the same time seeking outside markets for their surplus products. This industrialization process tends to develop first in the manufacture of

---

11   In 1922 the price of rubber in Malaya fell to less than 7d. per pound, but by 1926 the price had increased to 2s. 6d. per pound.

12   England imports 70 per cent of her cereals and 50 per cent of her meat.

the staples of general consumption, such as coarse textiles, shoes, etc., then advances to the production of the finer and more specialized articles for which the local resources are peculiarly suited. This tendency toward frontier industrialization has hit the pioneer centers of Europe, especially England. Her leading export industries, coal, steel, and iron products, shipbuilding and textiles, are all a condition of chronic depression.

Similarly, the Eastern trade frontiers established in the port cities of the Orient are passing from a pioneer to a settled condition, which is resulting in displacement of European population and services. Early trading with India, China, and Japan developed by the establishment of foreign colonies at the crucial points of trade advantage. The colonies were composed of the foreign managerial and clerical service required to carry on trade relations with peoples that had neither the knowledge nor the machinery for dealing with Western countries. As years passed, however, the people of the East have gradually learned the white man's technique and scheme of organization, with the result that there is a tendency to take over many of the services previously usurped by foreigners. The people of the Orient are gradually learning that they can run their own machinery with reference to importing and exporting, and the white foreigner is being considered an unnecessary and undesirable competitor.

Japan has made the great advance in this regard. She has practically eliminated all unnecessary foreign business enterprises. Despite her increasing contact with the Western world, her white population shows a tendency to decline rather than increase.[13]

Up to about thirty years ago, Japan's foreign trade was almost entirely carried on from the old treaty ports by foreign (non-Japanese) merchants, who imported such goods as Japan required and exported her products. These foreigners, most of whom were British, by their knowledge of foreign markets, helped to develop and extend her trade, and Japan's commercial prosperity was in no small degree due to these pioneers. Later the question of "direct trade," as it was called, acquired great importance and Japanese commercial policy consisted

---

[13]   The foreign population of Tokio was 3,562 in 1909 and only 2,051 in 1922.

principally in assisting the formation of a few Japanese firms who, with the indirect support of the government, would be in a position to compete successfully with the foreign firms. Gradually, however, with the success which attended her efforts at home, came a desire to extend her operations abroad; and now the large Japanese firms have ramifications all over the world, and, in addition to fostering the trade of their own country, they develop trade between countries in which Japan is not directly interested.[14]

The same condition is developing in the port cities of China, although at the present time the process is retarded on account of political instability. But many Chinese are quite conscious of the inutility of the foreign merchant who is performing a service and reaping a reward which might as well be in the hands of the Chinese. Practically the whole of China's foreign trade has in the past been handled in China by foreign (non-Chinese) merchant firms, amongst whom there is a perponderance of those of British nationality; but quite recent years there has been an increasing tendency on the part of Chinese merchants to enter into direct relations with manufacturers and exporters in foreign countries.[15]

This is the cause of much of the trouble in India and Egypt. However, in addition to the economic competition in these countries there is the political competition as well. Much of the anti-government attitude of the educated classes in India and Egypt is due to the difficulty in securing jobs. The only desirable white-collar positions are those associated with the government and are now held by the British.

Undoubtedly in the course of time the countries of the Orient will carry on their trade with the rest of the world in much the same way as the countries of Europe carry on trade with one another today. That is, each country will develop its own machinery with reference to finance and exchange so as to trade with as little loss to itself as possible.

Transformation Of Foreign Trading In Tientsin

During the past few years the number of trading firms has multiplied considerably, and naturally competition amongst them is ex-

14   *Report of Committee on Industry and Trade-Survey of Overseas Markets* (1926), p. 412.
15   *Ibid.*, p. 396.

tremely keen. Whereas a decade ago a few established hongs, doing business with heavy overhead expenses, manned with large staffs, and content with only large profits, had the trade of the port very much to themselves, they are now confronted with the competition of smaller firms that have sprung up recently. These latter firms have small overhead expenses and are content with a small margin of profit. Therefore, although the volume of the trade has increased, profits have decreased on account of the keen competition amongst firms. Of great importance is the rise of the Chinese capitalised firm carrying on business along foreign lines. These concerns do business directly with agencies abroad and thus eliminate "foreign middlemen"; they are naturally favourably situated for doing upcountry trade.[16]

The plantation type of frontier is the most difficult to wrench from foreign control. This is because of the large amount of capital involved and because the market is in the Western World. Even here, however, Western authority is beginning to lose its control. Many of the sugar plantations of Java and the East Indies are now under Javanese ownership and management. And the Chinese of Malaya, although slow to adopt corporate forms of business organization, are gradually getting control of an increasing monopoly of the tin and canning industries. Likewise, a considerable percentage of the tea and rubber plantations of Ceylon are now in the hands of the Sinhalese, and the textile mills of Bombay are practically a monopoly of the Parsees.

New Centers of Dominance

The world's centers of gravity are always in process of change. Old centers lose their relative importance as new factors enter to disturb the equilibrium. Some of these factors are temporary and accidental; others are associated with permanent trends. The world is gradually becoming a closed area. The pioneer conditions which gave economic unity to the British Empire are rapidly passing. New centers of dominance are arising and producing new combinations of regional interdependence which are often quite at variance with the existing political structure.

[16]   "Tientsin Customs Report, 1925," *Chinese Economic Bulletin,* October 9, 1926.

12

SPATIAL DISTANCE

1929

CHANGING SPATIAL distance, as measured by time and cost, is perhaps the most important factor in human affairs today. Human activities have a spatial base. Population and institutions are spatially distributed in relation to natural resources and other geographic factors. It is on this basis of physical distribution that all our maps are constructed. The distance between points is definite and fixed and is represented by a linear scale in accordance with the contour of the earth's surface. But such maps do not represent the more significant aspects of distribution. They fail to take into account the variations in distance between points as measured by time and cost. Distance conceived in terms of time and cost acquires a new meaning, and distribution determined by these factors varies accordingly.

Civilization is organized on a basis of fixity of location with mobility of goods and people. But while location is relatively fixed, *position*—the relation of one place to another—is variable due largely to the dynamic nature of time-cost distance. The world is shrinking with improved communications, but not evenly. Some places are coming closer together, others are remaining stationary or even becoming more remote. Each community struggles for advantage in time-cost distance over its competitors in the larger economy. We are now in the most romantic and significant period of world history with regard to changing distance. Not only do reports of new developments in transportation and communication

Reprinted from *Sociology and Social Research*, vol. 13, July, 1929.

whet our imagination but they also compel us to reflect on the fundamentals of existence as they connote changes in the distribution pattern that necessitate accommodation to new scales of distance and new forms of symbiosis. As long as human and animal energy were the prevailing modes of land locomotion the distribution pattern remained relatively stable, but when mechanical energy was applied to communications, distance became relative and space variable.

The most important differential in time-cost distance is between land and water space. Under present facilities of transport a unit of land space is about one-half the *time* distance but twelve times the *cost* distance of a unit of water space.[1] The significance of this time-cost differential in world organization is of tremendous importance. In the first place, as far as the cost of moving goods is concerned, ocean space is contracted to about one-twelfth of its physical size. Furthermore, the ocean provides an open highway to all the seaboard regions of the earth. It thereby serves as a unifying factor in the evolving world economy. No two places bordering on the sea are too remote to exchange products in this steamship age. The inner rim of the world economy is the seashore; the outer rim runs through the land masses and extends back from the seaboard as far as the prevailing facilities of transport permit the surplus products to be conveyed to an ocean port. Taking the route from Sydney to Liverpool—14,050 statute miles—as representing the maximum water haul, we find that the cost of tranporting a bushel of wheat this distance is about 18 or 20 cents; whereas by rail in the United States the same amount would transport a bushel of wheat less than 1,500 miles;[2] or by cart in China, 100 miles; or by carrier in China[3] or Africa,[4] about 30 miles. In other

[1]   There is of course a wide variation in shipping rates from time to time and on different commodities; but in general the rates seem to average about one-twelfth of rail rates.

[2]   Figures from Domestic Commerce Series, no. 4, U. S. Dept. of Commerce, 1927.

[3]   See John Earl Baker, *Explaining China* (1927), p. 202.

[4]   "Head porterage in an area where labor is plentiful and cheap works out at 2*s*. 6*d*. per ton mile; donkey transport at 11*d*.; camel transport at between 9*d*. and 10*d*.; while the railway takes baled cotton from

words, as far as cost is concerned Sydney is as close to Liverpool as it is to a point 1,500 miles inland by the most efficient rail system, or to a point 100 miles inland by animal cart, or 30 miles inland by coolie carrier. This places the most remote ports on the coast rim of the world closer together than inland points 1,500 miles distant by rail, 100 miles distant by animal-drawn vehicle, or 30 miles distant by human carrier. Moverover this is a conservative appraisal of the land and water differential. In most cases the contrast is even greater. Rubber, for instance, is transshipped from Western Europe to New York, a distance of about 3,500 statute miles, for $6.00 per ton; whereas the rail rate from New York to Akron, about 450 miles, is $9.40 per ton. Likewise tea comes from Yokohama to Seattle, a distance of 4,900 statute miles, for $12.00 per ton while the rate from Seattle to Fargo, 1,300 miles, is $30.00 per ton.[5] "Wool moves from Idaho Falls, Idaho, to Portland, Oregon, a distance of 782 miles at $1.14 per hundred pounds; it moves from Portland, Oregon, to Boston, by water, a distance of 7,019 miles, for 75 cents per hundred pounds."[6]

Furthermore the differential between land and water cost-distance continues to increase. The index of ocean freights, on a 1911–1913 basis, has dropped to 97, whereas the index of rail freight rates has risen to 150.[7] Not only is this increasing differential drawing foreign countries closer together in trade relations but it is shrinking national coast lines and stretching inland areas.

Before the war New York was 1904 cents away from San Francisco, while now it is only 1680 cents away. But a given Mid-West point, which was 2600 cents away from the Pacific Coast before the war, is today 3114 cents away. In effect this Mid-West point has moved 514 cents away from the Pacific Coast while New York has moved 224

Zaris to Lagos at under 2d. per ton mile" (Report by Hon. W. G. A. Ormsby-Gore, M. P. on his visit to West Africa, 1926, pp. 29–30).

5   From data compiled by Alfred H. Ritter, Transportation Economics of the Great Lakes-St. Lawrence Ship Canal, 1925.

6   Great Lakes-St. Lawrence Tidewater Association, February 9, 1929.

7   Rate on wheat; rates vary for different commodities (Year Book of Agriculture, 1927).

cents closer to the Pacific Coast. A similar calculation will show that in the same period this Mid-West point has moved 694 cents away from the markets of the Atlantic seaboard and South America.[8]

This differential in cost distance by water is producing a seaboard civilization. Population is massing in coastal regions. Most of the great cities of the world, especially those of nineteenth century origin, are located on the ocean rim or on sites accessible to it by navigable inland waters. Cost-distance differential in favor of seaboard places is further enhanced by the fact that freight rates between ports and important inland points are often the same or even lower than rates between intermediate points but a fraction of the mileage apart. This encourages manufacturing plants to group whenever possible on navigable water routes leading to the outside world.

But while the *cost* differential favors water space, the time differential favors land space. The recent gains in *time* distance relate largely to land transport. Trans-marine time has not decreased materially in the last two decades. The great ocean liners of twenty years ago traveled at about the same speed as the fastest ships do now.[9] However, in land movement, time distance has been revolutionize since the beginning of the last century as a result of the new facilities of transport, the straightening of routes, and the increased efficiency in dispatch. Even in rail transportation there has been considerable reduction in time-distance with respect to the movement of both goods and people. The Bureau of Foreign and Domestic Commerce states that "freight is delivered today in approximately one-half the time required seven years ago."[10] Passenger service has not achieved an equal ratio of time reduction but every year there is some decrease in rail time between the great cities at least. Of course the real revolution in land time distance has been brought about by the motor car and the airplane. The for-

[8]   Frank E. Williams, "The Geography of the Mississippi Valley," *The Annals of the American Academy of Political and Social Science*, January, 1928, p. 18.
[9]   In 1908 the Lusitania crossed the Atlantic in 4 days, 17 hours, and no boat beats that time today.
[10]   Commerce Year Book, 1928, vol. 1, p. 586.

mer has introduced a new scale of distance for local travel, the latter for travel between more distant points.

This time differential and the flexibility of land transport has increased the total mileage of land travel far out of all proportion to that of travel by boat. Peoples everywhere are responding to the introduction of new facilities of transport and increasing the volume of movement. In 1927 the per capita travel on railways in this country was 297 passenger miles. In the same year there were registered for passenger traffic alone over 20,000,000 motor cars. In addition, of course, there is the travel by airplane, which is just beginning to become important.

In general the tendency seems to be toward a water movement of goods, especially the basic products, and a land movement of people. Symbiotically the coast regions of the world are being drawn closer together due to the cost differential in water transportation, whereas sociologically the peoples on the continuous land masses are intermingling more and more freely as a result of the new facilities of transport.

But new modes of transport introduce changes in routes of traffic and travel that are almost as important from the standpoint of spatial pattern and human distribution as are the changes effected by the differentials in the time-cost distance. Every new form of transportation introduces changes in the routes of movement. The steamship follows routes that in the main are quite different from those pursued by the sailboat; likewise the railway evolved its own net of inland lines, and the motor highway follows a course quite different from the wagon road which preceded it. The airplane route, now in process of formation, is likely to introduce further changes in directing the streams of traffic and travel. The general tendency seems to be toward a more direct or geometrical system of routes between points distributed in space. The steamship, unaffected by ocean currents or winds, tends to follow the arc of the great circle. Every year canals, ferries, bridges, and tunnels straighten the inland routes for surface forms of land transport, and the airplane line is becoming a synonym for the nearest distance between two points. In addition to the straightening of the route there is a gradual tendency toward an elimination of breaks in movement between points of origin and destination. With the advance of engineering science an increasing number of the geographical barriers are being mastered, allowing movement to take place in uninterrupted fashion. It is not necessary to recount the progress made in recent years throughout the world in the construction of tunnels, bridges, canals, standardization of railway gauges, and facilities of transport, all of which imply an elimination of breaks in movement. Probably the greatest advance in this direction has come with the increasing use of motor cars. The motorization of short distance transportation has eliminated most of the transfers previously necessary for local travel and distribution service.[11] The airplane, unhampered by the usual breaks in travel, especially that between land and water movement, seems likely to effect further profound changes in distribution.

There is still another tendency relating to the route that should be noted, namely that of specialization of use. Specialization is taking place here as in all other forms of human activity. High-valued and perishable merchandise tends to move over the shortest time route while bulky and less valuable merchandise tends to move over the lowest cost route. Even in human travel there is a tendency toward specialization in the use of routes and facilities of travel. This is more pronounced in Europe and the Orient, where the gulf between classes is wide and the facilities of transport are adjusted to different degrees of economic status. In a word, the changes that are taking place in the direction and specialization of routes and in the elimination of breaks is introducing a new structural pattern of human distribution. The changes affect the smaller towns and villages more than the larger places. Chains of habitations come into being or disappear with the rise or decline of routes.

In this world of changing distance the problem of equilibrium is ever present. The market areas for most of the products of common use extend far beyond the regions of production. Usually many places compete in supplying the market with a given prod-

[11]   By eliminating the breaks that used to exist between urban and rural modes of transportation the motor car has erased the urban-rural boundary lines and given rise to the metropolitan region.

uct. In the competitive situation, change in distance, either time or cost, frequently is sufficient to determine the prosperity or decline of a region. This is why there is so much concern about the time schedule and freight rates.[12] Various organizations have been established for the purpose of stabilizing time-cost distance. The Interstate Commerce Commission attempts to stabilize railway rates within the United States. Ocean liner rates are usually fixed by conference agreement. But despite these and other stabilizing agencies rates fluctuate greatly and affect distance accordingly. Tariffs are the usual method of attempting to meet the competition of low water rates from foreign countries. They do not, however, counteract the differential between land and water rates within the domestic market.

Although the dynamic nature of time-cost distance is a disturbing factor in our economy of regional interdependence, the control that has arisen through the more definited delineation of space in time units has made possible an orderly system of exchange. Space can now be calculated definitely in terms of time and cost. One may go or consign goods from any place in the civilized world to any other place and know in advance the definite time of arrival and the cost of transportation. This has given a control over space the value of which is difficult to overestimate. It permits an orderly movement of goods and people over the earth's surface and makes possible a system of planning that was impossible in the premechanical age.

So far we have been dealing with distance as it pertains to the movement of physical objects—people or goods. The scope of this paper permits but a word to be said in regard to the transfer of intelligence. It is usually affirmed that wire and wireless communication have annihilated space and brought the civilized world into a single contact area. In actual fact, however, this is only a partial truth. Although the time factor has been largely eliminated, the

12   Note the recent agitation on the part of Puget Sound cities to obtain a sixty-three hour rail service to Chicago on the ground that the prevailing five-hour differential in favor of San Francisco and Los Angeles places the Puget Sound region at a disadvantage in competing for tourist and other travel.

cost factor still remains with its significant bearing. Seattle for example is $8.75 distant from New York by the minimum telephone charge and $57.00 from London, by the recently established trans-Atlantic telephone service. While telegraph and telephone rates tend to vary with distance, cable rates bear no such relation. According to the present schedule of cable rates the entire Pacific Coast of the United States is much more closely integrated with Europe than it is with Eastern Asia or South America. Seattle, by Western Union cable rates, is only 34 cents per word distant from England, 41 from Italy, 44 from Austria, while she is 77 cents per word distant from Japan, 92 cents distant from Shanghai, and 77 cents from Manila. In fact by cable rates Seattle is closer to India and Ceylon than to Yokohama or Manila. This differential in communications tends to give the entire Western Hemisphere a European as opposed to an Oriental orientation. Ideas, like goods, tend to flow along channels of lowest cost distance.

13

ECOLOGICAL SUCCESSION IN THE PUGET SOUND REGION

1929

THE PUGET SOUND region forms a link in the chain of habitation areas that extends along the Pacific Coast of America from Alaska to Mexico. The direct contact part of this civilization zone, lying between Vancouver, Canada, and San Diego, is about two thousand miles in length but only at a few points more than fifty miles in width. This strip of settlement is separated from all other regions and developed occupation by great distances; on the west, the broad Pacific lies between it and the settlements of Asia; on the east, a mountainous and arid zone of from four to six hundred miles in width separates it from the other population centers of the continent.

This north-south civilization, belt which a generation ago was but a frontier zone to the occupied sections of Eastern America, has rapidly evolved a civilization structure of its own and has passed from the position of a series of pioneer outposts to that of a metropolitan economy in which six great urban centers—Vancouver, Seattle, Portland, San Francisco, Los Angeles, and San Diego—integrate respective complexes of highly specialized sub-areas of production. Geographically this region falls into two distinct divisions as determined by topography and climate. The Siskiyou watershed at the southern boundary of Oregon divides the region into two supplementary zones. To the north extends an

Reprinted from *Publications of the American Sociological Society*, vol. 23 (1929).

evergreen forest belt that increases in density with the increasing precipitation northward. To the south extends the ever brown belt comprising the several great valleys of California, which, under modern methods of irrigation, have become regions of intensive agriculture with flourishing towns and cities. The geographical contrasts in these two sections of the Pacific rim have given rise to tremendous north and south movements of products and people. The basic products of these regions are supplementary rather than competitive. The north exports its lumber,[1] grain, and fish, for which the south exchanges its oil, sugar, citrous fruits, and early vegetables. Seasonal differences effect a similar supplementary exchange of population. The summer stimulates a northward flow of California's migratory laborers and tourists,[2] the winter months cause a reciprocal movement of people from Oregon, Washington, and Western Canada.

The Puget South basin, which is our subject of special attention, comprises one of the three major settlement units of the northern half of the zone just described. It is a natural geographic pocket formed by the Puget Sound inlet and the river valleys tributary thereto. Settlement is limited to a strip of territory approximately two hundred miles in length and varying from twenty to fifty miles in width. On the east and west sides it is sharply defined by geographical barriers, mountains or water. At the northern and southern extremities competition with adjoining habitation areas—the Fraser Valley on the north and the Columbia-Willamette Valley on the south—determines the margins of movement. The region is closely integrated with the Washington fruit

[1]   During the two years 1926 and 1927 the California market took about a third of all water-borne shipments of lumber from Oregon, Washington, and British Columbia, and this is a lower ratio than in former years, due to recent extensive shipments to the Atlantic Coast. On the other hand, California is the source of practically all the oil consumed in this lumber region. From California to Seattle, 90 per cent of tonnage and 50 per cent of value is gasoline and other oil (*Fort Warden Reports*, Seattle).

[2]   Definite statistics are not available, but 11,965 California tourists registered in Ranier National Park in the summer of 1928. This, of course, is but a small percentage of the number visiting the state of Washington.

and grain areas lying directly east of the Cascade range, but these sections are outside the immediate contact area and are only partly under the economic dominance of the Sound cities.

The Puget Sound habitation area as at present developed represents a highly integrated system of settlement units that have grown up in response to the changes that have taken place in the commercial and industrial activities of the region. The settlement web, owing to marked local differences in rain fall (85 inches in Aberdeen, 34 in Seattle, and 20 in Port Townsend), topography, and resources, represents almost as wide a variety of communal units as exists in the nation as a whole. In this narrow zone comprising a population of about one million[3] are to be found in close proximity, agricultural, fishing, mining, lumber, and amusement centers of a wide variety of types. The entire communal complex is integrated into a single economic unity with Seattle as the center of dominance and numerous subordinate towns and cities performing specialized functions.

The task of this paper is to trace what seem to be some of the important intervals of change in the process of settlement development. The fact that the region is young and that many of the pioneer settlers are still living somewhat simplifies the undertaking. Difficulties arise, however, in the use of statistical data. Census periods do not correspond with the intervals of most active transition, nor do enumeration districts coincide with the natural units of settlement. But even the crude data at hand bring into relief some of the salient features of the changing pattern of settlement resulting from industrial and commercial succession.

On the basis of census data the history of settlement may be divided roughly into three cycles of development: (1) from about 1850 to 1880, that is up to the coming of the railways; (2) 1880 to 1915, the period of aggregation and urbanization resulting from railway communications both local and national; (3) 1910 to the present time, the period of the motor car, market organization, and metropolitanism.

[3]   In 1920 the population of the fifteen counties embracing the region was 869,005; 65 per cent lived in cities of over 2,500 and 56.5 per cent in the six cities with more than 10,000 inhabitants.

I. *Period of Pioneer Settlement*

The first period, 1850–80, represents the pioneer stage in the process of settlement. During this time the region was but a frontier outpost of settlement elsewhere and more especially of the earlier developed districts in California and Oregon. This was a period of water transportation and rim settlement. The economic base was limited to one industry, lumber. Mills formed the nuclei of settlement and were widely dispersed along the shore of the Sound. It was a village economy stage, but each village was the creation of an economic need manifested in some distant place. The Puget Sound district never was a region of primary settlement in which production was mainly for local use, as was the case in early New England or even in the Willamette Valley of Oregon. From the beginning the products of the region were sold in distant markets, and most of the articles of consumption imported. There was but little contact among the mill villages of the pioneer period, partly on account of their relative inaccessibility, but chiefly because of the absence of any symbiotic urge. Each village sent its products direct by boat to outside markets and received its supplies direct by boat from outside centers.[4] During this thirty-year period the nuclei of practically all the present port cities were established, but there was no evidence of concentration or centralization. In 1880, Seattle, the largest town, had a population of only 3,533 and Tacoma, the next in size, 1,098.

II. *Aggregation and Urbanization*

The second period of regional succession began about 1880 when the Northern Pacific line reached Puget Sound (Tacoma, 1873; Seattle, 1886), soon to be followed by the Canadian Pacific Railway (1885), the Great Northern (1893), and a short while later by three other transcontinental lines. The influence of the railways is reflected in the growth and concentration of population.

[4]   F. S. Grant, *History of Seattle, Washington* (New York, 1891), p. 239.

TABLE I

POPULATION AND PER CENT INCREASE BY DECADES

| CENSUS* YEAR | PUGET SOUND REGION | | WASHINGTON STATE | | UNITED STATES |
	Population	Per Cent Increase since Preceding Census	Population	Per Cent Increase since Preceding Census	Per Cent Increase since Preceding Census
1880...............	29,951	131.4	75,116	213.6	26.0
1890...............	208,010	594.5	357,232	375.6	25.5
1900...............	300,787	44.6	518,103	45.0	20.7
1910...............	687,443	128.5	1,141,990	120.4	21.0
1920...............	869,005	26.4	1,356,621	18.8	14.9

* Census data.

[There were] two cycles of growth in the Puget Sound region during the five decennial periods under review. The boom following the introduction of the railways had subsided by 1900 with a consequent drop in the rate of aggregation. Also the decline in national prosperity (in regard to which the district always has been sensitive) during this period had its effect upon the region. The following decade, however, (1900–1910) shows an increased rate of growth resulting from the development of Alaska, and the expansion of industry and commerce in general. The last census period, which belongs to the third and present stage of settlement, shows a decline in the rate of aggregation, but the conditions associated therewith will be analyzed later.

The process of regional aggregation has been accompanied by a continuous rearrangement of local population. Every change in transportation and in the economic base has been reflected in a redistribution of inhabitants. Unfortunately census data fail to show the movements in adequate detail. Table II, however, indicates something of the local variations. The figures represent the per cent of increase per decade for each of the fifteen counties in the region divided by the per cent of increase for the same period for the region as a whole.

It is interesting to note that the greatest amount of local shift-

TABLE II

GROWTH INDICES: COUNTIES VS. REGION

Counties	1870–80	1880–90	1890–1900	1900–10	1910–20
Clallam	.43	.56	1.95	.16	2.59
Gray's Harbor	.99	1.52	1.38	1.06	.98
Island	.56	.10	.01	1.18	.63
Jefferson	.26	.65	− .72	.36	− .81
King	1.72	1.39	1.61	1.23	1.39
Kitsap	.77	.28	.97	1.25	3.33
Lewis	1.46	.58	.71	.87	.56
Mason	.92	.58	.78	.27	− .17
Pacific	.93	.28	.84	.85	.71
Pierce	1.03	2.41	.20	.91	.73
San Juan	.54	.19	.92	.18	.0004
Skagit	....	....	1.34	.81	.54
Snohomish	1.00	.86	3.94	1.14	.54
Thurston	.35	.33	.06	.6	1.03
Whatcom	3.71	.83	.62	.82	.08

ing of population occurred during the two periods of lowest regional increase—the decades 1890 to 1900 and 1910 to 1920. During these decades the average deviation of the county growth indices from the region's increase was 72.2 per cent and 71.3 per cent respectively, as opposed to 57.7 per cent for 1880 to 1890 and 33.5 per cent for 1900 to 1910, the two decades of most rapid regional increase.

The process of concentration and urbanization can be shown best by presenting census data for successive decades.

The tendency toward concentration is clearly revealed in Table III. Many ports of the pioneer period (prior to 1880) have remained stationary or have declined in population while new places suddenly appear in the communal constellation. Everett, Bellingham, and Bremerton (the United States Navy Yard) appear for the first time in the census as substantial cities. Seattle leads the group throughout; at first closely followed by Tacoma but gradually gaining in dominance over all competitors. During the last decade Seattle was the only Sound port whose rate of increase was greater than that of the region as a whole.

TABLE III
Growth of Ports on Puget Sound Inlet

CITY, TOWN, OR PRECINCT	POPULATION					
	1920	1910	1900	1890	1880	1870
Seattle...........	315,312	237,194	80,671	42,837	3,533	1,107
Tacoma..........	96,965	83,743	37,714	36,006	1,098	73
Everett...........	27,644	24,814	7,838	....	....	....
Bellingham.......	25,585	24,298	11,062	8,135	....	258
Bremerton........	8,918	2,993	....	....	....	....
Olympia..........	7,795	6,996	3,863	4,698	1,232	1,203
Port Angeles......	5,351	2,286	2,321	....	....	....
Anacortes.........	5,284	4,168	1,476	1,131	....	79
Port Townsend....	2,847	4,181	3,443	4,558	917	593
Blaine............	2,254	2,289	1,592	1,563	400	....
Port Orchard......	1,393	682	256	226	....	80
Port Blakely......	1,384	1,127	1,288	643	500	61
Mukilteo.........	1,077	724	104	92	56	....
Shelton..........	984	1,163	833	648	....	....
Port Madison.....	604	609	343	269	200	249
Port Gamble......	597	730	831	420	421	326
Steilacoom........	564	430	284	270	250	314
Friday Harbor.....	522	400	....	75	....	....
La Conner........	516	603	564	398	....	40
Port Ludlow......	479	639	399	236	212	259
Tumwater........	472	490	270	410	171	354
Port Discovery....	348	236	121	913	150	152
Coupeville........	343	310	495	513	90	....
Utsalady.........	267	511	460	207	187	100
Seabeck..........	174	436	235	257	266	150

Factors.—The increase and distribution of population within
the region is, of course, definitely related to the changing nature
of the economic base. . . . The two leading forms of agriculture at
the moment are dairying and poultrying. The former is a pioneer
industry and is highly developed throughout the region.[5] The latter is a recently developed industry but, owing to efficiency in cooperative marketing, has had phenomenal growth. The cooperative

[5]   In 1924 the value of dairy products sold amounted to about $15,-
000,000, and the industry has made substantial gains since then.

movement began in 1917, and in 1927 almost a million cases of eggs were handled.

Each industry has had its own peculiar effect upon population distribution. Coal, deposits of which were discovered in the seventies at points near Seattle and Tacoma, afforded the first stimulus to population concentration. Unlike the lumber industry, which, in the early period, distributed population rather evenly over a wide territory, coal tended to concentration near the points of production and shipment. Hence the rapid growth of Seattle and Tacoma about 1880 when coal-mining began. But the coal industry has had comparatively slight influence upon population during the last few decades. The competition of crude oil from California and the development of hydroelectric power have reduced greatly the local market for coal.[6]

The fishing industry has always been an important source of income for the region but it has not afforded a basis for town development. The twenty-seven canneries of the Puget Sound are scattered over a wide territory. The Alaska canneries, however, have influenced population concentration in Seattle as this city is their source of labor and materials as well as the port through which the products are marketed.

The lumber industry has had a profound influence upon the making and destroying of towns. Practically every city, town, and village of the region is to a greater or lesser extent dependent upon this industry. It is a double-headed industry—the logging camp and the mill town. In the beginning these two units had a common location with the result that when the local area was logged off, the mill was closed, and the villagers dependent thereon were forced to migrate unless a new economic base could be secured. This accounts for the decline of many incorporated places each decade,[7] also for the rise of new villages. In the course of time, however,

---

[6]   See Joseph Daniels, "The Fuel Mining Situation in the Pacific Northwest," *Transactions of the Canadian Institute of Mining and Metallurgy* 27 (1924).

[7]   Thirty-eight incorporated places declined in population between 1890 and 1920, and the region contains scores of deserted mill villages that never were incorporated.

the lumber industry has changed remarkably. With the development of transportation and technique the units of operation have
become larger. The logging camp of today, save for a few small
concerns, is usually quite remote from the sawmill, and the business office frequently is in a third place. As the mills have increased
in size they have helped to concentrate population. The five leading cities of the region are also the leading mill centers and ports
of lumber export.

While the concentration of the lumber industry has bunched
population at strategic shipping points and given stability to the
larger centers, the outer logging-camp rim is almost as mobile as
ever. Of ninety camps listed in Abbey's Register for 1921 only
forty-three appear in the 1927 edition.

Manufactures other than lumber so far have had but little
concentrating significance. While the total product is large, nevertheless, the units of production, with a few notable exceptions,[8] are
still small. The average number of employees per plant is but little
higher than it was twenty years ago. The recent rise of the pulp
industry at points along the western rim of settlement is causing
a rejuvenation of several decadent towns.

The changing nature and direction of commerce accounts in
large measure for the successive patterns of population distribution in the Puget Sound region. The unusually large number of
sizable cities in relation to the population of the region is due
to the bulky nature of the leading export—lumber, which, unlike
lighter and more valuable commodities, shows but little tendency
to concentrate for purposes of shipment.

In the early period of settlement, when the market was restricted and the boats were comparatively small, the leading ports
of export were located along the western rim of Puget Sound.[9] But

8   The six leading industrial centers of the region—Seattle, Tacoma,
Everett, Aberdeen, Hoquiam, Bellingham—contained 1,548 manufacturing
establishments in 1925, giving employment to 44,928 workers (*Biennial
Census of Manufacturers*, 1925).

9   In 1890, the Seattle *Post Intelligencer* gave a list of the thirteen
leading ports of lumber shipment from December 1, 1889, to November
30, 1890. The first seven appearing in the list are on the western water rim
but none is in the present list of customs ports (Grant, *History of Seattle*,
p. 251).

TABLE IV

FOREIGN COMMERCE BY CARGO PORTS IN
WESTERN WASHINGTON 1927*

Port	Imports	Exports
Seattle.............	$205,395,663	$60,089,926
Tacoma.............	18,438,250	42,372,089
Aberdeen...........	6,305	8,690,661
Bellingham..........	718,924	1,946,314
Everett.............	792,522	2,639,293
Port Angeles.........	1,221,054	458,084
Port Townsend.......	141,822	174,197

* United States Custom's Service, Bureau of Statistics, February 15, 1928, quoted in *Port of Seattle Year Book*, 1928.

While exports leave from many points, imports tend to concentrate. Table IV refers to foreign commerce only. The domestic commerce of these ports is greater than the foreign, but the relative port positions regarding imports and exports remains about the same.

after the railways came, most of the western ports declined and those on the eastern shoreline sprang ahead.

Agriculture has had considerable significance both in regard to distribution and selection of population. According to the 1925 census less than 3 per cent of the total area of the region was in harvested crops the previous year. The cultivated area is confined largely to the river valleys, lake shores, and tidal flats. The soil and climate favor truck farming as opposed to cereals. The limiting factor for this sort of agriculture has always been markets. Interesting successions in land utilization appear as settlement developed and as marketing organization became more efficient. In the nineties most of the land under cultivation in King and Snohomish counties were devoted to hop growing. Picking was done by Indians and Chinese. But as the cities grew, hops were displaced by dairy herds, not only to supply local needs but for a wider market. Condensaries were established in a number of valley towns, and many immigrants from the Netherlands came to the region as milkers or dairy farmers. In recent years, however, several new forms of agriculture are arising, largely as a result of cooperative marketing. Lettuce, berries, and especially eggs are becoming important products of shipment to outside markets. Dairy herds have gradually been pushed back from the cities and the land used in the production of vegetables and berries. The succession was accompanied by an invasion of Japanese, who first entered as laborers but gradually took up farming for themselves, specializing in lettuce and other truck corps.

Large-scale poultrying is a new industry in the region. In using the uplands it has not displaced any previous form of agriculture. On the other hand it is effecting a new distribution of the agricultural population. Several poultry villages have recently appeared on the logged off uplands,[10] the inhabitants being mostly newcomers from the middle western states.

III. *Centralization and Metropolitanism*

The third and present cycle in the evolution of settlement may be designated as the stage of metropolitanism. The period from 1910, or more accurately from the outbreak of the War to the present, differs from the preceding thirty years chiefly in regard to the rearrangement of local population and the reintegration of communal units. The influence of the motor car, the Panama Canal, Pacific trade, and the changing technique of business organization has been such as to effect a new cycle of regional development.

The most conspicuous feature of change during the last fifteen years is the increasing dominance of Seattle as a metropolitan center. Of the total regional increase in population for the decade 1910–20, 43 per cent took place within the corporate limits of Seattle. All available criteria of growth indicate that the same or even a higher rate of concentration has taken place since 1920.

Rearrangement of Centers.—The influence of the motor car and the new system of highways is reflected in the decline of many of the old communal centers and the development of new ones. Up to 1910, settlement was confined almost entirely to the salt-water rim and along the river valleys. Towns and villages were spaced

10   A good example is Alderwood Manor, a community of 1,500 people located on the logged-off uplands midway between Seattle and Everett.

from five to ten miles apart depending upon land utilization and topography. The settlements in one valley were quite largely isolated from those in a neighboring valley, frequently but a few miles distant. Towns along the Sound were united by boat or train, both of which followed circuitous routes. The coming of the motor car and highways immediately effected a new spatial pattern for the entire region. The motor highway, unlike the railroad, is not confined to the valleys nor does it slavishly follow the jagged coastline and meandering mountain streams. Every year the work of straightening and leveling the motor route progresses so that at present the Pacific Highway, which unites all the larger towns of the region, has become a comparatively straight line between centers.

Although the effect of motor transportation has been most pronounced during the last five years, its influence is discernible in the settlement changes that occurred in the decade 1910–20. During that ten year period, twenty-six incorporated places lost in population.[11] Nor were these logging camps that declined with the cutting of the timber. Many were agricultural villages located in valleys where production had steadily increased. A study of the map shows that many of the declining places are located within a ten-mile radius of a larger center of population. Most of the villages along the Pacific Highway decreased in population between 1910 and 1920. Likewise practically all the Cascade-rim villages declined. Branch highways serving as outlets to the larger towns along the Sound are responsible, undoubtedly for a considerable portion of this decline.

But aside from changing old towns and villages the motorization of the region is effecting a new pattern of population distribution and communal centers. The highways, of which there are at present 972 miles of cement pavement outside city corporations,[12] are assuming the characteristics of city streets. This is especially true of the Pacific Highway, along which homes and places of business have grouped with amazing rapidity. The following chart

[11]   As opposed to three for the decade 1900–1910.
[12]   In addition there are many miles of well-developed gravel and crushed-rock highways, also a few miles of asphaltic macadam.

gives a rough idea of the magnetic influence of this great thoroughfare of traffic. The Pacific Highway, in following almost a straight course between the leading cities of the Sound, traverses the logged-off upland and therefore fails to touch many of the intermediary valley centers. On the other hand it has occasioned the rise of a series of new minor centers located at cross roads and other strategic points.

The cities of this region are rapidly growing together. Topographic peculiarities—the Sound on one side and lakes and valleys on the other—are hastening the process by preventing lateral spread. The zones between cities are devoted largely to various forms of leisure-time enterprises. Tourist camps, golf courses, dance halls, road houses intermixed with a variety of supplementary types of business, such as service stations, garages, fruit, and "hot-dog" stands, form a series of successive zones leading out from each of the larger centers.

To a less extent all the other important highways of the region are serving the function of city streets and causing an outward movement of residence and business. Stage lines interlock practically all the communal units and every form of industry and business (bar logging, where the steam railway is still extensively used) is organized on the basis of motor transportation. Consequently all the old trade areas have been superseded by a series of wider zones. Milk and vegetables are trucked into Seattle daily from a radius of fifty to one hundred miles. And the free delivery zones of the leading stores of Puget Sound cities overlap and interlace making the entire region practically a single conurbation.

Integration and Dominance.—Coordinate with the changing scale of distance has come about a new pattern of communal integration. The region is becoming organized on the chain system with Seattle as the integrating center. Not only does this city contain the regional branch offices of business and social organizations having headquarters in New York, Chicago, San Francisco, or elsewhere, but it is also the business center of most of the great industrial and commercial enterprises originating within the region itself.

Chief among the factors making for business centralization and dominance is the recent development of market organization both in regard to the sale of basic products and in retail merchandising. So long as lumber, fish, and coal constituted the only important products of export, little attention was given to market organization. But when attempts were made to sell perishable agricultural products in distant markets, efficient organization became imperative.[13] Consequently within the last few years elaborate systems of market organization, both private and cooperative, have come into existence. And in nearly every case the central office is located in Seattle.[14] The general pattern is illustrated in the present system of marketing eggs and dairy products.

Even the lumber industry, where individualism is most pronounced, is now beginning to organize as a single marketing unit. In 1913, the Douglas Fir Exploitation and Export Company was organized to standardize and centralize the foreign export business in lumber. Today this organization handles about 90 per cent of the region's lumber exports. The head office is located in Seattle and the associated mills are distributed throughout the region from Canada to Oregon.

The chain system of merchandising is another important integrating factor. Local and national chains are spreading rapidly throughout the region, knitting together the communal complex. Practically every town in the region with a population of a thousand or over contains one or more branches of chain drug, grocery, hardware, and general merchandising stores.

The effect of these and many other forms of recent business amalgamation has been to make Seattle the financial and business center of the region and to increase its dominance in the communal constellation. This business centralization, however, is not accompanied by a corresponding concentration of industry. On the contrary, manufactures are distributed rather widely over the region

[13] This involves standardization of grades and methods of shipment, and centralized communication.

[14] The growth of Seattle as an office center is one of the striking characteristics of the present cycle of change. From 1920–25, 167 office buildings were erected in Seattle at a total cost of $10,494,240 in contrast to 12 office building at a cost of $2,023,200 for the two other cities of the region having more than 20,000 inhabitants.

and show but little tendency to segregate. Seattle ranks fourth as a center of lumber production and is exceeded by Tacoma, Everett, and Bellingham in the ratio of adults gainfully employed in manufactures.

Selection and Equilibrium.—The successive stages of regional growth have not only given rise to different patterns of population distribution but have also effected significant changes in population selection. The process of aggregation has always exceeded the genetic rate of increase. The region, therefore, has been a magnet constantly drawing to itself the population elements best adapted to its economic structure. Industrial succession has been accompanied by change in population composition. Space limitations forbid a complete survey of this interesting subject. A few facts, however, regarding changes in sex and age composition will serve to illustrate the process.

The region's ratio of males per one hundred females for successive decades is: 1880, 160; 1890, 188; 1900, 146; 1910, 140; 1920, 120. While the trend is downward, the curve follows closely the regional aggregation curve. The years of highest aggregation, 1890 to 1910, are also those of greatest disparity between the sexes. The sex ratio for 1910 is lowered somewhat by the urbanization process, but the seven rural counties having highest growth indices for this decade all show substantial increases over the previous decade in the ratio of males to females. The ratio of adult males (ages twenty to forty-four) to the aggregate population has always been high. The facts are not available for counties, but the data for the state and Seattle illustrate the situation for the region in general. The percentages are: (1) state—1900, 27.0; 1910, 27.8; 1920, 22.6; (2) Seattle—26.7, 32.5, and 26.0 respectively. The increase for 1910 is due to the more rapid aggregation during the first decade of the century.

The economic base of the region has always been very unstable. The basic industries are of the type in which seasonal and yearly fluctuations are pronounced. During the early stages of settlement, before agriculture and manufacturing developed, the problem of maintaining equilibrium was serious.

The region periodically suffered from a shortage or a surplus of labor. This is reflected in the high degree of mobility.[15] Population has always shuttled in and out of the region in response to economic change. But, as the economic base of the region becomes increasingly complex, the effect of fluctuations in the great basics is less drastic. The development of agriculture, manufactures, and commerce is increasing the stability of the region as well as changing the composition of the population and the character of the economic and social institutions.

While the region still bears many marks of the frontier, it is rapidly entering upon a metropolitan era, the future of which lies in the Pacific with its unknown possibilities.

[15]   According to the 1920 census only 22.9 per cent of the population of Seattle was born in the state of Washington. On the other hand the percentage of foreign born declined from 31.9 in 1890 to 25.7 in 1920.

14

THE RISE OF
METROPOLITAN
COMMUNITIES

1933

A STRIKING phenomenon of population change in the United States during the past half century has been that which may be described in general terms as a movement from the country to the city. Since 1880 the percentage of population classified as urban has nearly doubled, while that classified as rural has declined proportionately. This statement gives only a very rough idea of what has happened. Urban territory, under the census classification, includes all communities having 2,500 or more inhabitants. Thus Kenilworth, Illinois, with a population of 2,501 in 1930, falls into the same group as Chicago with 3,376,438; and Cooperstown, New York, with 2,909, is "urban" as well as Greater New York with 6,930,446.

More precise results may be obtained by subdividing "urban" communities into nine groups, beginning with those having populations between 2,500 and 5,000 and ending with those having 1,000,000 or more. By dividing our urban population into nine or more fractions according to the sizes of the communities in which it resides, it is possible to determine the relative degree of "urbanization" which prevails. But even this method has proved unsatisfactory because it does not give a true picture of the organization of our urban territory. We are coming to think of the city not only as an agglomeration of people but as a way of living, with an influence extending far beyond its own borders. It is the

Reprinted from President's Research Committee, *Recent Social Trends*, vol. 1 (1933).

growth of the metropolitan way of living which we now wish to trace rather than merely the increase of metropolitan populations; and it is to the tracing and analyzing of this growth that the present report is largely devoted.

With the increasing ease and rapidity of travel, particularly by motor car, the large city has not only brought under its sway much territory that was formerly rural, but has extended its influence far out into territory that is still classified as rural. Smaller communities within a wide radius of every urban center have lost much of their former isolation, provincialism, and independence. Even beyond the commuting area, the city reaches out with its newspapers, radio broadcasts, amusements, and shopping facilities. In this process the character of the city itself is somewhat altered. If the suburban and country districts are urbanized, the city is in a degree ruralized. Its people more and more go outside the corporate limits to live, to spend their vacations, and to find recreation. Thus the city of former days is really being replaced by a new entity, the metropolitan community, with a distribution of population shading off from extreme congestion to relative sparseness, yet with some uniformity of character.

Each great city has its sphere of influence. By laying out these spheres on a map of the United States, according to criteria which will be explained in the body of the chapter, it is possible to divide the whole nation into metropolitan regions which economically and sociologically have greater reality than the several states. Three dimnsions would be required in order to give a clear picture of this metropolitan organization of the country, for some of our metropolises are regional in character, some are interregional and one or two are international in their influence. Neighboring metropolises compete for trade and prestige, and the boundaries between the territories they control may be as fluctuating and as hotly disputed as though each were an independent principality.

At the same time each is likely to be affected in its life by one of the interregional metropolises, especially New York or Chicago. Each is increasingly aware of its economic and social unity, yet each tends to imitate the larger centers culturally. Thus the great cities preserve many differences arising from their history, their geographical location, the nature of their population and their sources of livelihood, but they also tend toward cultural uniformity. National advertising, motion pictures, and in recent years the radio play a large part in this latter process. There are also economic influences that cannot be so readily analyzed.

The metropolitan community is not a static thing, though it has some characteristics which are likely to distinguish it for a long time to come. It is a product of development and change and is certain to measure, in terms of recent trends, the manner in which our urban population is concentrating itself, the characteristics of the metropolitan region, the nature of the growth process within the region, the part played by regional planning and zoning, and the role of metropolitan governments.

It cannot be too strongly emphasized that the modern metropolitan community is practically a new social and economic entity, comparable in some respects with the city state of ancient and medieval times, but in other respects unprecedented. The metropolitan region is the child of modern facilities for transportation and communication. These facilities have created the situations and problems of social and economic organization with which the present chapter deals.

I. *The Trend toward Metropolitanism*

Recent developments in means of communication have so enlarged the scope of local life that the ordinary individual, in the pursuit of his daily activities of work and leisure, is no longer confined to a single village, town, or even city. The modern community usually embraces a number of centers of different size, each more or less specialized in its institutions and its services. In other words it is characterized by a geographical division of labor.

We shall attempt to sketch the rise of this community of multiple centers, to examine some of the important changes taking place in local institutions as a result of specialization and differentiation of function and, finally, to outline a few of the problems associated with this complex pattern of local activities.

Two outstanding factors in the changing character of the local community are: (1) the increase in the aggregate population of the community and the extension of the area within which local activities are carried on in common; (2) the increased mobility of products and people, resulting in a wider range of individual choice, more specialization of local services, and a more closely-knit community structure.

Concentration of Population.—Each of the last three censuses has reported an increasing geographical concentration of population. If the total population is divided into one-fourth, one-half and three-fourths, each fraction is found to be contained within an increasingly smaller area, as Table I clearly demonstrates.

TABLE I   POPULATION CONCENTRATION AS SHOWN BY THE SMALLEST AREAS[a] REQUIRED TO OBTAIN ONE-QUARTER, ONE-HALF AND THREE-QUARTERS OF THE TOTAL INHABITANTS OF THE UNITED STATES AT EACH OF THE LAST THREE DECENNIAL ENUMERATIONS, 1910–1930[b]

| Year | Total population | One-quarter of population | | One-half of population | | Three-quarters of population | |
		Number of counties	Area (sq. mi.)	Number of counties	Area (sq. mi.)	Number of counties	Area (sq. mi.)
1910............	91,972,266	39	23,243	312	264,868	1,068	887,829
1920............	105,710,620	33	19,270	250	224,944	992	856,820
1930............	122,775,046	27	14,431	189	170,517	862	767,403

[a] Table is computed on county units; independent cities are included.
[b] Compiled from U. S. Census reports.

This table understates rather than overstates the actual facts of concentration.[1] Counties are grouped according to rank in

[1]   The converse side of the concentration process, as indicated by Table 1, is reflected in the extent of territory that is declining in population. Out of a total of 2,955 counties whose boundaries remained unchanged during the last decade (the boundaries of 144 counties were changed), 1,220 had less population in 1930 than in 1920. The combined population of these decreasing counties constituted 18 per cent of the total population of the country in 1930. This stands in marked contrast to the extent of decreasing area in 1900, when only 368 out of 2,836 counties showed a decrease during the decade and the total population of these

population rather than density. This procedure was adopted be-cause the Bureau of the Census did not compute county densities prior to 1920. Occasionally, however, a county with a relatively small population has a high density; consequently, if the table had been based on density, the number of counties listed for each divi-sion of the population might be somewhat greater, but the number of square miles of territory would undoubtedly be considerably reduced.

Population in general is moving toward the areas of high dens-ity. In 1920 there were 265 counties[2] with a density of 100 or more per square mile. In 1910 these counties contained 45.1 per cent of the total population; in 1920, 48.2 per cent; and in 1930, 52.6 per cent.

Movement toward Deep Water.—There is a significant but by no means uniform movement of population toward the deep water rim of the country—that is, toward the Atlantic and Pacific Oceans, the Gulf of Mexico, and the metropolitan territory adjoin-ing the Great Lakes. Table II presents in summary fashion the facts regarding this population increase.

Population moving toward the deep water rim does not, of course, spread itself over this broad strip of territory. It concen-trates in the metropolitan centers leaving other sections equally near deep water to decline. The area contains 540 counties and the District of Columbia. Of these counties, 100 actually decreased in population between 1920 and 1930, and 195 others had rates of increase less than the national average. The movement, therefore, is not a mere drift toward open water, but a migration into metro-politan regions which for various reasons are near the water.

Points of Concentration.—Population is moving toward the great cities. Table III reflects this movement. The 1930 census lists 93 cities with populations of 100,000 or more. A number of

---

decreasing counties was only 7.7 per cent of the population of the nation. Nor has the recent declining territory been strictly rural. No less than 102 cities of 10,000 population or more showed declines in population dur-ing the last decade as against 57 cities of this class in the decade 1910 to 1920 and 31 in the decade 1900 to 1910.

[2]   Independent cities and the District of Columbia are included.

TABLE II POPULATION CONCENTRATION IN A ZONE EXTENDING APPROXIMATELY 50 MILES INLAND FROM THE SEABOARD AND THE GREAT LAKES, 1900–1930[ab]

Census year	Population within zone	Percent of total U. S. population in zone	Increase within zone since preceding census	Percent of total U. S. increase within zone
1900.................	27,842,288	36.6	5,495,234	42.1
1910.................	35,633,796	38.7	7,791,508	48.8
1920.................	43,865,221	41.5	8,231,425	59.9
1930.................	55,413,567	45.1	11,548,346	67.7

[a] Compiled from U. S. Census reports. The table is computed on county units—a list of which is available from the author on request.

[b] The area of the zone is 435,863 square miles, or 14.65 percent of total land area of the United States. It may be defined as a region approximately fifty miles wide which skirts the salt water rim of the country and the southern shores of Lakes Ontario, Erie and Michigan.

these are so close together, however, that they may be considered as parts of the same metropolitan community. By drawing an arbitrary circle, with a radius of from 20 to 50 miles, around the largest center in such groupings, the number of metropolitan regions may be reduced to 63.

As this table shows, about half of the population of the United

TABLE III TOTAL POPULATION IN 63 METROPOLITAN ZONES: 1900–1930[ab]

(Cities of 100,000 or more plus adjacent counties; approximately 20 to 50 miles, depending on size of city.)

Year	Total population in United States	Total population in metropolitan zones	Percent which population in zones formed of total U. S. population	Percent which net increase in zones formed of total increase in U. S. since preceding census
1900.................	75,994,575	28,044,698	36.9	46.4
1910.................	91,972,266	37,271,608	40.5	57.7
1920.................	105,710,620	46,491,835	44.0	67.1
1930.................	122,775,046	59,118,595	48.2	74.0

[a] Compiled from U. S. Census reports.

[b] Since this table was compiled the Bureau of the Census has published the 1930 report on Metropolitan Districts (U. S. Bureau of the Census, *Fifteenth Census of the United States, 1930, Metropolitan Districts, Population and Area, 1932*), in which 96 districts are outlined, each with a minimum population of 100,000. The 96 districts contained 44.6 percent of the total population of the nation—almost 4 percent less than the percentage found in the districts as outlined in Table 3.

States at the present time lives within daily access of a city of 100,000 or more. This is approximately the same percentage of the total population as was reported in the 1,208 cities of 8,000 or more in 1930, and only 8 per cent less than the total population recorded as urban. The metropolitan region cuts the population in a different way from the urban classification of the census, yet it cuts almost as large a slice.

A considerable proportion of the population included in this arbitrary definition of metropolitan territory would naturally be classified as "rural" by the Bureau of the Census. But such rural population is probably more urbanized from an economic and social standpoint than much of the so-called "urban" population living in small centers remote from the larger cities.

The Metropolitan Constellation.—Large cities seldom appear isolated. They are almost always surrounded by a cluster of smaller centers, varying in size, which are economically and socially intertwined. There are, to be sure, marked differences in the number of separate political communities that appear around the margins of individual cities. Geography, industry, and the degree of annexation that has occurred seem to be important factors in determining the number of political entities in a territorial grouping of population. But regardless of political boundaries the same general social and economic forces seem to be at work in every metropolitan region.

TABLE IV   PROPORTION OF TOTAL POPULATION IN DIFFERENT TERRITORIAL CLASSI-
FICATIONS, 1900–1930[a]

Territory	1900	1910	1920	1930
Total urban territory	40.0	45.8	51.4	56.2
Cities of 8,000 or more	32.9	38.7	43.8	49.1
Metropolitan zones (Table 3)	36.9	40.5	44.0	48.2

[a] U. S. Census reports.

Table V shows the number of incorporated places located within some of the main metropolitan districts as outlined by the Bureau of the Census. But the metropolitan district as delimited by the Census on the basis of density represents only a part of the area that is economically and socially tributary to each of these central cities. Had trading areas been used as the basis of calcula-

TABLE V   INCORPORATED PLACES OF SPECIFIED SIZE IN SELECTED METROPOLITAN DISTRICTS, 1930[a]

Size of place	New York	Pittsburgh	Chicago	Philadelphia	Boston	Los Angeles	St. Louis	Cincinnati	Detroit	Cleveland	San Francisco
Less than 2,500	112	57	59	43	10	10	27	23	13	24	14
2,500–4,999	49	26	16	25	14	13	4	9	11	5	6
5,000–9,999	49	23	15	14	17	13	8	7	6	4	8
10,000–49,999	48	27	18	7	30	16	7	3	8	5	7
50,000–99,999	8	1	5	1	5	2	1	1	4	2	1
100,000 and over	6	1	2	2	4	2	1	1	1	1	2
Total	272	135	115	92	80	56	48	44	43	41	38

[a] *Fifteenth Census of the United States, 1930, Metropolitan Districts.*

tion, the number of satellites for each of these cities would be greatly increased. The data presented, however, are sufficient to demonstrate the point that smaller cities tend to group themselves around larger ones somewhat as planets group themselves around a sun. They are, so to speak, within its gravitational field. A general analysis of urban statistics without reference to this fact is apt to be misleading. Population increases in the group of small cities are largely in areas exposed to the metropolitan influence. For example, the 78 small urban centers in the state of Illinois, falling in the 2,500 to 4,999 class in 1920, increased in population 32.2 per cent in the decade 1920 to 1930; but 93.4 per cent of this increase took place in the 25 towns of this size that happened to be suburbs of Chicago or St. Louis. Of the remaining 53 places in this group, located elsewhere in the state, 23 actually decreased in population during the decade. Likewise in Michigan: in 1920 the state contained 32 towns in the 2,500 to 4,999 class, with an aggregate population 117,178. By 1930 the combined population of these 32 places was 153,538, in increase of 36,360 or 31 per cent in the decade. But of the 32 places 4 were suburbs of Detroit, the combined gain of which was 34,009 or 93.5 per cent of the gross increase.

The location of places incorporated for the first time during the decade 1920–1930, shows the same trend. The 1930 census records 38 incorporations in Illinois, 26 of which are suburbs of Chicago or St. Louis; the same census lists 33 new incorporations in Michigan, 22 of which are suburbs of Detroit; Ohio is credited with 55 incorporations, 29 of which are suburbs of Cleveland. When the new incorporations suburban to other large cities in these three states are included, practically all the incorporations during the decade are accounted for.

These are random samplings and may not represent conditions everywhere throughout the country. They indicate, however, the tendency toward concentration in certain areas and suggest the importance of taking location into account when interpreting urban statistics.

The Metropolitan Unit.—The essential unity of the central city and surrounding settlement is generally recognized. For the last three decades the Bureau of the Census has published population statistics for the larger cities and their "adjacent territory." No attempt has been made to analyze the relationship existing between the smaller centers and the main city, but from data furnished in the 1930 Census of Distribution[3] it is possible to show certain aspects of commercial interdependence within a metropolitan region. The 37 communities around Chicago having a population of 10,000 or more, make an excellent illustration. Twenty-one of these cities are located within a zone scarcely ten miles wide lying between the outer limits of the political city and a circle with a 20-mile radius drawn from the Loop, or business center. Six fall within the second concentric zone, lying from

3   U. S. Bureau of the Census, *Fifteenth Census of the United States, 1930, Distribution* (Preliminary).

20 to 40 miles distant from the Loop. The remaining ten are located in a third zone, lying from 40 to 80 miles distant from the Loop. An analysis of the average number of persons to a store and the average expenditure for food, wearing apparel, and general merchandise in each zone, shows that the central city's influence gradually tapers off. In the first zone stores are relatively few in proportion to population, with an average of 102 persons each. In the second zone this average falls to 69 and in the third to 65. This is a statistical illustration of the common fact of experience that the nearer one lives to a city's shopping center the more likely one is to shop there.

Other data show that the shopping done in the city by residents of the outlying communities is somewhat specialized. Food makes up 34.1 per cent of all retail purchases in the first zone, 26.8 per cent in the second zone, 26.4 per cent in the third zone. Residents of the first zone spend an average of $26.96 on general merchandise and $25.98 on wearing apparel yearly in their local stores; residents of the second zone, $81.86 and $52.90 respectively; residents of the third zone, $70.93 and $58.38. For other things than food Zone I depends to a marked extent on the shopping area of the central city, whereas Zones II and III, though obviously not independent of the main shopping center, have gone further in developing local shopping districts.

The same tapering off of the metropolitan influence may be shown by analyses of newspaper circulations, of wholesale selling districts, and of the relations of banks with their correspondents. The financial functions of a great city may extend for hundreds of miles, or even be nationwide. More than 60 per cent of Chicago's wholesale merchandise buyers come from distances of 200 miles or less, but more than 12 per cent come 600 miles or more.[4] Sometimes the metropolitan influence seems to jump an intermediate territory and to be strong at a remote periphery. Thus the

[4]   "Merchandise Buyers Visits to Chicago" listed in the Chicago *Tribune*, January 1 to October 1, 1930, *Bulletin from the Business Survey*, no. 293, December, 1930 (mimeographed sheets for the use of *Tribune* staff).

banks of Chicago have more than three times as many correspondents among banks between the 1,600-mile radius and the Pacific Coast as they have in the 800–1,200-mile zone.[5] This and other evidence shows that the Pacific Coast cities are more closely integrated with New York and Chicago than are smaller points in intervening zones.

Factors in Metropolitanization.—The tendency of population to concentrate in large metropolitan communities is not wholly due to industrial development. The processes of concentration have been even more rapid during the last decade than formerly, although the total number of industrial wage earners in the country was actually less in 1929 than in 1919.[6]

The economic and social advantages of specialization and division of labor seem to apply not only to the production of goods but to most of our institutions and services as well. The larger the population with daily access to a common center of institutions and services, the more specialized and differentiated these tend to become. The individual has a wider range of selection, the institution or service a basis for increased efficiency. The great cities draw to themselves the leaders in business, the professions, the sciences, and the arts. Concentration breeds concentration. Functions that require access to numerous or highly selected customers are possible only in cities. As population concentrates spatially, a hitherto unparalleled degree of economic and social specialization and diversification becomes feasible. Herein seem to lie the main "attractions" of the city—attractions which evidently outweigh the discomforts and wastes of congestion.

The city dweller may not like crowds. He may, however, find it hard to dispense with the goods and services which crowds make possible. The dispersion of population toward the outer zones of metropolitan regions is obviously an attempt on the part of the city man to have his cake and eat it too.

[5]   An *Analysis of Banker's Balances in Chicago*, University of Illinois Bulletin, vol. 26, November 19, 1928, Bureau of Business Research, College of Commerce and Business Administration, Bulletin no. 21, pp. 16–17.

[6]   United States Bureau of the Census, *Census of Manufacturers.*

II. *Metropolitan Regionalism*

The larger cities of the country are becoming what might be termed regionally conscious. The mapping of metropolitan regions thus becomes important. Practically every city of more than 50,000 inhabitants has sought to delimit the territory which it considers to belong to it by virtue of proximity and functional relationship. While much of the mapping is still of a rather arbitrary nature—a sort of random staking out of territorial claims for advertising purposes—nevertheless there is a definite trend toward a more careful delineation of regional boundaries for commercial and administrative purposes. In addition to the efforts of the cities themselves to define their primary areas of function, numerous national organizations, including the United States Bureau of Foreign and Domestic Commerce, have sought to divide the country into logical trading areas and sales territories for different types of economic service.[7] In the preparation of such maps a city is always taken as the starting point, and its primary marketing territory is defined in terms of newspaper circulation, delivery zones, freight differentials, and the like.

A general though obviously imperfect picture of metropolitan regionalism in the United States may be sketched by mapping the areas dominated by the daily newspapers of the larger cities. This is done in Figure 1. The cities selected are the Federal Reserve Banking centers, main and branch, together with a few additional cities[8] included to complete the picture. The territory assigned to

[7]   *The Atlas of Wholesale Grocery Territories*, Domestic Commerce Series, no. 7, 1927, was the first attempt of the U. S. Bureau of Foreign and Domestic Commerce to delineate trade areas. Since then the Bureau has conducted a number of important regional commercial surveys in which trade areas have been mapped. Among the non-governmental organizations that have compiled data on trading areas the following should be noted: The International Magazine Company (Marketing Division), New York; The J. Walter Thompson Company, New York; The Editor & Publisher Company, New York; The Woman's World Magazine Company, Chicago; Major Market Newspapers Inc., Chicago.

[8]   Milwaukee, Sioux City, Des Moines, Albuquerque, Charlotte, and Louisville. This makes a total of 41 "metropolitan regions."

each of the selected cities is simply the area in which 50 per cent or more of the circulation of competing metropolitan papers comes from that particular metropolis. For example, if a marginal town, A, takes papers from two or more of the cities under consideration, it is assigned to the metropolitan territory of the city from which it receives over 50 per cent of its total outside circulation. Only one paper, the leading morning daily, of each metropolis was considered, and the circulation data were taken directly from the Audit Bureau of Circulations.[9] Parenthetically it may be added that only towns receiving 25 or more copies of a paper are recorded by the Audit Bureau of Circulations. In order to ascertain change in boundaries, the data were computed for two years, 1920 and 1929.

Figure 1 is presented merely to illustrate a method of determining zones of metropolitan influence. It goes without saying that the districts indicated are by no means of equal importance. Moreover, within each of these so-called metropolitan regions there are numerous smaller cities possessing daily papers that circulate in surrounding trade areas. Had the circulation territory of local papers been plotted, there would be a series of irregular figures appearing like islands within the present regions or cutting across their boundaries.

It will be observed that in the mountain region there is an area lying between Helena on the north and Denver on the south that is labeled "Chicago." In plotting the newspaper circulation of the cities surrounding this area it was found that there was a considerable territory which received no papers from any of the surrounding metropolitan centers, at least not in sufficient numbers to be listed by the Audit Bureau of Circulations. On further examination it was found that the towns in this region received the Chicago *Tribune* more than any other outside newspaper, due, perhaps, to the resort character of part of the area and to a carry over from mail-order days. Consequently this territory was credited to Chicago.

Metropolitan conciousness was recognized, and undoubtedly

[9]   Mimeographed *Audit Reports*, Audit Bureau of Circulation, Chicago, available to the newspaper trade.

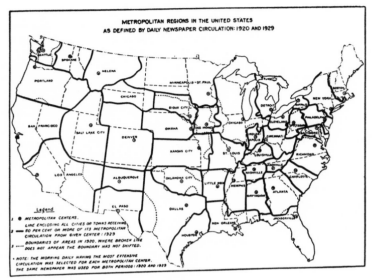

Fig. 1

stimulated as well, by the procedure of the Bureau of the Census in its preparation for the 1930 enumeration of metropolitan districts. About a year prior to the taking of the Fifteenth Census, the Bureau, through the cooperation of the United States Chamber of Commerce, invited each city of 50,000 or more to prepare a map of its own metropolitan district according to specific instructions. Among the factors proposed for the delineation of metropolitan territory were the following:

Commuting distance, including only suburbs from which not less than 10 per cent of the working population commute daily to the central city; power and light territory served from the central city; the phone service area of the central city; the territory served by the central city's water supply; the area in which the daily newspapers of the central city are delivered by the paper's own carrier; the area served by house connections with the city's sewer system; the residential membership area of social and athletic clubs located within the central city; the area of operation of local real estate companies in the surrounding region; the area covered by daily routes of solicitors, inspectors, and collectors, operating out of the central city as their headquarters.[10]

This worthy attempt to recognize the functional area as the appropriate unit for recording metropolitan statistics did not meet with complete success. The maps prepared by the different cities failed to reflect due care in following the Bureau's instructions, and the factors suggested for the construction of maps represented too wide a range of metropolitan services to insure the necessary uniformity required for statistical purposes. Consequently in the final tabulation of metropolitan statistics the Census Bureau was compelled to resort to a more standardized and on the whole less satisfactory procedure.[11]

In the 1930 Census the Bureau publishes figures for 96 metropolitan districts, the aggregate population of which is 54,753,645 or 44.6 per cent of the total population of the nation and 79.4 per cent of the total urban population. The combined area of the 96 districts is 36,577.87 square miles, the range varying from 2,514.11 square miles for the New York-Northeastern New Jersey

[10]   Abstracted from *Methods of Procedure in Defining Metropolitan District*, a mimeographed circular prepared by the Civic Development Department of the United States Chamber of Commerce.

[11]   "The metropolitan districts for the census of 1930 . . . include in addition to the central city or cities, all adjacent and contiguous civil divisions having a density of not less than 150 inhabitants per square mile, and usually any civil divisions of less density that are directly adjacent to the central cities, or are entirely or nearly surrounded by minor civil divisions that have the required density. This is essentially the same principle as was applied in determining the metropolitan districts for cities of over 200,000 inhabitants at the censuses of 1910 and 1920, except that the area which might be included within the metropolitan was then limited to the territory within 10 miles of the city boundary. At this present census no such limit has been applied, the distance to which the metropolitan district extends in any direction beyond the city boundaries being unlimited so long as the population density of the area meets the requirement of 150 per square mile" (U. S. Bureau of the Census, *Fifteenth Census of the United States, 1930, Metropolitan Districts, Advance Summary*, p. 1).

district to 52.77 square miles for the Atlantic City district.

An interesting feature of the 1930 enumeration is the number of hyphenated names appearing in the list of metropolitan districts; sixteen of the districts represent combinations of two or more central cities. About a third of these combinations were made at the request of the cities concerned.

The rising consciousness of cities as centers of commercial provinces is further indicated by the attention given to community advertising. In 1928 the Bureau of Foreign and Domestic Commerce made a nationwide survey of this subject and on the basis of its findings estimated "that the national bill for community advertising in that year totaled nearly $6,000,000."[12] Cities advertise to attract tourists, industries, and population in general. In a community advertising campaign it is customary for a number of neighboring centers to unite forces and pool budgets. In such cases it is the regional attractions and resources that are emphasized.

The emergence of regional consciousness seems to be a natural outcome of recent developments in transportation and communications coupled with their effect upon interregional competition. The expansion of the facilities of contact in the form of the motor vehicle, the metropolitan press, the telephone, and even the radio has tended to intensify movement and communication within the local area to an even greater extent than between distant sections. On the other hand, the increasing fluidity of commodities and people is exposing cities to new conditions making for growth or decline. Unlike the nation as a whole, which may build tariff walls and set up immigration restrictions to meet foreign competition, the individual city, so far as the domestic economy is concerned, has to meet competition in an open market. In intercity or interregional competition the larger the population group, or in commercial terms the larger the local market, the greater its competitive advantage. It is not surprising, therefore, that cities are devoting increasing attention to questions of transportation rates and routes, which in a sense are to cities what tariffs are to nations.

[12] U. S. Bureau of Foreign and Domestic Commerce, *Advertising for Community Promotion*, Domestic Commerce Series, no. 21 (1928), p. 5.

In the recent hearings conducted by the Interstate Commerce Commission with respect to suggested modifications of the freight rate structure in the middle western states—Western Trunk Line Territory—no less than "12,500 pages of testimony were taken and approximately 1,200 exhibits containing more than 12,000 pages were received."[13]

Margins of the Metropolitan Community.—The central city casts its influence over surrounding settlements in the form of traffic zones. This influence goes as far as distance and competition will let it. The boundaries, of course, are seldom definite stable lines which can be graphically shown on a map. They are rather, as has already been shown, tapering zones of influence, which vary with changing conditions of transportation and competition.

Two terms have come into common usage to designate areas of community influence: "metropolitan district" and "trade area." The term metropolitan district has come to signify the territory in which the daily economic and social activities of the local population are carried on through a common system of local institutions and services. It is essentially the commutation area of the central city and tends to correspond with the "built-up" area in which public services such as water, light, sanitation, and power become common problems.

The second concept, trade area, is used to designate a more extended territory of city influence. The term does not lend itself to precise definition, for different economic functions have different zones of influence. For practical purposes, however, a city's trade area may be defined in the words of John W. Pole, Comptroller of the Currency, as "The surrounding geographical territory economically tributary to a city and for which such city provides the chief market and financial center."[14]

Trends in the Size of the Commutation Area.—For the few cities having railroad commutation service it is possible to gain some conception of the trend in the volume and range of commutation traffic. According to the statistics published by the Interstate Commerce Commission there has been relatively little change

[13]   U. S. Interstate Commerce Commission, *Reports*, vol. 164, no. 17,000, May, 1930, p. 14.
[14]   *United States Daily*, January 3, 1931.

in the total commutation traffic on Class I railroads during the nine-year period 1922–1930, the time interval for which statistics are available. The volume of traffic, measured in terms of revenue passenger miles, increased about 8 per cent in this interim, and the average length of journey, as indicated by miles per passenger per road, increased from 14.28 to 15.20 miles.

Of course, the recent expansion of the metropolitan community is primarily a product of motor transportation. With the exception of a few cities of over a million population there has been a persistent decrease since 1920 in the number of revenue passengers carried by street railways and a correspondingly rapid increase in the use of buses and private automobiles. Statistics prepared by the American Electric Railway Association show that in seven cities of between 500,000 and 1,000,000 there was a decline of 10.4 per cent in the number of revenue passengers carried on street railways from 1920 to 1929, and 34 cities in the 100,000 to 500,000 class the decline was 27.6 per cent.[15] The data are not available for cities under 100,000 but it is reasonable to suppose that the decline in the use of the street railway would be even greater in these small places. According to figures published by the National Association of Motor Bus Operators there were in December, 1930, 222 cities of over 10,000 entirely dependent upon motor transportation.[16]

It is difficult to measure the radius of the motor city. Extensive studies of motor traffic made by the United States Bureau of Public Roads, though not pertaining directly to cities, suggest that the average distance of the local motor trip is relatively short. Various cities have prepared maps showing the flow of motor traffic at different points along arterial highways. Such maps invariably show a rapid tapering off of traffic beyond a ten or fifteen mile radius from the central business district. Certain cities, however, claim a considerable group of daily commuters coming distances ranging between 20 and 40 miles.

The small cities of the nation are tending either to become

---

[15]   Compiled for Miller McClintock, Director, The Albert Russell Erskine Bureau, Harvard University, for a chapter on Trends in Urban Traffic which appeared in the monograph relating to this report.

[16]   *Bus Facts for 1931.*

suburban to nearby larger centers or, if remote from large cities, to assume the role of embryonic metropolises to surrounding villages. The comparatively high rates of population increase in the small cities of the agricultural states in the west north central division suggest the influence of the motor car and paved highway on the extension of their tributary territory. In the seven states[17] comprising this census division there were, in 1920, 55 cities in the 10,000 to 50,000 class.[18] The combined increase of these cities by 1930 was 17.6 per cent as against only 6 per cent for the region as a whole.

Trends in the Size of the Trade Area.—Important changes are taking place in the marketing territories of most cities. The retail shopping areas of the larger cities, as measured by the daily free delivery service of central stores, have expanded greatly in recent years. It has become common practice for the larger stores throughout the nation to deliver their merchandise regularly within a radius of 30 to 50 miles. City department stores report not only an extension of their delivery systems since 1920 but also an increasing volume of trade from outlying territory. Some stores provide free telephone service to their suburban customers and some rebate fares, depending on distance traveled and volume of purchases. The outward movement of the higher economic elements of the population has been an important factor in the extension of the market areas of department stores. Several stores report a falling off of business within the inner zones; other report that the volume of the close-in business has been maintained largely as a result of the hotel and large apartment trade.[19]

Counter to the tendency toward increasing centralization as indicated by department store delivery practice is the rise of the chain store system of retailing, characterized by the centralization of management and warehousing functions in the regional city and the delivery of merchandise to towns and villages located within

[17]   Minnesota, Iowa, Missouri, North Dakota, South Dakota, Nebraska, Kansas.

[18]   Data supplied by P. K. Whelpton, Scripps Foundation.

[19]   Based on replies to a questionnaire sent to a selected list of department stores.

convenient trucking distance. In either case the city casts its dominance over surrounding settlement and changes the inter-relationships of nearby centers.

The enlargement of the marketing territory of the larger cities does not imply that the city's trade area is merely a magnified re-production of that of the small town. It represents rather the ten-dency toward greater specialization and division of labor among the different centers located within easy access of a large city. The increasing economic unity of the metropolitan region is chiefly the result of a transformation that is taking place in the field of market-ing. The small town is yielding many of its more specialized serv-ices to the city, while in turn it is acquiring new services such as the chain store and the motion picture theater. The role of the small center in the retail marketing complex is summarized in *Domestic Commerce* thus:

The Census of Retail Distribution offers, for the first time, a means of accurately determining the position of the small town and the coun-try store as outlets for various types of goods as compared with larger cities. By studying the figures for the state of California, the only com-plete state released to date, we find 37 per cent of the population located outside the cities of over 10,000 population, but only 32.7 per cent of the State's stores and 21.8 per cent of total sales.

The extent to which residents of small towns go to the larger cities for apparel, furniture and household goods, and items sold through department or general merchandise stores is evident in that such outlets in the small towns do only 7.7 per cent, 11.65 per cent and 15.2 per cent respectively of the total business done by these types of stores in the state.[20]

The general trend in wholesaling seems to be toward concen-tration and specialization. The small wholesaling center is sur-rendering most of its specialized merchandise. The tendency toward hand-to-mouth buying works in favor of the regional city as against the larger but more distant metropolis, especially with reference to staples. On the other hand, the large city, by giving increasing attention to overnight delivery by fast trucks and pack-age rail freight, is succeeding in maintaining its wholesale function

[20] Vol. 7, no. 18 (June 20, 1931), p. 199.

over a wide range of territory. In general, however, the tendency for regional cities seems to be toward smaller wholesale territories and more intensive coverage. This doubtless reflects the concentration and regional organization of population. An analysis of reports from 39 wholesale dry goods houses in the Gulf Southwest during the period from 1924 to 1928 showed a decrease in territory covered in the cases of 28 firms, while 11 reported increases. Of the firms doing over $1,000,000 worth of business a year, six were covering more territory in 1928 than they had covered in 1924, and 12 were covering less.[21]

The Motor Truck as a Factor in Economic Regionalism.— Modern economic regionalism is basically a product of motor transportation. As the passenger car determines the scope of the social community, so the truck is becoming the chief factor in determining the dimensions of the economic region. The truck is rapidly assuming a major role as a conveyor of local freight. Being a more flexible carrier than the railway as regards unit load, service, and routes, the motor truck tends to stimulate more intensive exploitation of regional resources and to establish a more direct and immediate relationship between the central city and surrounding settlements.

It is difficult to get reliable information regarding the trucking radius of a metropolitan center. Many factors are involved, such as the location of cities, the character and volume of freight, the condition of the highways, and the like. It is generally conceded, however, that the motor truck is still primarily a short haul agency of transportation. "Truck traffic on rural highways," reports the United States Bureau of Public Roads, "is predominately a short haul movement. While only about 6 per cent of all trucks travel less than 20 miles per day; 15.5 per cent travel from 40 to 59 miles; and 13.8 per cent from 60 to 79 miles per day. Nearly 50 per cent of all trucks, therefore, travel less than 80 miles per day, while 58.3 per cent travel less than 100. . . . While 80 miles is not usually considered a short distance, it must be remembered that this distance is the mileage per day on rural highways, and that

[21]   U. S. Bureau of Foreign and Domestic Commerce, Edward F. Gerish, *Distribution of Dry Goods in the Gulf Southwest*, Domestic Commerce Series, no. 43, 1931, p. 7.

it usually represents one or more round trips from origin to destination."[22]

The truck is still basically a private rather than a common carrier and as such the practice is to operate within a radius that may be served conveniently within a working day, including return to point of origin. "One large cartage company in Chicago, for example, offers a daily delivery to retailers in 125 cities or towns on 8 routes within a radius of 30 or 40 miles. Its delivery zone is limited by the distance a driver can cover and still get back to the Chicago headquarters within a normal working day.[23] This may be taken as typical of the trucking radius within the metropolitan area, especially with reference to merchandise.

But the motor truck plays a dominant role not only in the distribution of merchandise in the metropolitan region but also in the marketing of agricultural products. Los Angeles, according to a bulletin of the Bureau of Railway Economics, affords a glimpse of the division of labor between railroad and truck:

All of the lemons unloaded at Los Angeles were received by truck. Of the oranges unloaded, 98.6 per cent were received by truck; of the strawberries, 98.4 per cent; tomatoes, 98.3 per cent; grapes, 97.9 per cent; celery, 94.4 per cent; plums and prunes, 90.8 per cent; cabbage, 87.1 per cent; grapefruit, 79.1 per cent; peaches, 74.4 per cent; cantaloupes, 69.5 per cent; lettuce, 60.4 per cent; and sweet potatoes, 53.3 per cent.

Rail unloads exceeded truck unloads at Los Angeles for 5 of the 18 commodities. Of the combined rail and truck receipts of apples, 94.4 per cent were received by rail; white potatoes, 85.9 per cent; watermelons, 71.7 per cent; pears, 60.4 per cent; and onions, 55.9 per cent.[24]

22   *Report of a Survey of Traffic on the Federal Aid Highway System of Eleven Western States*, 1930, by the U. S. Bureau of Public Roads and the Highway Departments of Arizona, California, Colorado, Idaho, Nebraska, New Mexico, Nevada, Oregon, Utah, Washington, and Wyoming, p. 19.

23   R. E. Plimpton, "The Motor Truck in Distribution," *The Journal of Land and Public Utility Economics*, vol. 7, no. 3 (August, 1931), pp. 280–81.

24   U. S. Bureau of Railway Economics, *Unloads of Fresh Fruits and Vegetables at Sixty-six Important Consuming Markets in the United States, 1929*, Bulletin no. 39 (October, 1930), p. 11.

It will be observed that local products are transported to market almost exclusively by motor truck, while products coming from a distance, such as apples and sweet potatoes, are transported by rail.

The Metropolitan Region Comes of Age.—Large cities throughout the nation are gradually maturing in their commercial and industrial structure; in other words, they are "coming of age." As frontier conditions pass there is a tendency for each metropolitan area to become more nearly complete in its economic and institutional structure. In ten out of sixteen cities listed by Glenn E. McLaughlin[25] the number of industries increased between 1921 and 1927. The decline in certain cities, notably San Francisco and Pittsburgh, is in all probability due to the migration of industries into the suburban districts of the region. Diversification is no longer a characteristic of the larger cities alone but is spreading to the outlying regional communities. So far as local conditions permit there is a tendency in each case toward a complete industrial set-up. This tendency is, of course, subject to the limitations of accessible raw materials and markets as well as the more subtle ones of commercial and industrial traditions.

Within these limits, however, each large center of population tends to duplicate the occupational structure of similar centers elsewhere. This is particularly noticeable with respect to the manufacturing and mechanical industries. An exception to this rule seems to be the tendency for persons in highly specialized occupations, such as designers, artists, stock brokers, to concentrate in New York City. The New York region, so far as some of these services are concerned, is apparently almost nationwide.

The proportion of the nation's total bank business which it handles is perhaps the best single index of a growing city's maturity. Tables published by *The American Banker*[26] show some striking changes in this respect between 1923 and 1930. An outstanding feature of these tables is that, whereas New York City had 48.81 per cent of the country's bank deposits in 1923, it had

[25]   McLaughlin, "Industrial Diversification in American Cities," *Quarterly Journal of Economics*, vol. 45 no. 1 (November, 1930), p. 137.
[26]   January 21, 1924 and January 20, 1931.

only 32 per cent in 1930. Whether the latter figure reflects in part the unusual conditions prevailing in 1930 can only be surmised. It undoubtedly points to an increase in the financial maturity of the outlying regional cities. Chicago, Philadelphia, Boston, Cleveland, Los Angeles, Detroit, and Pittsburgh all gained during the period and San Francisco climbed from 5.94 per cent to 10.50 per cent. Oakland, across the bay from San Francisco, disappeared from the tables between 1923 and 1930, as did Brooklyn and Hoboken, satellites of the New York financial district. Eight cities —Atlanta, Dallas, Oklahoma City, Portland (Oregon), Cincinnati, Seattle, Syracuse, and Tulsa—made a showing in 1930, though they were not recorded in 1923.

The economic coming-of-age of the metropolitan centers of the nation, particularly those on the economic frontiers of the south and west, is unquestionably an important factor in intercity competition and in the development of regional consciousness. Cities, like nations, are seeking to develop balanced economies and to protect home industries and regional markets. There are natural limits, obviously, to this sort of development. The major industries of the country are still highly concentrated, and, considered from the standpoint of total output, there seems to be but a slight tendency toward industrial decentralization.

But in spite of this concentration of certain industries, the facts indicate that there will continue to be more intensive exploitation of local resources and more effort to build diversified economies on a regional basis. Thus there is the seeming paradox of regional communities growing more alike, yet growing also in independence and self-reliance.

III. *The Process of Metropolitan Growth*

The preceding sections have dealt with the rise of the metropolitan community as a population group and an economic entity, and with the interrelationships among such great communities. But certain changes are going on within the metropolitan community which have to be dealt with in order to present a rounded picture. Populations as well as individuals move about within the region, grow old, behave better or worse, become richer or poorer. The age distribution and sex ratio may change. The shifts of population from one locality to another within the city and its surrounding territory have economic and social consequences perhaps as significant as those of the more widely heralded rural-urban migrations.

The most conspicuous form of population shift within the metropolitan area is the so-called suburban or "outgoing" movement. This can be measured in terms of the proportion between the population of the central city or cities of a metropolitan district, as defined by the federal census, and the total population of the district. For the last three decades the Bureau of the Census has published figures for the metropolitan districts of the large cities. The change in procedure, already alluded to, in defining the 1930 districts would make strict comparisons over the twenty-year period impossible for the whole 96 districts. Fortunately the Bureau has adjusted the 1920 data for 85 districts to make comparison valid.

The rate of increase in the outside territory of these 85 metropolitan districts is a little more than twice as great as that in the central cities, and, as would be expected, the rate differentials tend to increase with the size of the districts. To be sure, wide variations are found in the relative rates of change for different districts, depending largely upon the practice of annexation. For instance, six of the 1930 districts show an actual decrease in population since 1920 in the territory outside their central cities; but in all save two, Duluth and Evansville, the decreases were due to recent annexations.[27]

The outside population in these 85 metropolitan districts constitutes 30.9 per cent of the total and is growing faster than the city proper. In eleven of the districts the population residing outside

[27]   When a city annexed a complete civil division between the two census periods, the Bureau of the Census added to the city's 1920 population the population of the annexed division at that date; but in most cases the annexed territory cut across civil divisions and therefore was not adjusted by the Bureau. The general effect of this is to reduce somewhat the actual rates of increase of outside territory.

the central cities is greater than that within central cities. In the Boston district it is over twice as great; in the Pittsburgh district almost twice that of the central city. Of course it is not claimed that the proportion of the population of a census metropolitan district that is found outside the central city or cities is a measure of the suburban drift. The metropolitan district, as defined by the federal census, usually represents a cluster or constellation of communities—villages, towns and cities—with varying degrees of dependency upon the central city. Some "satellites" are primarily agglomerations of commuters' dwellings while others are almost independent cities. Obviously the growth crests in the outer zones of metropolitan districts, in so far as they are the result of migration rather than of natural increase, represent the meeting in two opposite waves of movement—the overflow from the inner zones of the city and the inflow from outside territory. In a recent survey of Evanston, a suburb of Chicago, conducted under the auspices of the United Churches, it was discovered that of the 3,890 families giving information regarding last place of residence before entering Evanston, 47 per cent had come from Chicago, 7 per cent from communities just north of Evanston, and 46 per cent from places outside the general region.[28]

A clearer picture of the drift from the center may be obtained by a study of the movement of population within the city itself. This may be done only for those few cities in which enumerations have been made on the basis of census tracts, or small, constant territorial units. By means of these tracts it is possible to measure the changes of population in "zones" or belts of territory created by drawing concentric circles from the city's center.

Obviously the arbitrary concentric circle is useful only for purposes of comparison. It does not show the details of expansion, as growth is usually very uneven in different parts of the territory falling within a zone. This is particularly true in the outlying sections of the city, where growth is likely to follow radial lines.

[There is an unmistakable] tendency [for] the large city to lose

[28] See Albert G. Hinman, "An Inventory of Housing in a Suburban City," *The Journal of Land and Public Utility Economics*, vol. 7, May, 1931, p. 171.

population in its inner zones. It would seem that the outgoing tendency became somewhat accelerated during the past decade. Each of the four cities analyzed shows a widening range in which population is declining. Similar data for other cities, notably Philadelphia, Boston, St. Louis, and Detroit, though not directly comparable, tell a similar story. The economic depression seems to be causing considerable backwash to these lower rental areas, but in all probability this is but a temporary cessation of a general centrifugal process.

The motor car, bringing the country nearer in time, has caused an unprecedented development of outlying and suburban residential subdivisions. While this development pertains to families of a wide range of income, special attention has been given in the past decade to the promotion of exclusive residential districts designed for occupancy by the higher income classes. The lure of rural scenery is indicated by the extremely high rates of increase in suburbs bearing names denoting attractive physical features[29] such as heights, vistas, parks, and water frontage. Space does not permit a detailed analysis of this development but a few examples will illustrate the point. Here are some rather well-known suburbs with their percentage increases from 1920 to 1930: Beverly Hills, 2485.9; Glendale, 363.5; Inglewood, 492.8; Huntington Heights, 1000.4; Garfield Heights, 511.3 (suburbs of Cleveland); Grosse Pointe Park, 724.6; Ferndale, 689.9 (suburbs of Detroit); Webster Groves, 74.0; Maplewood, 70.3; Richmond Heights, 328.3 (suburbs of St. Louis); Elmwood Park, 716.7; Oak Park, 60.5; Park Ridge, 207.9 (suburbs of Chicago).

The movement, of course, is not always to sections outside of the city. This is indicated by the shift of the fashionable residence district in Manhattan from Riverside Drive to Park Avenue and by the rapid development of Chicago's Gold Coast and South Lake Shore territory. The famous Back Bay and Beacon Hill districts of Boston are losing many of their wealthy families to West Roxbury and Brighton, sections that have developed rapidly in recent years as high class residential areas. The movement of the wealthy class in Philadephia has been largely to the northern part of the

29   Too frequently in name only.

city, particularly to the Chestnut Hill and Germantown section; notable developments have also occurred in the northeast section. While 34 of Philadelphia's 48 wards showed an actual decline in population between 1920 and 1930, Ward 35 in the northeast corner of the city increased 314.4 per cent.

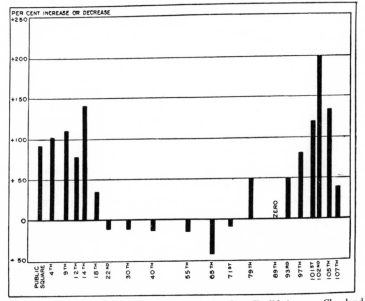

Fig. 2.—Percentage change in land value for blocks along Euclid Avenue, Cleveland, 1917–1930.

The general exodus of the upper economic classes from the inner sections of the city is creating serious problems by lowering land values and depriving the city of taxable wealth. The situation is well illustrated in the changes that have occurred in land values along Euclid Avenue, Cleveland, following the recent exodus of the wealthy residents from that street. Table VIII and Figure 2 show in part the effect of this migration.

These changing land values reflect the division of Euclid Avenue into three definite sections. First, extending from Public Square to East 22nd Street, a distance of about a mile, is the expanded downtown business area. The second section, running from East 22nd Street to East 71st Street, was once occupied by some of the wealthiest families of Cleveland, as a number of surviving mansions, put to various uses, testify. It is now a zone of decline. In the third division of the Avenue, from East 71st Street to East 107th Street, a secondary business center has sprung up around University Circle, and values are rising. Here are to be found some of the best of Cleveland's theatres and shops. Going still further east one comes to some of the city's most exclusive suburbs.

The history of land value movements along Euclid Avenue could be duplicated in many radial thoroughfares in other cities in the United States. The higher income levels of the city's population seek the more attractive outlying sections; the chain store, the branch bank, and the motion picture theatre follow them, and in the intermediate zones, of relatively little use to either the downtown section or the outlying nighborhoods, a trough in land values is created. Motor transportation and suburban development have accentuated this more or less natural aspect of city growth. Large cities everywhere are becoming keenly aware of the problem of the "blighted area" but little has been done as yet to cope with it. It is a complex problem involving factors of transportation, legal right to property, power of condemnation, and questions of finance.[30]

Age and Sex Selection.—Wide differences exist in the age-sex composition of the population in different sections of the city and in its various suburbs. As the city increases in size, segregation in its various forms—economic, cultural, biological—seems to become increasingly pronounced. Attention has frequently been called to the divergent character of suburban communities surrounding a common metropolitan center. It is commonly recognized that exclusive residential suburbs tend to have more females than males and less than the average number of children per family, while in most industrial suburbs the conditions are re-

[30]   See also discussion of blighted area in President's Conference on Home Building and Home Ownership, *Preliminary Reports*, VIII, 7, XXI, XXIII.

versed. By the use of census tract materials it is now possible to ascertain the make-up of the population as to age and sex by districts within the city itself.

An illustration of such a study is shown in Figure 3, prepared by Charles Newcomb of the University of Chicago. Newcomb measured the age and sex distribution for three successive decades in Oak Park, Illinois, and in six census tracts lying along Madison Street between Oak Park and the Loop district of Chicago, a distance of nine miles. The tracts selected are approximately 1.5 miles apart. Inasmuch as the population of a large part of this area is characterized by a high degree of mobility it is safe to assume that it has changed many times in the twenty-year interval shown. Yet the age-sex composition of the respective tracts has altered only slightly. In each decade an excessive proportion of adult males is found in the area lying close to the Loop, the main business center, with a tendency toward a more even age-sex distribution as one proceeds outward toward the fringe of the metropolitan area. The general tendency of women and children to withdraw from the central section of the city is quite apparent. So, too, is the decline in the proportion of children in the outlying tracts, although in interpreting this fact consideration must be given to the general decline throughout the city in the proportion of children to adults during the past two decades. Research on a more extended scale and in other cities may well show that this age-sex pattern is somewhat typical of metropolitan communities.

Delinquency Patterns.—The general wholesomeness of a city's environment, as measured by delinquency rates, seems to improve with distance from the main business center. In his extensive studies of juvenile delinquency, Clifford R. Shaw, of the Chicago Institute for Juvenile Research, found a definite tendency for rates to decline with distance from the center of the city.

Nationality and Race.—American cities have long been conspicuous for their concentrated colonies of nationality and racial groups. As immigrants have poured in from foreign countries and Negroes have migrated from the rural south, the newcomers have formed colonies within the cities where they have maintained, as far as possible, their traditional ways of living. Now that immigra-

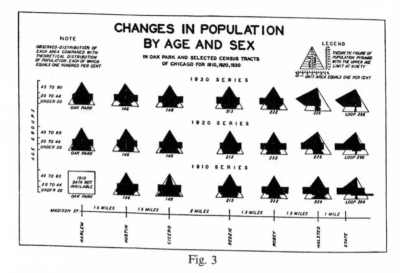

Fig. 3

tion has receded almost to the zero point[31] the question arises as to what will happen to the older immigrant districts found in almost every city. Not enough time has elapsed since immigration slackened to give a final answer to this question. A study of census tract statistics, in the few cities for which data are available for successive periods, indicates, however, a pronounced tendency for immigrants to abandon their colonies and disperse among the general population. Intensive studies made in the University of Chicago suggest that this process tends to occur in a successional manner. First there are the areas of initial settlement, usually located in the run down tenement sections near the center of the city and around the plants of the heavy basic industries; next there are the areas of second settlement, lying just beyond the zones of the first. In these areas the number of children per family is higher than is found in most other sections of the city. Finally there are the areas of third and subsequent settlement, as a rule too generally scattered to constitute colonies. As the immigrant moves up the

31   Emigration exceeded immigration in 1931.

economic ladder he moves out toward the periphery of the community. In this respect he is not unlike the native Bostonian, who has been described as a person who was born in the North End, lived in the South End, and died in the Back Bay.

Negro colonies have a somewhat different history. Instead of scattering, they tend with time to become more compact and racially more homogeneous. The pattern of Negro concentration varies too much to be considered here in detail. In some cities, notably New York and Chicago, the Negroes congregate largely in a single district; in others, such as Philadelphia and Washington, small colonies are scattered widely throughout the city. Local attitudes toward the Negro and local conditions of employment probably have something to do with these differences.

Ward lines too often cut across racial boundaries to make them satisfactory statistical units for our present purposes; nevertheless Table VI gives some conception of how the colored people are distributed within six large northern cities.

TABLE VI   CONCENTRATION OF NEGROES BY SELECTED WARDS AND STATISTICAL AREAS IN SIX NORTHERN CITIES, 1930ᵃ

City	Total Negro population, 1930	Percent increase in Negro population, 1920–1930	Total number of wards and statistical areas	Percent of Negroes to total population in each of the first four areas of highest Negro concentration				Percent of total Negro population of city in the four leading areas of Negroes
				I	II	III	IV	
New York (Manhattan)..	224,670	110.9	21	94.1	44.6	31.7	11.7	85.4
Chicago..................	233,903	113.7	75	94.6	91.9	88.7	16.5	82.4
Cleveland...............	71,899	108.7	40	72.4	70.2	58.2	42.1	78.4
Detroit.................	120,066	107.7	22	54.7	54.6	53.8	18.9	61.5
Pittsburgh..............	54,983	45.8	32	54.0	40.1	20.5	14.1	60.6
Philadelphia............	219,599	63.6	48	70.3	35.9	29.8	16.0	30.1

ᵃ Compiled from U. S. Census data.

The rapid growth of Negro population since the World War in many of the northern cities has naturally enlarged the colonies. Expansion usually takes the form of movement out along radial streets from the older centers of concentration. For instance, in Chicago, where the Negro population has increased from 109,458 to 233,903 during the last decade, the "Black Belt" has extended southward from the Loop district to 69th Street, a distance of nearly eight miles. In this expansion all other elements of the population have been displaced, the Negroes taking possession not merely of the apartments but of the churches, theatres, parks, and other institutions.

The Negro and the Oriental tend to build up cities within the city. They establish their own institutions—theatres, churches, stores, clubs, and dance halls. They come into contact with the general community life chiefly as employees and through their participation in politics. It does not appear, however, that the recent Negro migration has greatly disturbed the natural evolution of the northern cities. They came at a time when the outward drift of whites was at its height and, though they may have accelerated the movement in some localities, in many places they merely took over declining areas.[32]

Segregation a Characteristic of City Life.—The significance of segregation within the city has long been recognized by social workers and others dealing with welfare problems. It is being increasingly recognized by businessmen and administrative officials as a factor to be dealt with. More and more it is being realized that a city cannot be satisfactorily administered as a single population entity. More and more commercial firms and advertising agencies are beginning to analyze the economic and racial differences that exist in various sections of the cities and to deal with each district according to its particular characteristics.

IV. *Structural Change*

As the population distribution within the metropolitan region changes, so does the physical structure of the community and the way in which its various institutions function. As motor trans-

---

[32]   For other problems relating to Negro migration to northern cities, see *Preliminary Report* XXI of President's Conference on Home Building and Home Ownership for study of Negro housing.

portation permits the population to spread outward, the basic services follow it. All the public utilities—streets, water mains, sewerage facilities, electric lighting, gas and telephone services—show rapid rates of expansion in metropolitan regions within the past decade. This factor may be indicated by the expanding areas of street pavement, which generally carries with it the services mentioned. In 201 cities studied by Arthur H. Redfield[33] during the years 1925 to 1929 inclusive a total of 261,133,000 square yards of pavement were laid, the average laid each year increasing until 1927 and declining somewhat in 1928 and 1929. The rate of increase was greatest in cities of over 1,000,000 and next greatest in those of 500,000 or more, though perhaps too much significance need not be attached to this fact.

Redfield's figures applied only to pavement within the corporate limits of cities. But a city's street system actually reaches far beyond its political boundaries. The paved motor highway net encircling every city is really an extended street system. The physical base of the city, in the form of streets and other utilities, is no longer adequately described by statistics compiled for corporate areas.

This extension of city utilities has the effect of erasing many of the former boundary lines between urban and rural territory and of bringing within a single communal mechanism, with common problems of administration and finance, entire constellations of politically independent centers that were previously separated from one another by strips of rural or undeveloped territory.

Building Statistics as Indexes of Community Change.—Trends in building construction are here considered only as they indicate change in the organization and life of the community, not as they affect the building industry itself. Inasmuch as an increasing proportion of all buildings constructed in cities represents construction for sale or rent rather than for use by the owner, tendencies in construction are good barometers of the changing organization of the city. Buildings, like motor cars or household furniture, are

---

33   U. S. Bureau of Mines, *Street Paving in Representative American Cities, 1925–1929*, I. C. 6431, May, 1931, p. 7; names of cities given in this publication.

made for profit and, therefore, are responsive to the demands of the consumer. But the building differs from most other forms of consumers' goods in that it has a fixed location. Consequently, new developments in architecture and building equipment and in the platting and promotion of new districts and subdivisions tend to shift a city's population. If the consumer desires a new kind of motor car or living room furniture, he need not change his location to secure it. But if he wishes to live or carry on business in a new kind of building, he must go where that kind of building is. Building statistics reflect the relative shifts of emphasis from one class of construction to another, and thereby indicate, in a broad way, some of the major changes that are taking place in the physical structure and internal organization of the city.[34]

. . . Residential construction constituted more than half of the total floor space added to American cities in nine of the twelve years for which data are available. It gained in relative importance from 1921 to 1924, and held a position of over 60 per cent of the total through 1928, only to drop off sharply in 1929. Commercial construction, of which the chief subclass is office buildings, maintained about a uniform position throughout the twelve-year period. Factories dropped suddenly in relative importance after 1920, with a slight upward trend between 1924 and 1929 and is a pronounced sag in 1930. It is particularly significant that from 1921 onward the construction of educational buildings runs very close to that of factories. The effect of the depression is seen in the changing ratios of construction in the several classes of buildings in the 1930 figures when non-commercial classes—hospitals and institutions, educational and public buildings—gain in relative importance in the construction program. The shift will undoubtedly be much more pronounced in the 1931 figures.

Residential Construction.—In residential construction there are at least two general trends that are worthy of special attention. The first is the recent tendency for new residential space to increase faster than population; and the second is the tendency

[34]   See President's Conference on Home Building and Home Ownership, *Preliminary Reports,* I, VI, VII, XII, XXI.

toward multiple dwellings. In regard to the former, the report on *Recent Economic Changes* contains the following summary statement:

In the four years prior to the American entry into the World War, there was an average construction of 209 square feet per person added to the population. When the war years are included, this average drops to 205 square feet. The post-war boom of 1919 not only wiped out all the shortage created during the war but raised the average to nearly 221 square feet. Then followed another two years with a low construction record, which again brought the average below the level established in the four years from 1913 to 1916. But, beginning with 1922, construction began a consistent upward movement, and by the end of 1927 the average residential construction per person added to the population was more than 286 square feet.[35]

.   .   .   .

The Trend Toward Multiple Dwellings.—The rapid increase in the proportion of families provided for in apartments is strikingly shown in a compilation of building permits for 257 cities of 25,000 population or over published by the Bureau of Labor Statistics.[36] Between 1921 and 1928 the percentage of one-family dwellings, as indicated by the building permits, dropped from 58.3 to 35.2; the number of two-family dwellings rose from 17.3 in 1921 to over 21 per cent of the whole for 1922, 1923, and 1924, then declined to 11.1 per cent in 1928; and the percentage of multi-family dwellings climbed from 24.4 in 1921 to 53.7 in 1928. In 1929 and 1930 the percentage of one-family dwellings increased again, reaching 45.7 per cent in the last named year; and 1930 also saw the percentage of two-family dwellings climb to 12.1 and the percentage of multi-family dwellings fall to 42.2. But this interruption of the trend noted between 1921 and 1928 is probably only a temporary reaction caused by the economic de-

35   *Recent Economic Changes in the United States*, Report of the Committee on Recent Economic Changes of the President's Conference on Unemployment (New York, 1929), 1:63.
36   U. S. Bureau of Labor Statistics, *Monthly Labor Review* 31, April, 1931, p. 171.

pression. Despite fluctuations of varying degree the general long-time tendency in residential construction is definitely toward the multi-family dwelling.

A closer analysis of the building permit data, however, indicates that this tendency is a product of metropolitanism and is not characteristic of the housing movement in the smaller independent cities of the nation. Robert Whitten, analyzing the building permit data of the Bureau of Labor Statistics for 1921 and 1929 in connection with the President's Conference on Home Building and Home Ownership,[37] brings out this distinction clearly. In the fourteen largest cities, with populations of 500,000 or more, the permits for multi-family dwellings increased from 34 to 64.4 per cent of the whole. Increases for other urban communities were as shown in the following statement:

	1921	*1929*
31 Central metropolitan cities............	30.3	58.4
57 Suburban cities (population 25,000 or more)............	25.3	47.5
46 Independent cities (population 100,000 or more)............	11.2	19.9
65 Independent cities (population 50,000 to 100,000)............	8.8	15.9
64 Independent cities (population 25,000 to 50,000)............	10.1	10.4

In all the cities studied, except those in the third category, which were communities of 100,000 population or more outside of metropolitan regions, the percentage of two-family dwellings declined; in cities of that category it increased from 9.5 in 1921 to 13.4 in 1929. In general these figures reveal a much smaller percentage of apartments both at the beginning and at the end of the period in the smaller and independent cities than in larger cities or those included in metropolitan areas. Only within the metropolitan regions does the apartment seem rapidly to be changing the manner of life of the people.

[37] From an unpublished *Appendix*, prepared for the report of the Committee on Family Types and Community Relations as Determining Housing Needs. See also *Preliminary Reports*, I.

The Increasing Size of the Structural Unit.—"Large buildings," writes John M. Gries,[38] "have been the most distinctive feature of post-war non-residential construction. . . . Office buildings, department stores, hotels, apartment houses, and schools have tended toward larger units." Not only do a larger proportion of metropolitan residents live in multiple houses but the average size of structures both for dwelling and for working has increased. The growth of large apartment buildings, however, has been more conspicuous in the metropolitan regions than in the more scattered urban centers. . . .

Decreasing Size of the Dwelling Unit.—Although the size of the metropolitan apartment building and the amount of floor space per individual tend to increase, the family dwelling unit is growing smaller. This may be explained by the diminishing size of the family itself. Evidence regarding the trend toward smaller apartments is fragmentary but nevertheless suggestive. A. G. Hinman has summarized the records of the Chicago City Health Department as follows:

Of 293,045 apartment units constructed in Chicago, the period 1913–1928, 6 percent have one room; 12 percent, two rooms; 14 percent, three rooms; 29 percent, four rooms; 24 percent, five rooms; and 15 percent, six or more rooms. The average size of apartment units in the buildings constructed in the period 1913–1919 is 4.6 rooms and in those built since 1924, 3.5 rooms.[39]

The statistics published by the Regional Survey of New York show a similar tendency toward the smaller apartment:

In 1913 the average number of rooms per apartment in new construction was 4.19; in 1925 it was 3.63; in 1926, 3.49; in 1927, 3.39; in 1928, 3.34.[40]

Office Buildings.—The most conspicuous development in the large structural unit is the office building. Every year seems to

38   In *Recent Economic Changes*, 1:240.
39   A. G. Hinman, "An Inventory of Housing in a Suburban City," *Journal of Land and Public Utility Economics* 7, May, 1931, p. 174.
40   *Regional Survey of New York and Its Environs, VI, Buildings: Their Uses and the Spaces About Them* (New York, 1931), p. 238.

establish a new record in the height and floor space of the office structure. According to the annual surveys of the National Association of Building Owners and Managers, which cover old as well as new construction, the average rentable floor space per office building reported increased from 61,473 square feet in 1924 (23 cities—1,105 buildings) to 85,203 square feet in 1930 (43 cities—1,960 buildings). . . .

Vertical Expansion.—The increasing size of the structural unit is a result of vertical growth even more than expansion of the building site. American cities are reaching upward as well as outward. The vertical growth, like horizontal spread, is a natural structural response to the operation of economic forces under present conditions of technological culture. Recent developments in vertical transportation have been less conspicuous but almost as important as those in horizontal transportation. According to information furnished by the Otis Elevator Company, the total number of power elevators in the country increased from 138,756 in 1920 to 220,608 in 1929. But the increase in the number of elevators does not fully indicate the advance in vertical transportation. Although it cannot be shown statistically, the increase in the volume and mileage of vertical traffic has undoubtedly been very great in recent years.

According to Clarence T. Coley, operating manager of the Equitable Building, the 48 passenger elevators in that great structure carry on the average 96,000 people per day between the hours of 8 a.m. and 6 p.m. During the course of a year they will travel 275,000 miles, or 11 times around the earth at the Equator, each car carrying 6 persons for every mile. The building has 40 stories, 1,220,688 square feet of net rentable area and a permanent population of 12,000. The people passing in and out of its various portals each day number 135,000. The real estate management firm of Cushman & Wakefield has had a count made of the number of passengers carried by the elevators in sixteen office buildings under its management in the Grand Central Zone of New York City. The sixteen buildings had a combined height of 303 stories and were serviced by 75 elevator cars. During the year 1928, including 305 working days between the hours of 8 a.m. and 6 p.m., 36,089,850 persons were carried by the elevators. The 75 cars made a total of 4,960,170 trips equal to a total of 415,041 miles. These figures, inadequate as they are, give us some idea of the enormously heavy traffic carried by the "vertical streets" of New York City.[41]

While the tall building is still largely confined to a few of the great cities of the nation, it is beginning to appear in the smaller cities as well, where building regulations permit. In 1929 the Thompson Starrett Company, Inc., made a nationwide census of "skyscrapers," the result of which are summarized in the following table:

TABLE VII   CENSUS OF SKYSCRAPERS, BY SIZE OF CITIES, 1929[a]

Size of cities	Number of cities	Number of buildings 10 to 20 stories	Number of buildings 21 stories or more
1,000,000 and over..........................	5	3,009	295
500,000 to 1,000,000......................	8	399	40
250,000 to 500,000.........................	24	495	29
100,000 to 250,000.........................	25	303	12
Under 100,000.............................	12	80	1
Total.............................	74	4,286	377

a "A Census of Skyscrapers," *American City,* September, 1929, vol. XLI, p. 130.

This census, taken three years ago, does not depict the situation at the present time. New York City alone, according to its tax assessor's report which is summarized in the Chicago Sunday *Tribune,* March 13, 1932, has 493 buildings of over 20 stories, 93 of which have over 30 stories. "Four of the 93 tallest and a cluster of the lesser fry have been added to the total since the tax man was around last year."

The ratio between land area and rentable floor space is a determining factor in the economy of the skyscraper. The rentable floor space of the Empire State building is more than twenty-five times its ground area. In order to achieve this it had to be extended to 85 stories. For the Chrysler building the ratio is a little over

41   W. C. Clark and J. L. Kingston, *The Skyscraper, A Study in the Economic Height of Modern Office Buildings,* American Institute of Steel Construction (New York, 1930), p. 128.

twenty to one. For the Woolworth it is a little over sixteen to one. For the Metropolitan Tower it is under thirteen to one. But the ratio does not increase in direct proportion to height, largely because of the additional space that must be given to elevators in the higher buildings. There is, therefore, an economic limit of the height of city buildings and it is possible that that limit has been attained or even passed.[42]

Skyscraper Apartments.—Although high buildings are predominantly office and hotel structures, there are indications that the apartment has broken the tradition of the walk-up height, and is about to join the ranks of the skyscraper class. Probably because of building restrictions the number of skyscraper apartments is still comparatively small. The high apartment, as yet, is distinctly a metropolitan institution. It is found only in a few of the larger cities where land values make living near the business section prohibitive for all except the very wealthy and the very poor—those who accept the remnants of a passing residential economy. The recent sudden appearance of skyscraper apartment buildings close to the main business centers of New York City and Chicago may mark the beginning of a new historical phase in the residential use of some of the blighted areas of our large cities. There seems to be a growing desire on the part of business executives and certain professional groups to live close to their places of employment, and the skyscraper apartment is a structural accommodation to this interest. From an economic standpoint this type of building, designed for the use of the higher income brackets of the population, is able to compete with commercial services for high land-value sites. And from the social standpoint the size and prestige of the building are usually sufficient to overcome any stigma that may be associated with living in an area that is basically commercial in character.

[42]   Stewart Browne, President of the United Real Estate Owner's Association, is quoted in the New York *Times* (March 20, 1932) as predicting, "that during the present year [1932] all skyscraper buildings built during the past four years, except those owned by large financial institutions, will be foreclosed unless such buildings have already been foreclosed."

Furthermore, the introduction of the automatic control elevator into apartment buildings of medium height bids fair to initiate a new era in apartment living for a larger proportion of the city's population. The increase in the number of automatic elevators, which elevator companies report are confined largely to apartments, has been rapid in recent years. In 1924 there were only 830 automatic control elevators in the country; by 1929 the number had increased to 6,447.

The Significance of the Larger Structural Unit.—The most obvious effect of the increasing size of the structural unit is the change produced in the physical contour of the city. There is no doubt that the American city is beginning to assume aesthetic qualities which formerly it sadly lacked. The great tower, built for beauty as well as utility, has initiated a new era in American architecture. But it is outside the field of this chapter to deal with the architectural aspects of community change.

The large building is first of all a physical manifestation of the trend toward territorial concentration and functional differentiation of various types of economic and social activities within the city. It is generally known that as cities increase in size their different economc activities tend to group themselves, giving rise to financial, shopping, wholesale, amusement, and other kinds of districts. Locality specialization, whether in the form of districts or individual streets, has always been a distinctive feature of large cities, even those without modern facilities for transportation. The old cities of the Orient are renowned for their specialized streets, along which rows of small shops display similar or complementary wares for sale. The financial districts of London and New York are examples of old and seemingly permanent grouping.

The recent tendency in American cities is for the building, rather than the street, to become the physical unit for such complementary groupings of activities. The tall building is like the old specialized street, stood on end. By housing competitive or related services under a common roof, and by substituting vertical for horizontal transportation, a great saving of time is effected. The situation is well illustrated in the Chicago Merchandise Mart. This great structure, covering 200,000 square feet of ground, but having 4,000,000 square feet of rentable floor space, had listed on its directory of tenants in July, 1931, 1,258 different names, representing wholesaling, manufacturing, and advertising firms. Were these firms distributed on the old pattern they would require many times the ground space occupied by the Mart, and the customer would have to travel many miles of streets to obtain the selection of merchandise at present available in this single building.

The department store, which made its appearance in the 1890's, with the introduction of the electric street car, represented the beginning of the movement toward the large specialized building unit structurally designed to house a series of associated economic services. This type of building has now been widely imitated. Banks, theatres, hospitals, schools, and even churches are assuming the department store pattern of organization and conducting their operations in fewer but larger buildings, which are more systematically organized.

Of course the extreme expression of this tendency is the office building, the existence and the peculiarities of which can be partially explained by the fact that the managerial functions of a modern business can be carried on apart from its operative or productive functions. Management needs relatively small space and it is not tied down by problems of transportation. As R. M. Haig has said:[43]

The exercise of this managerial function of coordination and control is at first glance singularly independent of transportation. It does not require the transfer of huge quantities of materials. It deals almost exclusively with information. What is all-important is transportation of intelligence. The mail, the cable, the telegraph, and the telephone bring in its raw material and carry out its finished product. Internally easy contact of man with man is essential. The telephone is prodigally used, of course, but the personal conference remains, after all, the method by which most of the important work is done. Conferences with corporation officers, with bankers, with lawyers, and accountants, with partners, with fellow directors, fill the day. The work is facilitated when the time of the men whose time is most valuable is

[43]   R. M. Haig, "Towards an Understanding of the Metropolis," *Quarterly Journal of Economics* 40, May, 1926, pp. 426–28.

conserved. The district must be conveniently accessible and must be at the heart of the system of communication. It must be arranged so as to give the greatest possible ease of contact among men whose presence is desired in arriving at decisions.

V. *City and Regional Planning*[44] *and Zoning*

Up to this point attention has been focused on the natural processes of city growth as they find expression under prevailing conditions of direct competition or competitive cooperation. The two following sections, planning and government, deal with efforts to direct and control growth tendencies in the interest of the general welfare of the community.

While it is commonly recognized that the city is a sort of superorganism, which obtains its characteristic pattern from the interplay of competitive forces, still it is becoming increasingly apparent that unregulated competition may be destructive. It may distort the structural growth of the city and lead to waste, injustice and general inefficiency. In order to avoid these evils and direct the processes of city growth more in conformity with general welfare, the planning and zoning movement has developed throughout the nation.

The purpose of city planning and its more recent developments into regional planning is to make cities and regions convenient, healthful, and attractive places in which people may work, play, learn, and otherwise express themselves in well rounded living. This is an aim shared also by other civic endeavors; the special province of city planning is comprehensive treatment of the wide range of problems relating to the physical aspects of the city or other unit—its streets, railroads, waterways, public services; its public buildings, schools and other cultural centers; parks, recreation grounds and other open spaces; and the development of housing, industry, and other private property.

44   The material on planning in this section was prepared by Shelby M. Harrison (Director of Social Studies, Regional Plan of New York and Its Environs) and Flavel Shurtleff (Secretary of the National Conference on City Planning and the Planning Foundation of America.)

The city planning movement in the United States and its dependencies is dated from 1905. In that year three plans were
made: for Manila, P. I., San Francisco, California, and Columbus,
South Carolina. These are the earliest city planning reports of
which there is any record. One of the next important plans to be
completed was that from Chicago, which appeared in 1909. Significant trends from these beginnings are to be found in the legislation relating to city planning, in the setting up of planning commissions, and in the definite projects undertaken by cities, which
resulted in well considered reports.

Legislative Sanctions.—The first recognition in state legislation in this country of city planning as a function of a city department is found in the special act of Connecticut for Hartford in
1907.

The planning commissions in Milwaukee, 1908, in Chicago,
1909, and in Detroit, 1910, were established under city ordinances.
The Baltimore commission was appointed by authority of a special act of the Maryland legislature, passed in 1910. Most of the
other early planning commissions were established under local
ordinances.[45]

The first planning laws of general application were passed in
1909 for Wisconsin and in 1911 for Pennsylvania (cities of the
first class). In 1913 laws of this character were passed for all
New York cities and incorporated villages. Massachusetts in the
same year passed an act which made planning boards mandatory
in all cities and towns over 10,000 population. The states (other
than New York, New Jersey, Pennsylvania, Massachusetts, and
Wisconsin) which have since passed laws of general application
authorizing the creation of planning boards are as follows: 1915,
Nebraska, Ohio, California; 1918, Connecticut; 1919 Minnesota,
North Carolina, Oregon; 1921, Indiana, Illinois, Kansas, Nevada,
Tennessee, Vermont; 1923, Oklahoma; 1924, District of Columbia; 1925, Iowa; 1926, Louisiana; 1927, Maryland; 1928, Kentucky; 1929, Arkansas, Colorado, North Dakota.

[45]   For special discussions of planning in relation to housing, see Conference on Home Building, *Preliminary Reports*, VI, VIII, XII, XXIV.

Thus just two more than half of the states have enacted legislative sanctions or bases for planning in their cities. All sections of the country are represented, although the greatest activity was centered in the states along the Atlantic seaboard and in the middle west. The curve of developing interest during these two decades is fairly regular, with an indication of special activity around the year 1921. Many of these states have revised their first planning laws. Others have made them universally applicable where originally they applied only to cities of one class.

The following states have given legal sanction to a planning department or commission by special acts which apply only to certain-named cities or areas: 1917, Maine; 1921, South Carolina; 1923, Georgia, Florida; 1928, Virginia.

The earlier ordinances and acts set up advisory commissions or boards whose chief function was to study the needs of the city and secure a plan for its guidance. They had no authority to enforce their plans. Whether the plan was used or not depended largely on the character of the city's administration and its understanding of planning values. A more recent trend has been toward giving more power to the planning agency, culminating in the so-called master planning legislation passed by New York in 1926. This law and the *Standard City Planning Enabling Act* brought out by the Advisory Committee on City Planning and Zoning of the United States Department of Commerce in 1928, give a legal status to the master plan and a suspensive veto to the planning commission. California, Colorado and North Dakota, in 1929, and New Jersey in 1930, have enacted legislation rather closely following the Standard Act.

City Planning Commissions or Boards.—During the last two decades numerous official city planning commissions or boards have been established throughout the country. Their functions range from undertaking the preliminary survey work upon which later plans are based to drafting the plans and putting them into operation. Before 1914 there were 17 such official planning agencies. During the next few years the newly instituted agencies may be grouped as follows:

Years	Number of official planning agencies
1914 to 1922	207
1923 to 1926	161
1927 to (June) 1930	between 350 and 400

The total for the period of roughly twenty years is thus upwards of 735 official commissions or boards established as part of the local government machinery. In addition, numerous non-governmental city planning agencies have been instituted. The number of non-official agencies in recent years is proportionately less than formerly since the public has become somewhat better acquainted with city planning and it has seemed less necessary to get action started through an experimental venture. It is evident that the bulk of the development in official commissions has taken place during the last fifteen years, and that by far the most active period was from 1927 to 1930.

These official planning bodies may be grouped as to size of locality served. In the thirteen cities with a population of over 500,000 in 1930 there were 11 governmental planning agencies. In the 80 cities between 100,000 and 500,000 there were 70 official planning agencies. In the 283 cities having a population between 25,000 and 100,000 there were 205 official agencies. The approximately 500 remaining agencies were about equally divided between cities under 5,000 and the cities between 5,000 and 25,000, of which latter there were 1,457.

The effectiveness of planning agencies varies extremely widely among the different cities, depending on the composition of the commission, on the law or ordinance under which it operates, on the cooperation from other municipal agencies, and on other public support. Some indication of their place in the municipal scheme may be seen in the yearly appropriation received by the various commissions.[46] In those cities where separate appropriations to

[46]   To secure exact statistics is extremely difficult, if not impossible, for some cities which are effectively carrying out planning programs make no separate appropriations, the planning commission being considered a division of the public works department or the city engineer's office.

the planning commissions have been made over a period of at least three years the following facts may be summarized:

Appropriations of $20,000 and upward were made in 14 of the 18 cities which have a population of over 400,000.

Of the 75 cities between 100,000 and 400,000 population, 13 made appropriations of $10,000 to $20,000, and 13 made appropriations of $5,000 to $10,000.

Of the 1,740 cities in the country under 100,000 and over 5,000 there were less than 20 with appropriations of over $5,000 a year.

In other words, of the 93 cities with a population of over 100,-000, up to this writing 40 have specific appropriations for the planning commission's work ranging from $5,000 upwards. These appropriations are for the regular administrative work of the planning commission. They do not include amounts appropriated for specific planning projects, like the making of a topographical survey, a master plan, or the drafting of a zoning ordinance.

The experience of leading city planners points to the observation that the planning commission's work cannot be effectively carried out unless it has assigned to it a paid secretary-engineer. This official may have other duties; he may be the city engineer as he is in many cities. For the payment of his salary, or part of it, and for other administrative expenses of the commission there will certainly be required not less than $1,000 a year in the smallest cities and not less than $5,000 a year where the executive official of the planning commission gives his full time to that work. On this basis it is seen that a very large proportion of the planning commissions are as yet inadequately financed, less than 60 cities among the 1,833 with populations of 5,000 or over having seen fit thus far to provide at least $5,000 per year for this work. It should be added, however, that funds secured by a number of private, nongovernmental planning bodies would add considerably to this group of 60 cities. In a few such cases the total sums available have run into comparatively large figures, as in Philadelphia, where $500,000 has been raised for its Regional Plan and in New York, where the New York Regional Plan Committee has already spent more than a million dollars on its enterprises.

City Planning Reports.—Another indication of developments in planning is the number of cities which, through official or non-official agencies, have carried their planning projects to the point where a city plan report has been issued. Of the 93 largest cities of the United States, that is, those over 100,000 population in 1930, 77 have issued fairly comprehensive planning reports. Of the cities ranging between 25,000 and 100,000 population, reports have been prepared in 108; and of the cities under 25,000 about 150 have planning reports. In a few cases these are for the cities and their surrounding regions. Thus, of 1,833 cities of 5,000 or more, only a little over one-sixth have carried their interest in planning through the stage where a report has been published.

Of the 335 cities which have planning reports, 60 were made before 1916. These would now be considered hardly more than preliminary or sketch plans. They were not based on comprehensive studies of population, traffic movement or other local conditions, and in most cases were hardly more than suggestions for improvements made by the planner after a brief visit to the city. More than half the cities which had these early plans have since either discarded them entirely for more thorough and comprehensive reports covering all the items in a city planning program, or have supplemented them by comprehensive reports in one or more fields, such as streets, parks or zoning. Even in the 300 news or revised plans which have been produced since 1916 there is a great difference in the thoroughness of the basic surveys, and consequently in the completeness of the final plan; but only 125 of them are known to be grounded on substantial data secured by careful surveys. They would probably serve as "master plans" as defined by the planning laws of New York, New Jersey, California, Colorado and North Dakota.

These is fairly general agreement now among city planners that planning programs cannot be effective unless they are based upon reasonably complete master plans; and that master plans cannot be effective unless the relative importance of the various projects recommended is at least outlined. In other words, it is becoming increasingly evident that the city plan must include a financial as well as a physical program, and also a capital budget outlining long term improvements as well as a budget for current expenses.

The last ten or twelve years have seen the rise of regional planning, in which the principles and experience gained in city planning have been applied to a certain extent to larger areas. These areas in a few instances have been counties but more often include the suburban territory, the so-called commuting districts, around the central city, more or less regardless of political or governmental boundary lines. By 1931 at least three states had enacted basic legislation providing for planning on such regional or county bases.

Zoning.—The zoning of cities and other local areas, sometimes undertaken as a separate project but now more often, and more properly, as a part of city or regional planning, is here treated separately because many cities have been zoned which do not have even a preliminary plan, and in some cases not even a planning commission. Zoning regulations supplement the city plan by controlling the use which may be made of private land and buildings. They provide for three or four classes of districts, usually residential, commercial, industrial and unclassified; and then exclude from each district all uses regarded as undesirable.

Zoning dates back less than twenty years in this country. Before 1916 there were only five zoned cities in the United States, but by the end of 1930 there were nearly one thousand. The action taken by cities by periods of years may be summed up as follows:

	Cities zoned
Before 1916	5
1916 through 1920	30
1921 through 1925	438
1926 through 1927	210
1928 through 1929	221
1930	77
Total	981

It is evident from this summary that the period of greatest activity in zoning began in 1921. The annual increase in number of cities zoned since that date has been over 100, except from 1930 when the number dropped to 77. . . .

During the period since zoning began, there has been marked advance in the scope of zoning legislation and improvement in the technique applied to the drafting of zoning ordinances, just as there has been advanced in the scientific preparation of city plans. In some of the earlier ordinances cities were zoned for "use" only, that is, for the control of the uses to which the land should be put—commercial, industrial, residential, or other. Practically all of the ordinances since 1925 have been comprehensive, covering use to which land and buildings may be put, the height and bulk of buildings, or the area which may be covered.

A wide difference is to be seen in the administration of zoning ordinances. In some cities councils are easily prevailed upon to make amendments to the zoning ordinance, usually without referring the proposals to the planning commission or zoning board even for a report. In some cities the boards of adjustment or appeal, which are the quasi-judicial boards to hear zoning appeals, are very liberal in their interpretation of the ordinance or in permitting exceptions to them—too liberal in the judgment of leaders in this field for very effective community control of its land and building developments. In other cities, councils make no amendments without first getting the advice of the planning commission, and in the great majority of cases this advice is followed. In these latter cities, it is usually found that the zoning boards of appeal are strictly interpreting the ordinances and relaxing only in cases where decided hardship would otherwise result.

City Planning Instruction in Colleges.—Practically no attention was given to instruction in or training for city planning in any college or technical school in this country before 1909. The School of City Planning at Harvard University was established in the autumn of 1929. Twenty-five colleges or technical institutions are now giving either one or more city planning courses in connection with their departments of architecture, engineering, or landscape architecture. At least 50 additional colleges or technical schools give lectures on city planning in connection with courses in engineering, art, political economy, municipal government, political science, or sociology.

VI. *Trends in Metropolitan Government*[47]

The spread of urban population over vast areas surrounding our great cities has inevitably raised serious governmental problems. This population movement has not only disregarded existing units of government but has taken place with a rapidity far outrunning the normal expansion of cities by annexation. The modern metropolitan region, as indicated earlier in this chapter, frequently includes scores of towns and cities as well as the whole or parts of numerous counties, and certain regions intersect two or more state boundaries.

The problem which such a situation occasions are many and difficult. Some are due to the fact that the character of certain services such as planning, water supply, and sewerage naturally requires action on a broad scale. Others spring primarily from the inability of some or all of the individual units to finance the services required by their situation, as education, transportation, the institutional care of the poor and sick, recreation, and the ownership and operation of public utilities. Still others are caused by the impossibility of making a service such as police protection or health really successful in a particular unit in the absence of service of similar quality in its neighbors. One or more of these causes is involved in all the peculiar problems of the metropolis. Park sites, for example, are usually to be found only in outlying districts quite incapable of dealing with the problem on a metropolitan scale.

The historic method of reconciling urban needs and urban powers has been by annexation. Metropolitan development in the last twenty years, however, has been too swift for annexation. Furthermore, there has developed a notable opposition to annexation in well established satellite communities. Brookline will not submit to annexation by Boston, nor will Webster Groves join St. Louis. The forcible annexation of such suburbs by fiat of the state legislature is no longer considered politically feasible. The last great forcible annexation was that of Allegheny to Pittsburgh in

[47]   This section was prepared by Thomas H. Reed, Professor of Political Science, University of Michigan.

1907,[48] and its repercussions both in Pennsylvania and in the country at large have discouraged similar drastic action elsewhere.

Failing annexation, the one easily applicable remedy has been the establishment of special districts to provide particular services. There is nothing novel, of course, in this device. A metropolitan police district was established for New York as early as 1857, and the same method has since been used at intervals to meet special situations. The great majority of such authorities now in existence, however, date back no further than 1900, and in recent years they have been established at an average rate of more than one a year.[49] Some are governed by commissions appointed by the governor (Massachusetts Metropolitan Commission). Other commissions are made up of delegates elected by the authorities of the constituent municipalities (Montreal Metropolitan Commission), while still others are elected directly by the people of the district (Chicago Sanitary District). Some districts are financed by state funds; others by taxes levied directly by the governing body; others by assessments apportioned to the constituent municipalities on the basis of population, assessed valuation, or services rendered; others by loans secured on the earnings of enterprises.

Successful as many of these districts have been in providing essential public works, recreational facilities, and so forth, there has been a steadily growing recognition of the fact that they do not solve the metropolitan problem as a whole. To create enough of them to do so would inundate our urban centers beneath a flood of unrelated public authorities. Where, as in the case of the Massachusetts Metropolitan Commission, several functions are united under one board, we have something closely approximating a new unit of general local government. This indeed is what the situation seems to demand, and the last few years have seen deliberate attempts to solve the metropolitan problem by the establishment

[48]   In this case the legislature provided for a vote in both cities jointly, the result of which was a foregone conclusion. Pittsburgh had more than twice the population of Allegheny.

[49]   Fourteen are listed for the years 1915–1929 in Committee on Metropolitan Government of the National Municipal League, *The Government of Metropolitan Areas* (New York, 1930), p. 27. The list does not even pretend to be complete.

of new governmental units of metropolitan scope with specified powers, leaving all other functions to the existing municipalities within the area. What is more significant is that no other method has been prominently urged in any of the communities where vigorous campaigns have been conducted for the solution of the metropolitan problem. Though none of these attempts has been successful —and in one sense no trend of action established—they indicate the trend of thought upon which future solutions will probably depend. The first of these attempts was begun in Alameda County, California, in 1916. It was proposed to unite all the municipalities and some unincorporated territory on the eastern shore of San Francisco Bay in a single city and county of which the constituent municipalities were to be boroughs. In 1922 a proposal of this general tenor was rejected by the voters of the proposed city-county, actuated by fear of domination by Oakland. In 1923 the Pennsylvania legislature authorized the appointment of a Commission to study Municipal Consolidation in Allegheny County. This commission procured the adoption of an enabling constitutional amendment and after a thorough survey of conditions in the Pittsburgh area presented to the legislature of 1929 a charter which applied the name of City of Pittsburgh to Allegheny County, gave the new unit additional powers and a modernized governmental structure, but left present Pittsburgh and all the other municipalities of the county as members of this great municipal federation. This charter, seriously and harmfully amended by the legislature, received at a special election on June 25, 1929, a large popular majority in Pittsburgh and Allegheny County. But, although it carried more than two-thirds of the 122 cities, boroughs and townships of the county, it failed of adoption because the constitution required a two-thirds vote in a majority of these units. The movement goes on, and this year the legislature passed for the first time a constitutional amendment substituting a simple majority for the two-thirds provision.

After St. Louis had attempted unsuccessfully to annex St. Louis County in 1926, leading men in both city and county undertook to unite the two sections on a federated basis. An exhaustive study of local conditions prefaced the campaign, which had the support of prominent industrialists and business men. The enabling constitutional amendment, however, was defeated by the people of the state in November, 1930, in an election fatal to all proposals on the ballot.

In the meantime an organization was formed in Cleveland in the latter part of 1927 to study the metropolitan situation of that city, impelled largely by the realization that the best element of Cleveland's electorate was rapidly being lost to the city by reason of the outward movement of population. Amendments to the Ohio constitution sponsored by this organization, opening the way to metropolitan consolidation on the federated pattern, have failed to pass the Ohio legislature due to rural misunderstanding and opposition.

The assignment of powers to the Greater City or metropolitan government in several of the recently proposed plans of consolidation appears in Table VIII. All other powers in each case were left to the existing local governments.

These movements in several of our largest cities—so far unsuccessful but by no means extinguished—are a clear indication of the trend toward the federated city as a solution of the metropolitan problem. They have suffered defeat not because of opposition to the preservation of local autonomy but quite the contrary. The smaller units have feared that their autonomy was insufficiently protected. The office holders of the great city have objected to any diminution of their importance by the surrender of any of their functions to a greater city government. The only real hope of metropolitan consolidation, however, is recognized to be along the general lines of the Pittsburgh, St. Louis, and Boston projects. Annexation, even if possible, cannot be profitably undertaken for whole metropolitan areas because the poor but extensive remainder would be left to sink under the weight of impossible financial burdens. Probably the best solution is a metropolitan government for metropolitan needs, leaving local problems to the minor units much as they are today.

An interesting variation of this plan is the proposal, favored by some leaders in Chicago, of separate statehood for that city and at least its Illinois environs. There is little reason to believe

TABLE VIII PRINCIPAL POWERS ASSIGNED TO METROPOLITAN OR GREATER CITY
GOVERNMENT

Pittsburgh commission's plan	Pittsburgh legislative plan	St. Louis committee plan	Boston committee plan
Care of poor and insane..	....	Care of poor and insane.	
Making and enforcing health regulations directly when no local health authority existed.	Health regulation in less drastic form.	Health administration.	
Construction and maintenance of through-traffic streets.	Construction and maintenance of through-traffic streets.	Construction and maintenance of through highways.	
Planning...............	....	Planning.	
Zoning where zoning had not been undertaken at effective date of charter.	....	....	
Creation of special taxing districts for the purpose of supplying any work, utility, or service.	Creation of special taxing districts for the purpose of supplying any work, utility, or service.	Creation of special taxing districts for the purpose of supplying any work, utility, or service.	
....	....	Sewers and sewage disposal.	Main sewers.
Acquisition, construction, operation, etc. of water works.	Acquisition, construction, operation, etc. of water works.	Granting franchises......	Water supply.
Same as to transportation systems.	Same as to transportation systems.	Ownership and operation of any public utility.	Transportation systems.
Maintenance of metropolitan police apart from local police.	....	Maintenance of metropolitan police apart from local police.	The Port.
Powers of Allegheny County, including those relating to correctional institutions.	....	Correctional institutions.	
		Parks and recreation.....	Metropolitan parks.
		Public libraries.	

that the Illinois legislature would ever agree to give up the privilege of taxing Chicago property, but if it could be brought to pass, separate statehood would offer many advantages to the city itself. It would be relieved of taxation for down-state purposes. The relation of the metropolitan state government to local units would be more commanding than that of the Great City in the federated city plan. If it were possible to apply the principle of separate statehood to our three largest cities, giving them all their metropolitan extent regardless of existing state lines, a great task of simplification would be accomplished.

Short of a redressing of state lines, the only practical method of solving metropolitan problems where more than one state is concerned is by the method employed in the creation of the Port of New York Authority—a treaty approved by Congress. The success achieved by this Authority naturally leads to the query, cannot the same principle be applied to the creation of a joint metropolitan authority dealing with several functions of government? Cannot such a treaty be international as well as interstate, solving the problems of Detroit-Windsor or of the Niagara frontier as some of the problems of New York and New Jersey are now solved?

This dislocation of normal relationship between population and units of local government is not, strictly speaking, a new phenomenon. London had a metropolitan problem in the latter part of the eighteenth century and has never ceased to have one. Philadelphia had one in the second quarter of the nineteenth century, temporarily solved by consolidation with Philadelphia County in 1854. Boston had one partially taken care of by the Sewer and Water Districts established in 1889 and 1895. The creation of Greater New York in 1897 for the moment brought that metropolis under a single local government. But what was occasional has now become universal. At the same time the proportions of the problem have been enormously increased. Two decades have witnessed a revolution, and there is not a considerable city in the country today which has not its metropolitan problem. Annexation has failed as a remedy. The expedient of special districts has been increasingly invoked, but it is admittedly a mere expedient. The growing intensity of the evils of disjointed local government has forced the consideration of municipal expansion on an unprecedented scale, inevitably upon the federated pattern.

VII. *Summary and Conclusions*

It is now possible to take a bird's eye view of population movements in the United States as far as they are reflected in the growth and expansion of the metropolitan community. Fully one-half of the people of this country now live within an hour's motor journey of a city of 100,000 or more. Three-quarters of the national increase in population between 1920 and 1930 took place within the immediate orbits of these larger cities. The census classification of all incorporated places of 2,500 or more as urban is increasingly less significant than a classification based upon whether population is or is not contained within the sphere of influence of a metropolitan center. The trend toward the metropolitan community and the reaching out of such communities over an increasingly large expanse of territory are the outstanding phases of the recent "drift to the cities."

The censuses of 1910 and 1920 showed a concentration of population based largely upon the centralization of industry. In other words the population followed the factories. The census of 1930, with supplementary evidence now available, indicates that the factors involved in metropolitan growth during the past decade were primarily commercial and institutional, with industry playing a relatively smaller role. The metropolitan community, at least until the advent of the depression of 1929, offered an increasing variety of jobs as well as more steady employment. It also offered a wider variety of economic and cultural services. It took on more and more the aspects of a coherent economic and cultural state, more realistic in many ways than the existing political states.

The supercommunity, or city region, is largely a product of modern means of communication, developed more extensively in local areas than throughout the nation as a whole. Assume that the boundaries of an ancient or medieval city were largely determined by the distance a man could walk in two hours. This would give a practicable radius of eight miles and a diameter of sixteen miles. The introduction of the motor car would at once multiply these limits at least six times, extending the practicable city radius to at least fifty miles. The case of the modern supercity is not quite so simple as this, since transportation by horse drawn stages, by steamboats where waterways were adjacent and by steam railways, extended the urban radius long before the coming of the automobile. But the illustration is pertinent. Measured in time rather than linear space the old boundaries of cities have shrunken, and vast new areas have been brought within the city influence.

The supercommunity, therefore, absorbs varying numbers of separate local communities into its economic and cultural organization. Large cities everywhere are becoming conscious of themselves as centers of commercial provinces and are attempting to devine and delineate their primary trade areas. The evidence at hand seems to indicate that the influence of the central city over these areas tends to diminish with distance outward. There is usually a line—not easy to determine since some influences of the central city are more potent and more far reaching than others—at which the territory of one center meets that of another. We can, in fact, draw a map tentatively allotting the entire territory of continental United States to a comparatively small number of supercities.

These supercities throughout the nation appear to be becoming more nearly uniform in their economic and institutional structure. The frontier type of city is gradually developing into a more mature type of metropolis. This is shown in physical structure—in the growth of skyscraper office buildings. It is shown also in the growing complexity of the industrial and occupational pattern of the larger cities throughout the nation—by the tendency toward wider distribution of talented or highly skilled persons in the more specialized occupations. This increasing diversity within the city and uniformity among the cities results in a higher degree of local autonomy. The regional city tends to become more self-sufficient. But this self-sufficiency is limited by the concentration of certain industries and of certain raw materials, and by a counter-tendency toward a closer functional interrelationship of the metropolitan centers of the nation. Just as communities within a metropolitan region preserve a certain degree of independence and local identity, yet are closely bound within the economic and cultural network of the central city, so the regional communities themselves are independent in many things, yet are parts of a national urban system.

But while the role of the great city in the nation at large has been growing in importance and changing in nature, even more radical and important changes have taken place within the city itself. In the first place, every large city has experienced rapid shifts in its local population since the end of the World War. The suburban drift has not only increased in volume but has altered in character. The outward movement in recent years has been largely among the white-collar classes, who have created a definite new problem by removing themselves to an increasing extent from the political city while remaining within the sphere of influence of the economic and cultural city. They have drawn after them a number of local institutions, business outlets, and municipal services, creating a real *rus in urbe* in the suburban territories. Industry likewise has tended to migrate outward, not for the same reasons but because increasing congestion in the more central districts has hampered its activities and added to its production costs. The heavy industries go first and farthest; the lighter ones and those which are most dependent on proximity to their metropolitan customers do not go so soon or so far; but the tendency in nearly every case is centrifugal.[50]

When individuals, businesses and industries move out in this way, at the rate which has recently marked these migrations, they leave a partial vacuum. The general effect of this drift, coupled with the more intensive use of land brought about by large structural units, is to hasten the obsolescence of much of the older pattern of the city. This applies to practically every type of institution and service. Every large city is confronted on the one hand with the problem of increasing congestion in certain areas and, on the other, with that of revitalizing its blighted areas. The deteriorated districts are rarely rehabilitated by private enterprise, though in some cities, notably New York, blighted areas have been restored, at least partially, by the erection of high class apartment houses. But these areas are always in competition with newer subdivisions which offer a more inviting field for private enterprise. Usually lying close to the main business center of the city they become the habitats of the vicious and criminal elements of the population.

[50]   Detailed studies on this point for the early post-war years are to be found in volumes IA and IB of the *Regional Survey of New York and Its Environs* (New York, 1928).

Without the economic incentive toward repair or replacement, buildings are allowed to deteriorate. Land values decline, assessments are lost to the city, transportation problems are aggravated by the fact that residence is further removed from business. This actual misuse and underuse of land creates a difficult situation for the city planner, the city assessor, the health department, the police department, the transportation managers and the housing and welfare agencies.

While the deteriorated areas are largely allowed to go to waste, there is an intensive exploitation of certain other areas within the city and toward its periphery. There result problems of transportation and traffic which are among the gravest that confront any modern city. In some cities the growth of private transportation by motor car has tended to disorganize the mass transportation facilities originally existing and has at the same time created a new traffic problem. There are many intricate details and differences among cities in this field, which cannot be dealt with adequately in this chapter but will find their rightful place in the accompanying monograph. It may be pointed out here, however, that the loss of business by rapid transit lines to motor transportation has not been universal. Nearly everywhere the surface street car line has lost ground. In New York City, however, in normal times, the rapid transit facilities of all kinds have never been adequate to the demands put upon them.

Nearly every one of the new problems of great cities comes home sooner or later to the governmental agencies. The last decade has witnessed an unprecedented expansion of all types of municipal utilities and services. At the same time many of the governmental functions have failed to keep pace with the economic and cultural expansion of urban life. The multiplicity of separate governmental and taxation bodies in every large metropolitan aggregation constitutes one of the most serious difficulties confronting the metropolitan community today. Because city planning is by definition limited to the obsolescent political city, it is now being rapidly superseded by regional planning. But regional planning on a scale commensurate with actual needs is thwarted by the large number of politically independent communities with which planning bodies have to deal.

The development of the new supercity points, therefore, to the need of some sort of supermetropolitan government. This problem and the steps already taken to cope with it were presented in the preceding section. It is quite apparent that the old procedure of annexation of surrounding territory by a central city is no longer a satisfactory solution. The spread of population under the influence of motor transport is far too rapid and too extensive to be dealt with adequately by annexation, even if annexation were not vigorously resisted by most of the outlying communities of most cities. Some plan of coordination of governmental functions must be developed before the political unity of the real functional metropolitan community can be achieved.

To sum up, the past decade has definitely witnessed the emergence of a new population and functional entity—the metropolitan community or supercity. So far as can be seen this new entity will characterize our national urban life for an indefinite time to come. The next decade may be expected to bring about further efforts to digest it into the economic governmental and cultural pattern of the nation.

The Bibliography of Roderick D. McKenzie

"The Neighborhood: A Study of Local Life in the City of Columbus, Ohio," *American Journal of Sociology,* 27; pts. 1 and 2: September, 1921, pp. 145–68; pts. 3 and 4: November, 1921, pp. 344–63; pts. 5, 6, 7, and 8: January, 1922, pp. 486–509; pts. 9, 10, 11, and 12: March, 1922, pp. 588–610; pts. 13 and 14: May, 1922, pp. 780–99.

"The Ecological Approach to the Study of the Human Community," *American Journal of Sociology,* 30 (November, 1924): 287–301.

"The Scope of Human Ecology," *American Journal of Sociology,* 32 (July, 1926): 141–54.

"Movement and the Ability to Live," in *Proceedings of the Institute of International Relations,* pp. 175–80. Riverdale, Cal., 1926.

Oriental Exclusion. New York: Institute of Pacific Relations, 1927.

"Spatial Distance and Community Organization Pattern," *Social Forces,* 5 (June, 1927): 623–38.

"The Concept of Dominance and World-Organization," *American Journal of Sociology,* 33 (July, 1927): 28–42.

"A Sociological Point of View," *Scientific Monthly,* 26 (June, 1928): 537–39.

L'Évolution économique du monde. Paris: Albert Kahn Foundation, 1928.

"Spatial Distance," *Sociology and Social Research,* 13 (July, 1929): 536–44.

"Ecological Succession in the Puget Sound Region," *Publications of the American Sociological Society,* 23 (1929): 60–80.

"Migration in the Pacific Area," in *American Foreign Relations, 1930,* ed. C. P. Howland, pp. 315–42. New Haven: Yale University Press, 1930.

"Cultural and Racial Differences as Bases of Human Symbiosis," in *Social Attitudes,* ed. Kimball Young, pp. 136–65. New York: Henry Holt, 1931.

"Human Ecology," *Encyclopedia of the Social Sciences,* 5 (1933): 314–15.

"Oriental Immigration," *Encyclopedia of the Social Sciences,* 11 (1933): 490–94.

"The Rise of Metropolitan Communities," in *Recent Social Trends: Report of the President's Research Committee on Social Trends*, 1: 443–96. New York: McGraw-Hill, 1933.

The Metropolitan Community. New York: McGraw-Hill, 1933.

"Industrial Expansion and the Interrelations of Peoples," in *Race and Culture Contacts*, ed. E. B. Reuter, pp. 19–33. New York: McGraw-Hill, 1934.

"Demography, Human Geography and Human Ecology," in *The Fields and Methods of Sociology*, ed. L. L. Bernard, pp. 52–66. New York: Ray Lang and Richard R. Smith.

Readings in Human Ecology, ed. Roderick D. McKenzie. Ann Arbor, Mich.: George Wahr, 1934.

"The Ecology of Institutions." Lecture delivered to Alpha Kappa Delta, University of Cincinnati. Cincinnati, 1936.